Performing Prose

Performing Prose

The Study and Practice of Style in Composition

CHRIS HOLCOMB AND M. JIMMIE KILLINGSWORTH

Southern Illinois University Press
Carbondale

20 19 18 17   7 6 5 4

Cover design by Mary Rohrer

Library of Congress Cataloging-in-Publication Data
Holcomb, Chris.
Performing prose : the study and practice of style in com-
position / Chris Holcomb and M. Jimmie Killingsworth.
    p. cm.
Includes bibliographical references and index.
ISBN-13: 978-0-8093-2953-3 (alk. paper)
ISBN-10: 0-8093-2953-0 (alk. paper)
ISBN-13: 978-0-8093-8576-8 (ebook)
ISBN-10: 0-8093-8576-7 (ebook)
1. English language—Style. 2. English language—Compo-
sition and exercises. I. Killingsworth, M. Jimmie. II. Title.
PE1408.H6647 2010
808'.042—dc22   2009030705

Printed on recycled paper. ♻

Contents

Preface

Welcome to Teachers and Scholars in Rhetoric and Composition

Our oldest and most durable vocabulary for talking about style emerged in the context of performance: the oratory of ancient Greece and Rome. Rhetoricians of the time invested considerable energy in cataloguing verbal devices they heard from both bema and rostrum, as well as from poet and rhapsode. Their primary aim was not to generate a vocabulary for literary analysis (although the terms they devised work very well for such purposes). Rather, they were assembling a repertoire, a collection of verbal moves orators could weave into their choreographed productions. Ideally, this stylistic repertoire would work in concert with other resources for performance: not only strategies for developing subject matter (the topoi of invention, for instance) but also, and more importantly, techniques for manipulating voice and gesture, the province of oratorical delivery. Cicero, for instance, saw style and delivery as a united effort. While he recognized the traditional division of rhetoric into the "five canons" (invention, arrangement, style, memory, and delivery), he grouped the third and fifth parts together under a single heading, "manner of speech," which he says, "falls into two sections, delivery and use of language [*in agendo et in eloquendo*]" (*Orator* xvii.55). What unites these two canons is their preoccupation with identifying performative set pieces, whether linguistic or gestural: substituting part for whole, for instance, or juxtaposing contrasting phrases, modulating vocal pitch, or sweeping the arm upward across the torso. Richard Schechner would classify all of these actions as "restored" or "twice-behaved" behaviors—that is, "strips" or units of behavior that "people train to do, that they practice and rehearse" (22). Presumably, the goal of such training and practice would be to help orators tap the rhetorical power of these behaviors and use them for orchestrating relationships among themselves, their listeners, their subject matter, their opponents—in short, the entire communicative scene.

Since antiquity, the study and teaching of style as performance has gradually declined, owing in large measure to the advent of print, which encouraged viewing style as a static object rather than a dynamic interaction among writer, reader, language, and subject matter (see Carpenter 187). *Performing Prose* rejoins the two concerns, and it does so at a moment when style is experiencing a modest revival in rhetoric and composition studies. As part of this renewed interest, scholars have begun reconstructing the history of verbal form in our discipline's recent past. The consensus has it that in the field of English composition, style was a casualty of the process movement (Connors; Carpenter; Clements). According to William J. Carpenter, "Style has existed in writing instruction for close to thirty years as an unwanted child, a reminder of past product-based pedagogies, brought out for exercise only when the real work of writing—the inventing, the organizing—had been done" (185). In a field dominated by the writing process, any attention to verbal form looked too much like the older product-oriented paradigm (Rankin). Rather than amend or enrich that paradigm's conception of style, the process movement diminished it further, presenting it as a minor part of an already minor part of the composing process: editing and proofreading.[1] If, however, we reconceptualize process as performance, then style again finds a more central place in composition studies.

Performing Prose participates in this reconceptualization by drawing on the stylistic vocabulary of classical rhetoric (with its all-but-forgotten orientation toward performance) and on more recent developments in sociolinguistics, discourse analysis, and performance studies. Throughout this book, we assume that writing is not just a social act (a way to make one's mark on the world); it is also, and more fundamentally, a social interaction, an encounter between writer and reader. And in written or printed text, where writers lack access to the communicative resources of oral delivery, style must shoulder much of the interactional load. For this reason, it must be part of the composing process from start to finish and not just during the "mop-up" operations of editing and proofreading. Invention, for instance, is not just a time for generating subject matter. It's also an opportunity for writers to consider what kind of social interaction they want to initiate and oversee. In fact, there is no such thing as "raw" subject matter. It must always assume some form—a sample of freewriting, an idea cluster, a shaky first draft—and in assuming that form (rather than another), it is already placing the writer into some kind of relation with the broader rhetorical scene—it is, in other words, already a set of choices about which words to use, already an incipient performance and an opportunity for creativity.

Performing Prose is itself a prose performance, and in recognizing that, we have worked to cultivate a style—a mode of social interaction—accessible and engaging to students in advanced writing, rhetoric, and literature classes. We hope the book is also suitable for graduate students in introductory courses on rhetoric and prose analysis, and for scholars and teachers in rhetoric and composition who want to reinvigorate their approach to style by a review that also weaves in recent theory and the theme of performance. Another audience includes editors and students of editing who need not only to be able to correct errors and revise effectively but also to explain their decisions to fellow editors and to the original authors of the passages on which they work. Throughout we strive to avoid contrived examples and, instead, feature samples of prose from real writers—authors of literature, creative nonfiction, journalism, and even blogs and advertising copy. Our aim in selecting these samples is not only to illustrate key concepts but also to bolster our claims that what we are presenting is, in fact, part of a larger cultural repertoire of style.

Welcome to Student Readers

We wrote this book for our own students, to be used in the classroom in courses on style and rhetoric. We wrote it because we could not find the book we needed—a book that would integrate instructions on *how to analyze prose* in close reading with guidance on *how to improve one's own style* by following the best practices of modern English-language authors.

We drafted chapters toward the book we envisioned and tested those early efforts in our classes, listening closely to our students' responses and revising accordingly. Other teachers used the manuscript, too, and reported on their students' responses. More revisions followed. The book you are reading is the result of that extensive engagement with students in active communities of learning.

It is a relatively short book (our students told us to keep it short), but it has a big ambition. It aims to show that in the best writing, language is not a dead thing, inky letters printed on a page, but a living force. Good writing does not merely make sense or passively convey information. It performs. It brings people together in acts of participation and observation—like a dance or a song.

To get a quick sense of language as performance, think about all the courtships that take place on our electronic networks today in various forms of writing. In email, instant messaging, Facebook, and cell phone texting, people meet and make plans, flirt and entice, break up and come together again. In all of these exchanges, what substitutes for tone of voice, for body language, for the well-timed touch of one human being to another? What substitutes is the thing we call style, or prose performance.

Have you ever been irritated by an email that was too short, that seemed curt or haphazardly dashed off, as if you weren't worth the time it would take to send a more considerate response—not by the meaning the message conveyed, but by the way it was delivered? Have you ever known someone injured by a rude remark or a racist slur? Then you know that words can hurt. The main premise of this book is that words can also heal—and perform in myriad other ways. The choices we make, even at the level of word and phrase, guide our written encounters with others. Through these choices, we present ourselves (or take on various roles) and orchestrate our relationships with readers, with the subjects under discussion, with the entire scenes of our interactions.

When you learn to read closely, paying careful attention to the ways words work, you can identify patterns that over time have come to be recognized as special organs of behavior in the living body of language. Such patterns include figures of speech like metaphor—a way of saying that something is what it literally is not, in order better to communicate what it really is, or how it works in a social context. When we say, for example, "His touch was electric," we are using language to act out our sense of the power we feel in someone's presence. The word *electric* may not convey new information about the touch so much as it concretely dramatizes an emotion we experience. The writer uses the phrase to focus the reader's attention and invite a more intimate, intense response. If it works, if the reader deepens his or her participation, knowing that the writer is investing more emotion into the written text, a new relationship between reader and writer begins to come alive. In this way, style adds drama to writing; it adjusts, adds nuance, colors, enhances, cools, or heats the language we use. It performs.

Once you recognize these patterns of action, you can begin to enact them in your own writing. The chapters offered here are devoted to identifying different kinds of patterns; they show you new ways to read and think about written prose. The exercises at the end of each chapter give you an opportunity to put your new observations into practice. The book is designed so that if you want to learn about style as an aid to analysis, you can concentrate on the chapters; if you want to work on improving your own written style, you can add the exercises. In addition, the appendix provides a review of basic English grammar that covers much of the language used in the chapters to describe word forms and sentence structure.

We recognize that students, as well as teachers and scholars, have different needs and desires in taking up such a book—hence the division into chapters and exercises. But we also want to stress the ultimate need of truly deep literacy to integrate reading and writing into a single unified practice that we call "performing prose."

Acknowledgments

The collaboration that made this book possible goes well beyond the interchange of the two old friends who are the coauthors. In addition to students at the University of South Carolina and Texas A&M University who read through and responded to various drafts in our advanced writing and rhetoric classes, we would like to thank several colleagues who used portions of the draft text in classes they taught and provided suggestions and encouragement: Monika Shehi of the University of South Carolina, David Johnson of Washington State University, and Elias Dominguez-Barajas of Texas A&M. Our thanks also go to Jacqueline Palmer and Sarah Hart of Texas A&M who read and commented on many parts of the manuscript. We are grateful to Kristine Priddy, to the anonymous reviewers of the manuscript, and the staff at Southern Illinois University Press, a publisher known for its outstanding contributions to the study of writing and rhetoric, for seeing this book into print and maintaining throughout the process the spirit of collegiality in which it was originally conceived. We would also like to thank SIUP for permission to adapt some of the material appearing in the sixth chapter of the present volume from Jimmie Killingsworth's *Appeals in Modern Rhetoric*.

Introduction

Most books on style concentrate on either how to analyze prose or how to improve your own writing style. *Performing Prose* blends the two concentrations. It equips you with a vocabulary for analyzing prose style while making you more aware of the choices available as you plan and write sentences, paragraphs, and papers. We contend that analysis and performance are complementary and mutually reinforcing: analysis feeds performance, and performance feeds analysis. When you analyze a sample of writing, you identify its various verbal devices and interpret their effects. By explicitly articulating what these devices are and how they operate, you make them available in your own writing repertoire where you can draw upon them and fashion them for fresh purposes. Practice in writing will, in turn, enhance your powers of analysis. By experiencing the writing process from the inside—as a participant with the awareness of an analyst—you increase your sensitivities to the challenges that writers face and the options they have. You learn to question an author's choices in light of how you might have composed a different kind of sentence or chosen a different word.

Toward achieving these two goals—insightful analysis and better writing—consider three interrelated terms describing different levels of written prose: grammar, style, and performance. These terms are difficult to pin down because they have been defined in so many ways, and there is some overlap, yet the following will serve as workable definitions:

- *Grammar* is the set of rules by which a language functions.
- *Style* comprises the choices a writer makes within that system.
- *Performance* is the moment when language goes into action, when the writer puts the stylistic repertoire to use with a rhetorical awareness of audience and context.

As the system of rules by which language functions, *grammar* allows writers to assemble sequences of words into meaningful combinations: "The cat is on the mat," but not "Mat the on is cat the." Children begin internalizing these rules at an early age, and by the time most begin formal schooling, they are able to produce hundreds of utterances that are grammatical. By the time they are young adults, their knowledge of the language has increased exponentially. The problem, from the perspective of stylistic analysis and performance, is that much of this knowledge is intuitive. Young adults may be able to produce thousands of grammatical utterances, but they may not be able to articulate why they are grammatical. Although we assume in our readers a rudimentary command of grammatical terms and concepts, we've provided an overview of English grammar in the appendix in case you need a quick introduction or review. Our aim in the main chapters is to build upon grammatical knowledge to create a strong sense of style and performance.

The big difference between grammar and *style* is that while grammar involves compliance, style depends upon a writer's decision making. Identifying style with choice implies that there are different ways of saying the same thing. To put it more abstractly, it implies that meaning is somehow independent of style, that there are meanings held in the mind or out there somewhere that can be realized in multiple ways. Such a proposition holds only in a general sense and ignores an important fact about language: any change in the manner of expression will have consequences for the meanings expressed. Linguists Geoffrey Leech and Michael Short capture this aspect of language (and avoid the pitfalls of assuming that content and form are independent) by distinguishing between *stylistic variant* and *stylistic value*. Stylistic variant refers to alternate expressions for roughly the same thing, while stylistic value refers to the consequences (what is gained and lost) by choosing one alternate over another. Consider the following sentences (adapted from Leech and Short 34):

1. After dinner, the senator made a speech.
2. When dinner was over, the senator made a speech.

3. When dinner was over, a speech was made by the senator.
4. The senator delivered a postprandial oration.

All of these are stylistic variants, but they differ in the stylistic values they communicate. The difference between 1 and 2 is negligible, although 2 may sound slightly more emphatic because it begins with a full clause ("When dinner was over") rather than a prepositional phrase ("After dinner"). The difference between 2 and 3 is more significant. In 3, the verb is voiced as a passive; it thus alters the emphasis. Sentence 2 presents the senator as its topic—that is what the sentence is about. It treats the making of a speech as new information (as we'll see, readers generally expect new information to come at the end of sentences). Sentence 3 reverses this arrangement, presenting the speech as the topic and its delivery by the senator as its news. Of all the stylistic variants, sentence 4 differs most significantly from the other three. Most noticeable is the Latinate diction ("delivered," "postprandial," and "oration"), which bumps this sentence up into a more formal, more learned level of style or register. It's still a stylistic variant of 1 through 3, but it carries a very different stylistic value.

So why do writers choose one stylistic variant (with its accompanying stylistic value) over another? Or, to place ourselves in the writer's shoes, why would we choose one variant over another? Decisions of this sort are often conditioned by other factors: not only grammatical rules but also the elements of rhetoric: the situations in which the writing takes place, the selves that writers hope to project, their attitudes about the subject matter, and the readers they hope to influence. Writers cultivate styles that both accommodate and shape these factors, but not always in equal measures. Some styles tip the scales toward accommodation, adapting language to reflect already accepted definitions of the situations, people, events, and things they address. Other styles lean more toward shaping circumstances. To take a simple example, when our students refer to us as "Professor," they are making a stylistic choice that accommodates the institution in which they find themselves. When they refer to us as either "Jimmie" or "Chris," they nudge circumstances in a new direction, defining their relationship to us as one of parity. On many occasions, we invite our students to call us by our first names, but in doing so, are we still exercising institutional power by determining our students' stylistic choice? They may even resist such efforts and, despite our invitation, prefer to call us "Professor," thus defining their relationship to us institutionally rather than familiarly.

In discussing how style embodies or defines relationships between people, we are already talking about an important component of *performance*—that is, how stylistic choice interacts with the people involved in a linguistic exchange. But a full treatment of style as performance requires that we attend to other kinds of interaction as well: not only the interaction between stylistic choice and other people, but also its interaction with other words and verbal patterns and with broader practices and meanings. We can begin to describe all of these interactions by considering stylistic choice in terms of three arenas of action:

- textual arena
- social arena
- cultural arena

Imagine these arenas as three concentric circles with the textual arena circumscribed by the social one, which is itself circumscribed by the cultural one (see figure 1).

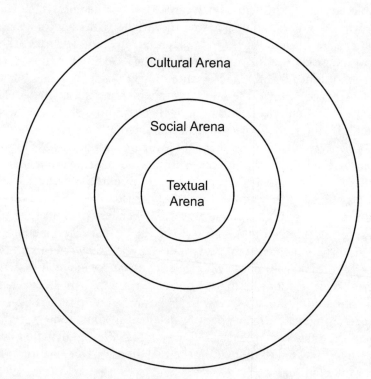

Fig. 1. The Arenas of Action

The arenas are thoroughly interdependent. A single decision about word choice or sentence arrangement (textual arena) can have a rippling effect and radiate out, affecting interaction between writer and reader (social arena) as well as their understanding of broader meanings and practices (cultural arena). Reciprocally, a writer and reader's understanding of these broader meanings and practices and their experiences with language and how it shapes social interaction can affect the choices that a writer makes (and how readers interpret them) at the level of text. Let's consider each of these arenas more fully so we can better see how an awareness of them can improve your own writing, while enriching your analyses of the writings of others.

Textual Arena

When you consider style within the textual arena, you are interested in how all the words on the page interact with one another to form patterns and meanings. Some patterns are so thoroughly a part of our expectations that we hardly notice them, like the conventional word order of the English sentence (subject-verb-object, as in "The dog chases the cat"). What we do notice are patterns of unusual regularity or patterns that depart from expectations, both of which arrest our attention as we observe words (even parts of words) interact (Leech and Short 48). Consider alliteration, or the use of the same consonant at the beginning of words in close proximity: "Meteors occasionally streaked the sky, and satellites cruised more stately orbits" (Raymo 148). The recurring "s" sounds (a pattern of unusual regularity) does not emerge from a single word or part of a word, but from the interaction among words with similar beginnings across a segment of text.

Even when it may seem that a verbal device concentrates into a single word, it's usually the case that the pattern only becomes visible in combination with other words. David Quammen, for instance, uses a metaphor while defining "glacier": "When a tongue of ice flows down a mountain valley, we call it a glacier" ("Strawberries" 197). The word "tongue" seems to carry the metaphor here, but this turn of language is actually the result of "tongue" in combination with other words in the sentence. Compare: "She stuck out her tongue at him." Same word, but here it is used non-metaphorically—that is, literally. How do we register the difference? By noting how "tongue" interacts with the words around it. In Quammen's sentence, the primary clue is "ice": we don't usually think of ice as a tongue. This departure from expectation, together with the more powerful expectation that it must make some kind of sense, invites us to interpret the combination metaphorically. With the second sentence, we call upon our understanding of human anatomy and behavior, knowing that some "she" could very well have "stuck out" a "tongue" at some unsuspecting (or well-deserving) "him."

In many cases, larger patterns emerge from the interaction of smaller ones. Consider a passage from Cynthia Heimel's "Fantasy Kills." The essay begins with an autobiographical anecdote: Heimel and several of her friends are sitting at a bar when an attractive man walks in and gives Heimel a smile—a "big, 'Hi there, cutie' smile." This friendly gesture stirs Heimel's imagination, and she begins spinning an elaborate fantasy about herself and the man, a fantasy which she prefaces and presents as follows:

> And here's what, I swear, immediately went through my head: "He looks too clean cut for this place. Too . . . nice. That's ok. That's really good. I want nice. He looks open. Maybe too open. Just a touch of the sensitive vegetarian. But definitely intelligent, definitely. . . . I'll twist around just a little, show him I'm interested. . . . Where would we live? This guy, I can tell, likes plants. Big leafy plants. Trees, in fact. A big loft downtown? The country? Will I have to move to the country? I'll probably have to make him wheat-germ shakes for breakfast. Will he want a banana in it? Does he want children soon? It will have to be soon." (148–49)

Taken together, all of these words and their arrangement add up to a stretch of writing that imitates a highly colloquial and somewhat frenetic style—just the kind of thing we might expect to hear (or express ourselves) when caught up in a moment of acute excitement. How do we know that this style is colloquial and fast paced? From the cumulative effect of many smaller patterns and devices: contractions, repetition of words, short sentences, sentence fragments, ellipses, strings of questions, frequent revisions of thoughts as they rush forward (for instance, "This guy, I can tell, likes plants. Big leafy plants. Trees, in fact")—the kinds of things we will explore more fully in the chapters that follow. The net effect is a dramatic reenactment of the fantasy, supposedly just as it occurred. Heimel could have *chosen* to represent her thoughts indirectly ("I thought he looked too clean-cut for this place"), while also tidying up the departures from standard written English ("I decided to twist around just a little to show him I'm interested"). These revisions would have produced a slightly more formal style, one that distances readers from the details and excitement of the fantasy. Instead, Heimel opts for the unmediated version, and by doing so, she invites readers to experience her fantasy with her—to experience it vicariously.

Social Arena

Our final observation in the previous section—how Heimel's style invites readers to participate in the fantasy as it unfolds—marks a place where the textual arena blurs into the social one—that is, where our interest turns from interactions among words and structures to interactions between writer and readers *through* those words and structures. Indeed, style is a powerful medium of social interaction. It allows writers to present a self or take on an already established role (storyteller, expert, client, supervisor, journalist, friend, confidant, lover). Writers also use style to assign roles to their readers (a writer who takes up the storyteller role, for instance, might cast his or her readers as an attentive and credulous audience). More generally, we can say that style is an important resource for managing relationships among writers, readers, subject matter, and the relative positions of all these elements within a broader situation. It works in ways very similar to what Erving Goffman calls "footing," which he defines as the "alignment" or attitude (which literally means the way a person faces something, a position of the body, a stance) a speaker takes up with respect to his or her listener and the circumstances of their interaction (128). Footing describes not only social position and distance (superior to subordinate, for instance, or friend to friend), but also emotional distance—that is, how writers make their readers feel about their interaction and how they orchestrate their emotional experiences as they read a text.

Extending Goffman's notion further and applying it to writing, we can say that writers use style to establish certain "footings" with their readers and their subject matters. In the passage quoted from "Fantasy Kills," Heimel assumes at least two footings with respect to her readers: a narrator reflecting back on a past experience, and a character within that narration who, in this case, happens to be in the throes of a fantasy. These two alignments toward readers are signaled in several ways. First, and perhaps most obviously, are the quotation marks, which typographically mark a dividing line between these two personas. Second, there's a downward shift in style: Heimel delivers her fantasy in a style that is markedly more colloquial and quirky than the writing that surrounds it. By using this more intimate style, Heimel creates the illusion that readers are with her on that barstool in that bar on that evening, eavesdropping on her thoughts. As narrator, Heimel takes up a different footing, one that distances her (and her readers) both spatially and temporally from the events she is about to narrate. Note especially her use of the past tense rather than the present: she doesn't tell us what "goes" through her head, but what "went" through it. This distance gives Heimel greater latitude in how she reflects back on and evaluates the events of that evening and, by implication, how she defines her relationship with readers. The parenthetical aside "I swear" is particularly revealing. It suggests that Heimel is taking up an ironic footing towards what she's about to write, that she can hardly believe that these were the thoughts that raced through her mind. As a result, the "I swear" invites readers to assume a similar footing towards the fantasy and gives them permission to laugh with Heimel (the narrator) at Heimel (the fantasizer).

Understanding what's happening within the social arena often requires, as a preliminary step, that we cycle back to the textual arena—that we get a firm grasp on the interactions between words and structures so that we can better see how they influence interactions between writer and reader. Let's consider Heimel's essay again. As the fantasy races towards its climax with Heimel imagining herself living with the man who smiled at her and bearing his children, things come to a screeching halt: a woman enters the bar and snuggles up to the object of Heimel's affection; the man responds in kind, embraces the new woman, and thus signals to Heimel that he's already spoken for. Heimel describes the woman's entrance in this way: "Through the crowd a sinuous long-haired girl snaked" (149). What's going on within this sentence? We might first notice the alliteration ("sinuous . . . snaked") and the unusual verb ("snaked"): it's actually a noun that Heimel has transformed into a verb by placing it after the grammatical subject and adding the past tense inflection–*ed*. Moving out a bit, we might also note the sentence's inverted arrangement. The English sentence typically moves from subject to verb to object, complement, or adjunct. Thus the more conventional way to write this sentence would be, "A sinuous long-haired girl snaked through the crowd," where the subject is "A sinuous long-haired girl," the verb is "snaked," and the adverbial adjunct (which tells us *where* she snaked) is "through the crowd."

Why does Heimel opt for the inverted syntax over the more conventional word order? There seem to be several reasons. The first concerns the interface between the textual and social arenas: that is, the inversion helps preserve cohesion within the text while meeting readers' expectations about the staging of information within a sentence. Readers expect (and prefer) that known information appear first in a sentence and that new information appear last. Readers already know that Heimel is in a crowded bar, but they (like Heimel at the time of the events she narrates) don't know about the girl. The inverted sentence thus allows Heimel to accommodate readers' expectations by placing the known information first ("Through the crowd") and reserving the end of the sentence for the new information ("a sinuous long-haired girl snaked"). The inversion also allows Heimel to move the sentence's most interesting and arresting word, "snaked," to a position of stress—the end of the sentence. If Heimel had chosen the more conventional word arrangement ("A sinuous long-haired girl snaked through the crowd"), the verb would still grab our attention (it is, after all, a noun turned into a verb), but placed in the middle it would risk getting lost in the syntactic shuffle.

A second reason for opting for the inverted version is more squarely about the footing Heimel wants to establish between herself and her readers. The "snaked" sentence signals a shift from the fantasy that precedes it, a change in alignment between writer and reader. While delivering the fantasy, Heimel creates the illusion of unmediated access to thoughts that seem on the brink of spiraling out of control. With the "snaked" sentence, Heimel resumes the role of narrator. She's back in the driver's seat, so to speak. No longer in the throes of a fantasy, Heimel is reflecting back on the culminating event of that night (snake girl's arrival), actively and authoritatively shaping her readers' responses to it, including how they feel about it. Heimel could have chosen a more neutral introduction for snake girl, in terms of both word arrangement and diction: "A woman walked through the crowd." She doesn't. She's not interested in simply documenting an event (the arrival of the other woman). Instead, she uses the resources of style to portray it, to color it in a particular way, to make her readers feel about it as she does. The inverted, serpentine syntax and the hissing alliteration of the "s" sounds build toward and reinforce the final image delivered by the unusual (and unusually placed) verb—"snaked." The overall effect is that this "sinuous long-haired girl" is nothing shy of *sin*ister itself.

Cultural Arena

As we move from the textual through the social into the cultural arena, we are interested in how verbal devices interact with broader cultural meanings and values. In other words, a particular device may have, independent of the message it expresses, significance to some larger community of language users. Try to imagine, for instance, a political or religious address without patterns that balance phrases or clauses ("We observe today not *a victory of a party* but *a celebration of freedom*, symbolizing *an end* as well as *a beginning*" [Kennedy 11]), or try to imagine one without emphatic repetitions ("I have a dream" [King 81–87]). It's difficult to do because these stylistic devices have become an essential ingredient to such performances;

they elevate them and grant them dignity, solemnity, and power. To take a more homey (or homely) example, consider how frequently puns appear in the titles and lyrics of country music songs ("Pour Me," "Don't Rock the Jukebox," and "Walking the Floor over You"). Why this predilection for puns? What purposes do they serve and what meanings do they bear for writers and fans of country music? Are they signs of verbal sophistication, or do they allow these writers and fans to identify with a particular lifestyle and region—say, a hillbilly ethos? What about those who look down upon country music, preferring more urban (or urbane) strains? Would the punning music title only confirm what they see as a backward and backwater culture (the pun being one short step away from a malapropism)? A stylistic analysis of the pun as cultural performance would answer such questions. It might even consider the history of word play in other forms of popular entertainment, perhaps stretching all the way back to the pervasive punning in the dramatic works of Shakespeare, an author who wasn't above a little rustic revelry himself.

Examining style within the cultural arena means looking for verbal patterns that circulate in, and gain resonance from, the broader cultural context. In chapter 9, we call these patterns rituals of language. Some of these are fixed sequences of words—like proverbs, idioms, and clichés. Others are not tied to specific words placed in fixed sequences but consist of conventional grammatical structures and word forms like antitheses, metaphors, and analogies. Consider, for instance, the first sentence from the Heimel passage: "And here's what, I swear, immediately went through my head." It contains at least one ritual of language, the parenthetical aside "I swear." It's a phrase that we've probably all heard, seen, or even uttered or written before. In courtrooms and congressional hearings, it has a special, legally binding significance: "I swear to tell the truth, the whole truth. . . ." In less formal settings, it serves as a stylistic set piece that can convey a range of possible meanings—from intensifying our commitment to (or conviction about) what we are saying, to reassuring skeptical listeners and readers, to undercutting what we are saying by dramatizing a measure of self-doubt or irony. In Heimel, as we have already seen, it serves something close to the latter purpose. It marks a distinction between Heimel the narrator and Heimel the fantasizer, opening up a space for Heimel the narrator to reflect back on, evaluate, and laugh at a former version of herself.

Heimel's inverted sentence, "Through the crowd a sinuous long-haired girl snaked," is another ritual of language. Heimel didn't invent the pattern; instead she borrows it. First used by poets to fit the requirements of meter and rhyme, syntactic inversions in prose often suggest a poetic, archaic, even gnomic feel (think of Yoda from *Star Wars,* who almost always delivers ancient Jedi lore through inverted sentences). In Heimel, the inversion sharpens the contrast between the quirky, conversational style of the fantasy and the event that disrupts it: the arrival of snake girl. As part of a broader cultural repertoire, the inversion also helps signal a change in the narrative's emotional tone. We sense, as did one of the witches from Shakespeare's *Macbeth*, that "something wicked this way comes" (IV.i.44).

Topics in Other Chapters

Such are the topics that we deal with in this book, the overall aim of which is to increase your capability to recognize and articulate patterns of repetition and trends of language use and then apply your awareness to your own written performance. In our other chapters, we expand the discussion somewhat more deliberately, isolating elements and movements of stylistic variation and moving through them one step at a time.

Chapter 2, "The Motives of Style," discusses the general strategies authors use to vary their style and the reasons for their choices—such as manipulating subordinate clauses in sentences to emphasize one part over another, or making the style of the prose reflect the reality it represents (choppy sentences to reflect a rough ride over a dirt road, for example). By increasing your awareness of the motives, you should be able to improve both your analysis of style (moving beyond identification of a feature like inverted syntax or metaphor to say why someone might choose such a feature) and your own writing (by multiplying and organizing the strategies in your repertoire of stylistic variations). We discuss the ways that the motives affect different elements of any discourse—language, subject matter, writer, and reader.

Chapter 3, "Convention and Deviation," covers the common guidelines that too often get presented as "rules" for style in textbooks on how to solve problems in your writing. Instead of taking the usual course of showing how to heal these diseases of bad prose—such as passive voice, jargon, and wordiness in writing which may be grammatically correct but is somehow troubling for many readers (especially English teachers)—we consider stylistic features that (within most contexts) improve reading speed and comprehension. The overall aim of readability conventions is to produce prose that prefers familiar over arcane language and that is active, flowing, organized for emphasis, and concise. But we don't stop there. We go on to show how conventions set the stage for deviations, shifts in expectation, the kinds of performances in prose that some analysts believe to be at the heart of style—whether an individual's personal style or a community style that identifies special kinds of thinking and knowing.

Chapter 4, "Distinction: From Voice to Footing," picks up where chapter 3 ends, with the way people use the word *style* to confer distinction upon certain writers—Hemingway's telegraphic style, Faulkner's breathlessly long sentences, or E. B. White's whimsical tone. The word that often gets associated with a distinctive style is *voice*, as in the expression that teachers sometimes use: "That student really found her voice on the last paper." What does this expression mean? Our aim in this chapter is to demystify the concept of voice by considering such topics as the relation of oral and written language and the use of tone in writing. An excellent alternative is suggested by performance studies—the idea of stylistic "footing" that we introduced briefly in this chapter, a description of the way a writer establishes a tone, attitude, or special perspective on the subject matter and audience of a particular discourse.

Chapter 5, "The Rhetorical Tradition," considers style as one of the five "canons of rhetoric" in ancient times (the others being invention, arrangement, memory, and delivery). We place particular emphasis on the sometimes misunderstood concept of "levels of style," exploring contemporary applications of Cicero's contention that different levels of style are appropriate for different purposes—plain style for teaching, the grand style for moving an audience, and a middle style for entertaining audiences or maintaining the forward momentum of a discourse.

In chapters 6 and 7, we continue to pursue topics with long-standing significance in the rhetorical tradition—the patterns of language known as figures of speech—which have accrued further significance in modern times with attention from linguists, literary critics, anthropologists, psychologists, and language philosophers. Chapter 6 deals with tropes, the alternation of words' common meanings in expressions such as metaphor, metonymy, synecdoche, and irony. Chapter 7, "Schemes," introduces strategies for varying the conventional structure of sentences.

Chapter 8, "Images," covers the many ways that writers try to engage the senses of readers. Modern literary criticism has expanded the meaning of "image" to include not only the visual but all the senses or ways that language appeals to the bodily experience of the author and audience. The topic is further expanded by recent work in "body criticism" and the "rhetoric of the body." The question is how a writer can restore some sense of the physical in a medium of communication often considered to be "disembodied." In discussing imagery in style, we not only deal with issues of descriptive writing but also approach the ways that imagination gets worked out in language.

Chapter 9, "Rituals of Language," uses the concepts of convention and deviation to explore patterns of language use so common as to attain the status of a social or cultural ritual. The suggestion in this chapter that style has its ultimate effect on the formation and perpetuation of culture becomes the foundation of chapter 10, "Style and Culture." Here, by way of conclusion, we explore the meaning of style beyond its linguistic confines, considering the ways that language connects to styles of various kinds—in clothing, technology, music, and architecture, for example.

At the end of the book, you will find some additional help. The "Appendix on Grammar" provides a grounding in standard terminology and key concepts. It covers matters of word form (morphology) and sentence structure (syntax) and hints at changes that English has undergone over history—changes that not only have affected stylistic choices but some that have been caused by authors' (conscious and unconscious) experiments with language in action over time.

We also provide exercises at the end of each chapter. The exercises give opportunities for practice in analysis and writing that will help you move from understanding the performances of others to enhancing your own verbal performances.

Throughout the book we will insist that the study of style goes beyond the mechanical manipulation of language, beyond fixing errors, beyond formulas and rules of thumb. The implications of stylistic investigation and practice are wide and varied. Though we may start with a narrow consideration of a word's form or a sentence's structure, ultimately we must expand outward, as the latter chapters of the book suggest, toward the widest possible applications of human perception, preference, and action.

Exercises

1. Start keeping a *commonplace book*, a regular practice among many writers who have come to be known for their style. Henry David Thoreau, for example, kept one that grew to enormous proportions during his relatively short lifetime. A commonplace book is an informal record of your reading in which you copy out sentences and slightly longer passages that you find striking or well written, along with your own comments about the quotations. You can also practice your own prose performance by varying, parodying, or imitating the passages you copy.

To keep a commonplace book that focuses on style—one that records passages you like as much for the way they are written as for what they say—is a good way to advance your study of style, for at least two reasons. First, just the act of writing down the passage forces you to slow down and look at it more closely; the words and the patterns are more likely to impress themselves upon your mind. Second, as your commonplace book grows, you are building what the linguists call a *corpus* (literally a body) of samples you can use in stylistic study. You can begin your analysis by informally commenting on the passage.

You can keep your commonplace book in either a paper notebook or a special computer file. (We recommend the paper notebook because the physical act of copying a passage by hand often reveals features of style missed when merely transcribing it into a computer file.) Select entries from any reading you do—from course textbooks or research projects, novels or magazine articles, blogs or emails from friends, even advertisements. Leave space to add comments and variations as you go.

Below are some sample entries from a commonplace book developed for a research project on the style of nature writing. All the quotes come from the anthology *Nature Writing: The Tradition in English*, edited by Robert Finch and John Elder, 2nd ed. (New York: Norton, 2002). To make your commonplace book useful as a corpus of study materials, by the way, you should always note down page numbers and bibliographical information, at least in short form, so that you can find the information when you need it.

> To enjoy a thing exclusively is commonly to exclude yourself from the true enjoyment. —Henry David Thoreau (187)

> Our winged thoughts are turned to poultry. They no longer soar. —Thoreau (203)

> Thoreau . . . took man's relation to Nature and man's dilemma in society and man's capacity for elevating his spirit and he beat all these matters together, in a wild free interval of self-justification and delight, and produced an original omelette from which people can draw nourishment in a hungry day. *Walden* is one of the first of the vitamin-enriched American dishes. —E. B. White (442)

> Our boat is the Park Service boat, a thirty-four-foot diesel work-horse. It has a voice like a bulldozer's. —Wallace Stegner (507)

> The smell of Funk Island is the smell of death. It is probably the source of the island's name, which in various languages means "to steam," "to create

a great stench," "to smoke"; it may also mean "fear." The island certainly smells ghastly. No battlefield could ever concentrate such a coalition of dead and dying. —Franklin Russell (609)

You will find the flora here as venomous, hooked, barbed, thorny, prickly, needled, saw-toothed, hairy, stickered, mean, bitter, wiry, and fierce as the animals. Something about the desert inclines all living things to harshness and acerbity. The soft evolve out. —Edward Abbey (621)

Beneath the plane, the elephant mass moved like gray lava, leaving behind a ruined bog of mud and twisted trees. —Peter Matthiessen (634)

. . . my faithful Land Rover . . . gave a hellish clang and, dragging its guts over the stone, lurched to a halt. —Matthiessen (637)

Picked up by the scruff of the neck, [the bear cubs] splayed their paws like kittens and screamed like baby bears. The cry of a baby bear is muted, like a human infant's heard from her crib down the hall. —John McPhee (685)

Mountain lions coo like pigeons, sob like women, emit a flat slight shriek, a popping bubbling growl, or mew, or yowl. —Edward Hoagland (692)

The continent is covered by an ocean of engine noise. —Wendell Berry (724)

I know here a grandfather, a man as bald as if a cyclone wind had taken his scalp—something witnesses claim has happened elsewhere [in tornado country]—who calls twisters Old Nell, and he threatens to set crying children outside the back door for her to carry off. —William Least Heat Moon (777)

The thought of crossing paths with a thousand-pound grizzly who hasn't eaten or taken a shit for six months, and may have hungry cubs bothering at her side, is enough to convince me that we should change our plans. But I'm reticent to say so, not wanting to appear lacking in courage. —Alison Hawthorne Deming (938)

At the Nevada state line we cast aside Utah's wholesome aura for its nemesis. Behind: Leave It to Beaver. Ahead: Sodom and Gomorrah. —Ellen Meloy (952)

I am going to go out on a limb here, and guess that the kind of nest these blue jays are making has never provoked anyone to an encomium to nature's symmetry and perfection. —Emily Hiestand (961)

I can feel the grass underfoot collecting its bashful energy. Big Bluestem, female and green sage, snakeweed, blue gramma, ground cherry, Indian grass, wild onion, purple coneflower, and purple aster all spring to life on a prairie burned the previous year. —Louise Erdrich (1045)

2. Don't try too hard to comment on the passages in your new commonplace book before you develop your vocabulary for stylistic analysis. Instead, try this exercise. Write variations or parodies of one or two of the quotes. Take the original and your variations to class, and in a small group of your classmates, read them to one another. Discuss how the changes in language alter the tone and meaning of the passage. Ask the simple question, "What is lost and what is gained (if anything) in the variation?" Here are a couple of examples:

Original: Our winged thoughts are turned to poultry. They no longer soar. (Thoreau)
Variation: Our best thoughts never get off the ground.

Original: *Walden* is one of the first of the vitamin-enriched American dishes. (E. B. White)
Variation: Thoreau gave America a powerful new energy drink, caffeine for the intellect and protein for the soul.

2

Motives of Style

The previous chapter took Heimel's "fantasy" passage through the textual, social, and cultural arenas, detailing various verbal features and interpreting their effects. The goal of that exercise was threefold:

- To present a framework for examining writing as performance: writing is a dynamic process, a series of interactions among textual features, writers and readers, and the cultural contexts they inhabit.
- To model stylistic analysis: one way to learn how to do analysis is through imitation—that is, by studying the methods and practices of other analysts of style.
- To make certain stylistic strategies visible so that you might add them to your own writing repertoire: for instance, using syntactic inversion to move an important word, such as "snaked," into a position of stress.

This chapter moves you closer toward these goals. It does so by giving you insider knowledge of the motives that often drive analysis and performance.

Each motive offers a general strategy—a line of argument, so to speak—that allows you, when analyzing others' work or considering your own options, to move from stylistic description ("This is a metaphor") to stylistic interpretation ("This is how the metaphor may function"). This move is crucial. Too often students of style complete the first step (they describe or identify a stylistic feature) and think their work is done. It's not. You need to push beyond description and interpret how a stylistic feature functions in context. The motives of style will help you bridge this all too common gap between description and understanding.

Although we feature the term "motive" throughout this chapter, we are not interested in recovering the intent of an author—in fact, we believe that intent is ultimately inaccessible, even to authors themselves. Instead, we survey the various ways writers and analysts explain stylistic behaviors to either themselves or others. Typically, these explanations will name, or at least imply, an orientation toward one of the elements of the rhetorical situation: language, subject matter, writer, or reader. All of these elements are at play in every stylistic decision, but as we suggested in chapter 1, any specific choice may focus on one more than others. Accordingly, we will use them to organize our discussion of the stylistic motives.

Motives Focused on Language

Language-focused motives emerge from the linguistic code itself and include the meanings and functions we conventionally associate with word classes (nouns, verbs, adjectives, and so on) and phrase and clause types. Of all the motives we survey in this chapter, these are the most specific in focus, requiring us to examine the word-by-word decisions a writer makes and the reasons that might inform those decisions. These motives are also the most varied and numerous. As a result, we can only provide a sampling here.

Let's start with a very familiar word class, definite and indefinite articles: "the," "a," and "an." Although articles can serve a number of functions, one of their most important is to tag a piece of information as *new* or *already known* to readers. Consider these three sentences from Alice Munro's short story "The Moons of Jupiter":

> A small screen hung over his head. On the screen a bright jagged line was continually being written. The writing was accompanied by a nervous electronic beeping. (*Selected Stories* 307)

In the first sentence, the indefinite article "a" tags the "small screen" as information that is new to the reader. Once Munro mentions "screen," however, it becomes known information, and she labels it as such in the second sentence with the definite article "the." Similarly, Munro presents "bright jagged line" as new information, but when she refers to it again in sentence three, she tags it as known: "The writing."

The choice of definite and indefinite articles may seem a small matter, hardly worthy of note: use definite articles when readers are already familiar with a piece of information; use indefinite articles when they are not. Most native writers perform this action almost automatically. A skilled stylist, however, can play on this linguistic convention to create interesting effects. For instance, writers of modern literature (including literary nonfiction) often use definite articles, among other devices, at the beginnings of narratives to create the illusion that readers already share knowledge of the world they are about to enter (Traugott and Pratt 280). Writers can also pair them with indefinite articles to highlight certain bits of information while backgrounding others. Observe how William H. Armstrong uses definite and indefinite articles in the first paragraph of his novel *Sounder*:

> The tall man stood at the edge of the porch. The roof sagged from the two rough posts which held it, almost closing the gap between his head and the rafters. The dim light from the cabin window cast long equal shadows from man and posts. A boy stood nearby shivering in the cold October wind. He ran his fingers back and forth over the broad crown of the head of a coon dog named Sounder. (1)

Through the first three sentences, Armstrong uses definite articles to present every bit of information (except "long equal shadows") as if it were already known to readers: "the man," "the porch," "The roof," "the two rough posts," and so on. Even though we have never encountered this particular man and the porch he stands on, the definite articles foster the illusion that we have. In this way, they draw us into the narrative, creating the illusion that we are part the fictive world of the novel, listening to the story like an observer present on the scene, while also raising questions we can only answer by reading further. In the second half of the passage, however, a shift occurs. "A boy" and "a coon dog" appear in the scene. The indefinite articles mark these two characters as new information and thus cast a spotlight on them. In other words, their newness makes them stand out to readers, while the presumed familiarity of the man seems to push him into the backdrop along with the porch and its sagging roof and rugged posts.

Articles are only one of eight word classes recognized by most grammarians. The others include nouns, verbs, adjectives, adverbs, pronouns, prepositions, conjunctions, and interjections. If space permitted, we could catalogue conventional functions associated with each word class and discuss how they serve as motives for stylistic choice—how writers make strategic use of them while crafting their own prose and how analysts often refer to them in interpretation. But for now, we'll limit our discussion of the micro-motives of style by considering phrase and clause types, one example of each.[1]

Prepositional phrases often serve as modifiers: as either adverbs or adjectives. In these roles, they add specificity and precision to the verbs and nouns they modify. Collectively, they establish the circumstances under which actions (and the participants involved in them) occur (Halliday 149ff.). Notice the prepositional phrases in the following sentences:

Gulls loop above the boardwalk in jazzy little arcs. (Fagone 86)

An eagle with a bum leg will starve to death. (Ehrlich 185)

Strider sprang from hiding and dashed down towards the Road, leaping with a cry through the heather. (Tolkien 204)

The prepositional phrases in the first sentence act like adverbs: "above the boardwalk" tells us *where* the gulls looped, and "in jazzy little arcs" tells us *how* or in what *manner*. In the second sentence, "with a bum leg" works like an adjective, modifying "eagle" (What kind of eagle? One with "a bum leg"). Strip these sentences of their prepositional phrases, and you rip them out of time and space, leaving readers wondering about the circumstances in which they happened:

Strider sprang and dashed, leaping.

Is this Strider (aka Aragorn), son of Arathorn, descendent of Isildur, and future King of Gondor, or some lunatic? Without those prepositional phrases, it's hard to tell.

As for clauses, we can consider them by themselves or in relation to other clauses. Clauses can be short and emphatic, or long and diffuse; they can be declarative, interrogative, or imperative. They can be actively voiced and deliver their information from the perspective of the agent of action ("The dog chased the cat"), or they can be passive and focus on the recipient ("The cat was chased by the dog"). We can also find motives in the ways writers form relationships between and among clauses. English recognizes two primary ways to connect one clause with another: coordination and subordination.[2] In essence, these two relationships constitute a mechanism for ranking information. Coordinate clauses—that is, clauses joined by "and," "but," "or," or a semicolon—rank the information presented in each clause as equal in importance or emphasis. Subordination, by contrast, ranks one clause beneath another (the word "subordination" comes from Latin and literally means "to place under").

Subordination can serve the relatively practical motive of highlighting certain pieces of information while backgrounding others. Consider this passage from Bill Bryson's *Short History of Nearly Everything:*

> Although everyone calls it the Big Bang, many books caution us not to think of it as an explosion in the conventional sense. It was, rather, a vast, sudden expansion on a whopping scale. (13)

In the first sentence, Bryson subordinates the first clause, "Although everyone calls it the Big Bang," to the second, "many books caution us not to think of it as an explosion in the conventional sense" (the tip-off is the subordinate conjunction "although"; other subordinators include *when, if, because, while, whereas*). Why did Bryson choose to rank the first clause under the second? To ensure that the most important information receives the emphasis. The main point in this context is not what everyone calls the origin of the universe (most readers already know it as the Big Bang); rather, the point is that this name fails to capture what most scientists think really happened. This mismatch between name and event is the most important information, and Bryson codes it as such by making it the main clause in the sentence. This ranking has the additional benefit of setting up the sentence that follows, a sentence that tells readers what the event really was: "a sudden expansion on a whopping scale."

Beyond using coordination and subordination to highlight and background information, writers can use these two devices to specify relationships between clauses. The coordinating conjunction "and" is our most neutral connector. It joins two structures without saying much about how they are related. The conjunctions "but" and "or" supply a little more information: "but" signals a contrast; "or" introduces another possibility. Subordinate conjunctions provide even more information, specifying such relationships as time *(when, after, before)*, cause-effect *(because, so)*, and condition *(if)*. In the hands of a skilled stylist, these conjunctions help shape and filter the experiences that writer is describing. More specifically, writers who favor a more coordinate style present the world as a stream of loosely connected events, leaving it up to readers to figure out how those events relate to one another (in some cases, the point may be that there are no connections; only ones that we impose). Writers favoring a more subordinate style, by contrast, play a more active role in interpreting events, making the relationships among them explicit.

Ernest Hemingway is well-known for his insistent coordination even when subordination may seem the more natural choice:

> One hot evening in Padua they carried him up to the roof and he could look out over the top of the town. (139)

We might expect a subordinate conjunction between these clauses to express purpose ("they carried him up to the roof *so* he could look out over the town") or causation ("he could look out over the town *because* they carried him up to the roof"). We're given neither and, as a result, are left either to infer the relationship ourselves or to meditate on a why the narrator chose to join a sequence of events by only the loosest of connectors. Contrast the Hemingway sentence with this one from Paul Crenshaw:

> While my father and uncles and grandfather watched the storm, my mother herded my brother and me down the stairs where, in a little room at the bottom, my grandmother and aunts and cousins sat quietly in the light of a kerosene lamp, their shadows thrown large on the wall. (22)

There are three clauses in this sentence depicting three actions (four if you count the absolute phrase at the end), and Crenshaw uses subordinate conjunctions to specify and interpret relationships between them, relationships of time (*while*) and location (*where*). We could *Hemingway* this sentence by switching the subordinate conjunctions to coordinate ones:

> My father and uncles and grandfather watched the storm, and my mother herded my brother and me down the stairs to a little room at the bottom. There my grandmother and aunts and cousins sat quietly in the light of a kerosene lamp, and their shadows were thrown on the wall.

The difference is striking and illustrates how something that seems as incidental as a conjunction can have big consequences.

Except in highly specialized studies, the language-focused motives are usually a means to an end rather than an end in themselves. For analysts of style, they often serve as a point of departure or intermediary step between identifying verbal features and advancing broader interpretive claims about the works in which they appear. We could, for instance, use our observations about the first paragraph of *Sounder* to build an interpretation of the novel in general—how the definite and indefinite articles foreshadow the man's separation from his family for most of the narrative, in contrast to the boy's central position in both the narrative and the family circle. For writers, these motives are the building blocks of any stylistic repertoire. Like a musician who is thoroughly versed in scales, arpeggios, and melodic structure, writers with a deep (if only intuitive) understanding of the language-focused motives can claim command of their medium.

Motives Focused on Subject Matter

Subject-oriented motives are in play when analysts and writers focus on relationships between style and the experiences, actions, or phenomena to which it refers. This section introduces you to two of these motives. The first involves how writers use style to mirror or imitate subject matter. This motive is often found in analyses of literary style where the degree to which style works in harmony with its subject matter is taken as a measure of artistic value. The second motive involves the way writers use style, not to imitate subject matter but to organize, structure, or even create it.

The first subject-focused motive is so common in stylistic analyses—and presumably, so pervasive as a motive driving writers' stylistic choices—that scholars have coined a term for it: "iconicity" (Leech and Short 233). According to them, style is iconic when its "textual forms" imitate, reflect, encode, or dramatize the "meanings" they express (233). We drew on this motive of style in our analysis of Heimel's "snaked" sentence: "Through the crowd a sinuous long-haired girl snaked." There we interpreted the inverted syntax and hissing alliterations as an imitation or "icon" of the sentence's central image: snaking.

There are many other possibilities for iconic styles. To take a somewhat pedestrian example, consider the linearity of prose—how one word must come after another. It often mirrors chronological order: "if A comes before B in [time], then A comes before B in the text" (Leech and Short 234). Every writer and reader of recipes knows that "crack two eggs into a bowl, mix, and combine with dry ingredients" is not an arbitrary syntactic sequence, but a chronological one. The order of its clauses imitates the order in which readers are to execute its instructions.

Verbal form might also imitate objects in motion and become a *simulation* of the movements it reports (Tuft 253). As an example, consider this sentence from James Joyce:

> He watched their flight; bird after bird: a dark flash, a swerve, a flash again, a dart aside, a curve, a flutter of wings. (192)

The structure and rhythm of the sentence "reflects the erratic motion of the birds in their darting, curving flight" (Tuft 253). Annie Dillard uses similar techniques to dramatize her experience flying through the mountains in a small plane piloted by a stunt pilot:

> We came back for another pass at the mountain, and another. We dove at
> the snow headlong like suicides; we jerked up, down, or away at the last
> second. . . . Pitching snow filled all the windows, and shapes of dark rock.
> I had no notion which way was up. Everything was black or gray or white
> except the fatal crevasses; everything made noise and shook. (185)

Dillard's style not only simulates the sudden and violent movements of
the plane ("we jerked up, down, or away"), but also dramatizes her mental
and physical responses to them, particularly how disoriented and fright-
ened they made her feel—the emotion reflected in the jumbled syntax in
"Pitching snow filled all the windows, and shapes of dark rock" and the
heavy repetition: "Everything. . . . everything," "black *or* gray *or* white."

The imitative potential of style need not be limited to simulating temporal sequences and movement. Writers can also use it to dramatize major
concepts or themes running throughout an entire work. In his "I Have a
Dream" speech, Martin Luther King Jr. calls for racial and social justice,
and one the main devices he uses to present that theme is parallelism, or
the stringing together of grammatically equivalent items:

> I have a dream that one day . . . little black boys and black girls will be able to
> join hands with little white boys and white girls as sisters and brothers. (237)

> I have a dream that one day every valley shall be exalted, every hill and
> mountain shall be made low, the rough places will be made plain and the
> crooked places will be made straight. (237)

> With this faith we will be able to work together, to pray together, to struggle
> together, to go to jail together, to stand up for freedom together. (237)

> When we let [freedom] ring from every village and every hamlet, from
> every state and every city, we will be able to speed up that day when God's
> children—black men and white men, Jews and Gentiles, Protestants and
> Catholics—will be able to join hands. (237)

The syntax here does not just describe King's hoped-for future—it enacts it.
The insistent parallelism, with various social groups and actions expressed
as grammatical equivalents, reinforces and dramatizes the equality King
envisions.

The next subject-focused motive is the obverse of the previous one.
Instead of mirroring a situation, experience, or theme, the style structures
or creates one. Let's stick with parallelism. The following sentence comes

from an essay written by Garret Keizer, a self-described liberal who defends gun ownership:

I own a fire extinguisher, a first-aid kit, and a shotgun. (140)

The parallelism here organizes the items listed in a particular way: that is, the grammatical equivalency (a series of noun phrases) suggests that they all belong to the same class of things—things designed for home- and self-preservation. We can imagine an alternate grouping in which the first two items belong to the class of things that save life, while the third belongs to things that take it. If we wanted to convey this alternate grouping to readers, we would pick a syntactic form that organizes the items by a principle of contrast rather than similarity:

Although I own a fire-extinguisher and first-aid kit, I also own a shotgun.

In addition to arranging objects into different categories, syntax can also control the tempo and tone with which details are presented. While traveling through central Africa with a convoy of truckers, Ted Conover and his companions stop for lunch at a roadside barbecue shed. They enter:

Beams of light slipped in through the slats, illuminating sides of goat hanging from hooks on the back wall. Hosts of flies jumped from the meat to us and back again. A man with a cleaver stopped hacking away at a beef carcass long enough to hear Malek order three skewers. The flies landed. He started hacking again. The flies took off. (317)

The last three sentences focus the reader's attention in what is presumably a wave of sensory input. They also slow time down. Conover could have written:

The flies landed, but when he started hacking again, they took off.

But this variant, by combining all three events into a single sentence, seems to diminish the impact they had on Conover. Instead, he wants his readers to register each event individually, to dwell on it, and to share his concerns over possible cross-contamination. So he picks a syntactic form that organizes his subject matter accordingly. The more general point here is that syntactic forms are templates that writers impose on the subjects they discuss, organizing those subjects and defining relationships among them in particular and often strategic ways.

But syntax is not the only stylistic resource writers use to organize their subject matter and fashion realities. Word choice performs similar work. When a writer uses a word to name a person, place, object, idea, feeling, or action, he or she selects from a range of alternatives. And selecting one alternative over others often entails either highlighting certain attributes of the thing named while concealing others, or arguing (if only implicitly) for a particular definition of, or attitude toward, the thing named. Is the place where you live a "house" or a "home"; the thing that you drive a "car" or an "automobile"; do you "eat" or "dine"? In some cases, a single word or phrase can carry a tremendous load and imply a particular stance on a larger, more complex issue. Is the organism produced by the fertilization of a human ovum a "fetus" or an "unborn baby"? Who is the U.S. military fighting in Iraq—"terrorists," "insurgents," or "freedom fighters"? Do we call people crossing U.S. borders "illegal aliens" or "undocumented workers"? Terms such as these have become shorthand for entire visions (and versions) of reality.

Words used figuratively can also shape subject matter. When Mathew Quirk calls the Air Guitar World Championships an "orgy of heavy metal camp" (33), the term "orgy" constructs the event as one of unbridled excess, while "camp" suggests bad taste (a different writer might have settled for a "convergence of heavy metal enthusiasts"). Similarly, the mention of "lobsters" by itself might conjure thoughts of fine dining or succulent, butter-soaked morsels, but when David Foster Wallace calls them the "garbagemen of the sea" (254), he casts them in a decidedly different light.

Matters get especially tricky when literal and figurative meanings begin to blur, when someone tries to pass off a figurative expression as a literal one (is the "War on Drugs" really a war, and are "Mathletes" really athletes?), or when figurative expressions compete. Take, for instance, a politician who alters his position on an issue. He might say that he had a "change of heart" or, to minimize the significance of the change, that he has "refined" his views. His opponent will surely say that he "flip-flopped" (maximizing its significance), while a political analyst, who sees all politics as raw maneuvering to secure votes, might describe the change as a "pivot" either to the left, right, or center. The news media calls this "spin"; we call it "prose performance."

The two motives that we covered in this section—to imitate subject matter or create it—imply two different perspectives on language and its relationship to meaning. The first motive privileges meaning over form: style can deliver meaning in a more or less unadorned fashion without the imitative effects ("An attractive woman walked through the crowd"), or it can give that meaning an added boost or presence by imitating meaning in the act of presenting it ("Through the crowd a sinuous long-haired girl snaked"). In either case, style is working in the service of meaning either as a neutral delivery mechanism or as a medium that mirrors its message (see Fahnestock 20–23 on "value-added theories" of style). The second motive reverses this power relationship and grants style the primary role in shaping or even constructing meaning. Pushed to its extreme, this perspective maintains that there is no meaning independent of forms that express it. Our sympathies lie with the second position, but that doesn't mean we have to abandon the style-imitates-subject motive. Instead, we can "refine" our understanding of it. Style can still imitate something, but what it imitates is not reality. Instead, it imitates our conventional understandings of the world, understandings that have already been shaped and constituted through language (Attridge 138).

Motives Focused on the Writer

"Style is the man himself," or so says Georges Buffon, eighteenth-century naturalist and writer (quoted in Kinneavy 362). Implicit in Buffon's adage is a motive of style, one that has fueled writers' aspirations and informed stylistic analyses for years. It suggests that a writer's true or authentic self is somehow expressed by, or (from the standpoint of analysis) recoverable through, the decisions he or she makes at the level of style. For writers, it offers the promise of distinction, a way to set themselves apart from other contenders on the field. For analysts of style, it offers an angle of approach, the possibility of examining a sample of prose and excavating from it the personality or psychology of its writer—what makes him or her tick. As a method of analysis, however, this motive is all but obsolete, owing in large measure to changes in how we understand identity. In its place, analysts interested in relationships between style and writers draw from a different motive of style—what we call *performing a conventional self.* According to this motive, style still conveys information about the writer, but what it delivers is not an authentic or true self. Instead, it presents the writer playing any number of available social roles or showing particular group affiliations. If there is such a thing as a distinctive self expressible through style, it is through a singular combination of the conventional selves the writer performs. (We return to this important topic in chapter 4.)

We have many resources for presenting ourselves to others: the way we dress, the things we do, the way we walk, the things we own, the company we keep. But of all of these, one of the most powerful (and versatile) is language. And it's not just a matter of *what* we say (although commanding various subject matters is important when performing certain roles); it's also a matter of *how* we say it. To put it more directly, many social roles that we encounter or take on—journalist, teacher, pastor, bureaucrat, parent, gourmand, skate punk—come with their own stylistic repertoire, a set of verbal features that give evidence to others that we are performing this role rather than another one.

Consider, for example, the language used in Winegeeks.com, a community Web site where members access articles and resources on, not surprisingly, wine. We can start our analysis with the title of the site. Why "Winegeeks" rather than "Wine Lovers" or "Wine Connoisseurs"? Self-identifying as "geeks," the authors of the site may be acknowledging their medium (that is, people who use the Web, even wine connoisseurs, must be geeks). Or maybe they are using self-irony to muffle the snobbishness normally associated with the epicurean wine lover. This approach could make the site seem less intimidating to users uninitiated into the mysteries of wine appreciation. If that is the aim, however, the style of the site undercuts it, as we can see in reviews posted by members of Winegeeks, which suggest another reason why they identify as geeks: they display an unabashed and obsessive concern with the object of their delight (in the same way that computer geeks, car geeks, game geeks, and geeks of all kinds seem to relate only to other geeks who share their passion and to the objects of their passion).

In the following passages from four short reviews written by four different wine geeks, pay attention to the stylistic similarities and consider how each writer draws from roughly the same repertoire of language to perform the role of wine connoisseur:

> This white from the Savoie region of France, and particularly the village of Abymes, features a crisp, fresh acidity with notes of peach, strawberry and lime. A touch of chalk and river stones soften the acidity, and the wine ends with a mid-finish. . . . Some will say to pair this with Thai, and I agree, but I think this is a perfect pairing with mac 'n' cheese! (http://winegeeks.com/wines/2309)

> A very fruit forward, soft, and exquisite wine. The grapes used to make this beautiful ruby colored wine, which smells of raspberries and blackberries, are gathered by hand. It is a truly well balanced wine, fruity and smooth, with just the right amount of tannins and a long finish in the mouth. . . . This wine [is] a perfect companion to poultry and white meats. (http://winegeeks.com/wines/2304)

> The nose is perfumed and deep, with hints of lavender, black fruits and espresso roast. The palate is big, broad and expansive, with ripe black fruits,

a little rich topsoil nuance and a blend of spices that range from roasted herb to a little tobacco and tea leaf. Very well balanced, yet big enough to take on all comers. (http://winegeeks.com/wines/2298)

The nose is just about as perfumed as it gets, with lovely rose petals, lilac and lavender. Add to this a mix of fresh red fruits, licorice and a fr[e]sh pine note and you have a soft and easy-going aroma that I could smell for days. The palate is very fresh and minty, with gobs of fresh black raspberries and cherries. So silky and elegant that it is almost Burgundian in feel, but not without chewy tannins and tingly acidity. Long and lush. Cellaring will reward you, but I know that I would have a hard time waiting. (http://winegeeks.com/wines/1093)

Look at the overall structure of the reviews. Each writer organizes his or her post into three parts: first, a general statement that either identifies the wine's place of origin or makes a broad claim about the wine's overall quality; second, a description of the wine that also tries to recreate the experience of drinking it (note how the descriptions tend to move from the wine's smell or "nose," to its taste or "palate," then to its "finish"); finally, advice on how to store, use, or "pair" the wine with foods. That all four writers adopt the same organization suggests that this structure and the three moves it contains are part of the performative repertoire of writing reviews for this site.

But beyond mastering this three-part organizational scheme, the wine geek must also command several vocabularies:

- Technical terms describing the wine's chemistry: "tannins" and "acidity."
- Terms for regions where grapes are cultivated and the wines produced: Savoie, Abymes, and Burgundy.
- Adjectives that evaluate the wine ("exquisite," "well balanced," "lovely") or try to capture its characteristics ("smooth," "crisp," "fresh," "soft").

Perhaps most interesting are the metaphors and nouns the writers use to create an aroma and flavor profile for each wine. Several of these metaphors appear in more than one review; they thus seem to work as an extension of the technical vocabulary mentioned above: a wine can sound "notes" and has a "nose," "palate," and "finish." The fourth review merges the metaphors with the technical vocabulary to form expressions such as "chewy tannins" and "tingly acidity." As for the nouns, they name items from natural settings to which flavors are compared. Fruits are a favorite (particularly varieties of berries) as are herbs and other forms of vegetation: peach, lime, raspberries, blackberries, licorice, pine, tobacco, and tea leaf. And let's not forget the chalky river stones and rich topsoil (if you're licking rocks and eating dirt, maybe it's time to put down the bottle!).

Throughout all four reviews, wine offers the writers a vehicle for performing a self. Ostensibly, the wine is the centerpiece, and many of the stylistic choices bear this out. The anatomical metaphors we mentioned earlier (nose and palate) displace the connoisseur's sensory apparatus (his or her capacity to smell and taste) onto the wine: it's the wine, and not the taster, that has a "nose" and "palate." Similarly, with the catalogues of fruits, herbs, rocks, trees, and so on, the wines seem to absorb everything that surrounds them. But this is very much a prose of self-display. An interest in wine and gourmet food—as opposed to, say, beer and fried corn snacks, or yogurt and granola—communicates information about the writers, as does each writer's familiarity with the conventions of a wine review (its organization and style). Beyond making these credentials evident, however, the writers seem eager to display the sensitivity and refinement of their own tastes. The more smells and flavors each writer can discern (and the more unusual, rare, or esoteric they are) the better, for they all serve as clues to the readers, inviting them to infer from each review the highly cultivated sensibility that penned it.

The passages from Winegeeks.com are relatively pure samples of a style performing a self. That is, their writers largely stick to playing one role, although there is the occasional modulation into other roles—for instance, the reviewer who recommends pairing a white wine with "mac 'n' cheese" may be trying to convey that he is a regular guy after all. More usually, the selves that we perform in writing, like the selves that we perform in everyday life, are more fluid. We move out of one role into another and then back again, or we play several simultaneously. What usually dictates such movements is the writer's desire either to accommodate a given situation or to nudge it into a new direction.

Motives Focused on Readers

As the wine reviews we just examined suggest, taking on a particular social role is often indistinguishable from interacting with readers. Writers playing the role of wine connoisseur implicitly call upon their readers to share their appreciation for wine and to witness the reviewer's discerning tastes. To put it more generally, when writers use style to assume various social roles, they invariably assign roles to their readers. They invite them to *participate* in the performance. We can divide the focus on readers into three more specific varieties:

- To engage readers' emotions.
- To enlist readers as collaborators with the text.
- To establish footing between writer and readers.

We return to these motives again and again (especially in chapters 4 and 8), so for now, we only briefly introduce them.

Recognizing a link between style and the emotions is as old as the study of style itself. In ancient Greece and Rome, rhetoricians saw verbal forms as triggers to the emotions, and they went to great lengths to identify which form triggered which emotion. Here's how the process was supposed to work: a speaker who wanted to stir some emotion in his audience would pick the form that best expressed it; the audience, caught up in the speaker's display of passion, would begin to feel it on their own—they would, in other words, "vibrate in sympathy with him" (Vickers 295). Using short choppy sentences, for instance, might convey a sense of panic: "I tried to feel my heart. I could not feel my heart. It stopped beating" (Jerome 5). Repeating a word again and again could communicate grief or anguish: "Reputation, reputation, reputation! O, I have lost my reputation! I have lost the immortal part of myself, and what remains is bestial. My reputation, Iago, my reputation!" (Shakespeare, *Othello* II.iii.281–84). Understatement might suggest a sense of calm or bravado especially when circumstances seem to demand a different response: "It's just a flesh wound," says the Black Knight in *Monty Python and the Holy Grail* after having his limbs hacked off. But it's important to remember that, in spite of rhetoricians' best efforts, there are no absolute or guaranteed links between a given form and a given feeling. Short choppy sentences might also communicate a steadfast determination: "I marched up to his door. I knocked twice. I demanded my money back." The key is context. A given form may be conventionally associated with a particular emotion but it need not always be (Fahnestock 21).

Writers also use style to enlist their readers in collaborative relationships. It's as if style can induce a kind of rhetorical hypnosis and carry readers along before they realize where they are going. Have you ever laughed at a joke and then thought, "I can't believe I laughed at that" because it was either excessively silly or offensive? What probably happened was that you became complicit in the joke's form: that is, in order to appreciate (or at least, understand) the joke, you let down your guard and let the joke's own internal logic—its verbal puzzles, word play, ambiguities—carry you forward to its desired end—an outburst of laughter. Other, nonhumorous verbal devices can encourage similar outcomes. As Kenneth Burke, a twentieth-century rhetorician and literary critic, observed, "Once you grasp the trend of the form, it invites participation regardless of the subject matter" (*Rhetoric* 58). To illustrate his point, Burke quotes and then interprets a relatively famous statement made during the "Berlin crisis" of 1948:

> "Who controls Berlin, controls Germany; who controls Germany, controls Europe; who controls Europe, controls the world." As a proposition, [this statement] may or may not be true. And even if it is true, unless people are thoroughly imperialistic, they may not want to control the world. But regardless of these doubts about it as a proposition, by the time you arrive at the second of its three stages, you feel how it is destined to develop—and on the level of purely formal assent you would collaborate to round out its symmetry by spontaneously willing its completion and perfection as an utterance. (*Rhetoric* 58–59)

In other words, writers often enlist their readers' participation at the level of form so that they may be better disposed to accept whatever propositions those forms are conveying. This motive of style seems especially at home in political speeches (as in the example above) and in advertising, where the form of some catchy slogan may induce potential consumers to suspend other modes of reasoning and buy the product advertised.

Finally, writers use style to establish various "footings" with their readers. We introduced this term in the previous chapter to describe how writers position themselves with respect to readers, subject matter, and circumstances in general. Here we'll develop that concept more systematically with respect to writer-reader relationships (and in chapter 4, we elaborate even further). We can think of those relationships in two interrelated ways. The first is vertically: does the writer position him or herself as superior, equal, or inferior to his or her readers? The second is horizontally: does the writer maintain a high degree of distance from readers, or does he or she assume a relationship of familiarity? These are not absolute positions but extremes along two intersecting continua that we can represent visually (figure 2, based on Tannen 28).

Using this graph, we can chart relationships between writers and readers for almost any piece of writing. In business communication, for instance, where people's positions in an organization's hierarchy are relatively fixed

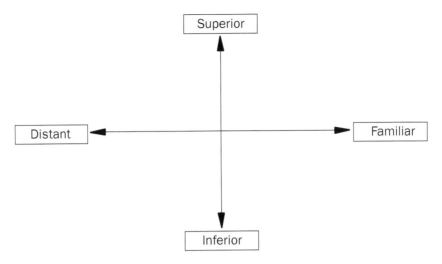

Fig. 2. Writer's Position with Respect to Reader (based on Tannen 28)

and where formality is the norm, we would expect the footing between writer and reader to trend toward the distant end of the horizontal axis, and we would expect it to be variable along the vertical axis depending on who is addressing whom: low for inferiors addressing superiors, and high for superiors addressing inferiors. By contrast, letters, emails, and instant messages exchanged between friends would trend toward the familiar end of the spectrum and hover right on top of the x-axis (that is, neither high nor low, but equal).

Often after reading a sample of prose, we may have a good feel for where it would fall on this graph. But we should be able to confirm these initial impressions by pointing to specific features in the text that confirm or, in some cases, cause us to readjust our initial placement. Reciprocally, as writers aiming for just the right mixture of relative rank and distance, we should have as part of our performative repertoire the stylistic resources to hit the right mark.

In this chapter, we have examined each of the motives individually, but we want to stress that in actual prose performances, they overlap. We can often discuss a single verbal feature in terms of several, if not all, of the motives. For instance, when we examined definite and indefinite articles in the first paragraph of *Sounder*, we focused primarily on the effects in language: how the author uses articles to label information as new or already known. But even with this description, we're already venturing into the territory of subject matter, as we can see by shifting the focus ever so slightly (that is, by looking at how the articles *construct* that information to suggest a version of reality). Or we might shift attention to how the author uses the articles to shape the experience of readers—what they are presumed to know and not know—as they enter the world of the novel. In fact, we couldn't help but hint in this direction in our original discussion of this opening paragraph.

In short, if you want to treat style as a medium of performance, then you need to think about it in terms of all of the motives if only as a preliminary step to analysis and composition. As you add elements to a diverse repertoire of stylistic moves—other points of entry into writing and analysis—you need to keep in mind this complexity: each choice and each change has a rippling effect and brings other elements into play.

Summary of Motives in Chapter 2

Description of Motive	Brief Example
Motives Focused on Language (not an exhaustive list)	
Using indefinite articles to label new information.	A small screen hung over his head.
Using definite articles to label known information.	On the screen a bright jagged line was continually being written.
Using definite and indefinite articles to background and highlight information (or to suggest some other relationship of contrast).	The tall man stood at the edge of the porch. . . . A boy stood nearby shivering . . .
Using prepositional phrases to establish the circumstances under which actions (and the participants involved in them) occur.	Gulls loop above the boardwalk in jazzy little arcs.
Using coordination and subordination to rank clauses in order of importance or prominence.	Although everyone calls it the Big Bang, many books caution us not to think of it as an explosion in the conventional sense.

Using coordination to leave relationships between clauses unspecified (readers must interpret them for themselves).	One hot evening in Padua they carried him up to the roof and he could look out over the top of the town.
Using subordination to specify relationships between clauses (the writer interprets them for readers).	While my father and uncles and grandfather watched the storm, my mother herded my brother and me down the stairs where, in a little room at the bottom, my grandmother and aunts and cousins sat quietly . . .

Motives Focused on Subject Matter	
Imitating subject matter	He watched their flight; bird after bird: a dark flash, a swerve, a flash again, a dart aside, a curve, a flutter of wings.
Organizing or constructing subject matter	I own a fire extinguisher, a first-aid kit, and a shotgun.

Motives Focused on Writers	
Performing a distinctive self	**
Performing a conventional self	This white from the Savoie region of France, and particularly the village of Abymes, features a crisp, fresh acidity with notes of peach, strawberry and lime.

Motives Focused on Readers	
Engaging readers' emotions	Reputation, reputation, reputation! O, I have lost my reputation!

Motives Focused on Readers (*continued*)	
Enlisting readers as collaborators	Who controls Berlin, controls Germany; who controls Germany, controls Europe; who controls Europe, controls the world.
Establishing footing between writer and reader	Addressing a social superior using her title and surname ("Dr. Jones"); addressing a social inferior by first name alone ("Marcy").

Exercises

1. This exercise offers you an opportunity to become an expert on one of the word classes we didn't cover under motives focused on language: nouns, verbs, adjectives, adverbs, pronouns, prepositions, conjunctions, and interjections. From this list, pick one and catalogue its possible functions. Push beyond a general definition of that class: for instance, don't just stop at "a noun names a person, place, or thing." Instead, list its various subclassifications (not just nouns, but concrete nouns, abstract nouns, proper nouns, and so on), and for each of these subclassifications, assign a possible use (or uses). We encourage you to research the word class you choose. You can begin with the "Appendix on Grammar" in this book. A grammar handbook is also a good place to start, as are several online sources. For more in-depth treatments, we recommend:

- Anita K. Barry, *English Grammar: Language as Human Behavior*, 2nd ed. (Upper Saddle River, NJ: Prentice Hall, 2002).
- Martha J. Kolln, *Rhetorical Grammar: Grammatical Choices, Rhetorical Effects*, 5th ed. (New York: Longman, 2007).
- Sidney Greenbaum, *Oxford English Grammar* (Oxford: Oxford University Press, 1996).

After you have compiled your catalogue of functions, write a paragraph on a topic of your choosing in which you try to make strategic use of the word class you researched. Follow that paragraph with another in which you analyze what you wrote. In this self-analysis, be sure to point to specific instances of your chosen word class and explain what effects you were trying to achieve.

2. Pick a relatively well-known social role. It can be a generic one such as politician, hip-hop artist, academic, journalist, gamer, pastor, interior designer, and so on. Or it can be a specific person or character: Rachel Ray, Darth Vader or Yoda from *Star Wars*, Simon Cowell from *American Idol*, etc. Jot down a few notes detailing the behaviors and attitudes that are conventionally associated with that role or person, and then explore (again in your notes) how you can express those behaviors and attitudes through style.

Now write a paragraph as if you were that person (your subject matter should be appropriate to the role you are playing). Follow that with another paragraph in which you analyze your performance. Here refer back to your list of behaviors and attitudes, and be sure to point to specific stylistic choices you made in order to embody that role or persona in writing.

3. Drawing on the motives of style, write a brief comment about two of the quotations in your commonplace book. Be prepared to discuss your examples in class or in a small group. Here are a couple of examples from the sample commonplaces given in the exercise for chapter 1:

> *Quotation*: You will find the flora here as venomous, hooked, barbed, thorny, prickly, needled, saw-toothed, hairy, stickered, mean, bitter, wiry, and fierce as the animals. Something about the desert inclines all living things to harshness and acerbity. The soft evolve out. (Abbey, quoted in Finch and Elder 621)
>
> *Comment (motive focused on language)*: Abbey uses a long list of adjectives that all describe more or less the same attribute of desert things: they are dagger-like and poisonous. The number of adjectives suggests the many ways they are harmful to the human body. And they all hint at the kind of tough people who live in the desert (like Abbey himself): harsh and acerbic.

> *Quotation*: The thought of crossing paths with a thousand-pound grizzly who hasn't eaten or taken a shit for six months, and may have hungry cubs bothering at her side, is enough to convince me that we should change our plans. But I'm reticent to say so, not wanting to appear lacking in courage. (Deming, quoted in Finch and Elder 938)
>
> *Comment (motive focused on the writer)*: Just as she hides her fear from her hiking companions, Deming tries to cover over her worry about grizzlies just out of hibernation with tough colloquial language, expressions like "taken a shit." She tries to embody a kind of feminine machismo. Interestingly, the scary bear of her imagination is also female, an overwrought, hungry, constipated mother with bothersome cubs.

3

Convention and Deviation

Conventions are patterns mutually recognizable to performer and audience, crystallizations of audience expectations in certain rhetorical situations: beginning a musical production with an overture, ending a Catholic mass with a benediction, structuring a pop song by alternating between verse and chorus. In written media, it is conventional to begin a letter with the greeting "Dear Somebody," for example. Other conventions include the kind of guidelines given in any editorial style guide: whether to place a comma before *and* in a series, whether to use single or double quotation marks, whether to capitalize all words or only the first word in titles, and so on. These conventions amount to rules but vary from style to style (American to British, or MLA to APA, for example). They also change over time, sometimes from year to year.

Even more variable are the conventions of rhetorical style, which many authors seem to ignore altogether. Such conventions include the use of the passive voice in scientific writing, the use of overview paragraphs at the beginning of news stories, and the use of "once upon a time" to signal the beginning of a fairy tale.

Stylistic conventions help writers manage their relationships with readers, placing them in a comfortable frame of mind by meeting previously established expectations. But in many genres of writing, such as the personal essay, readers expect not only to be comforted but also to be surprised occasionally by what the author says and the way it is said. Surprise involves violating, transgressing, or suspending other expectations. As we will see in chapter 6, figures of speech often violate the conventional meaning of a word's denotative, dictionary definition. Love is not a rose, after all, despite what poets and country singers say. To take another example, some authors of historical narratives create a sense of drama, a you-are-there intensity, by slipping into the present tense even though convention requires the use of past tense. Autobiographers usually narrate in the first person, but a few famous examples, such as *The Education of Henry Adams*, use third-person "he, she, or they" instead of the conventional "I" to create an odd sense of pseudo-objectivity. The Mexican writer Carlos Fuentes narrates his novella *Aura* in the second person "you" to create a creepy feeling of personal investment for the reader. The word linguists use for such stylistic adventures is "deviation." For some, deviation from a linguistic norm is the definition of style itself, at least in the literary or rhetorical sense.

This chapter invites you to think about style as the interplay of convention and deviation. How you follow convention and deviate from it in prose performances will largely determine the tone of your work—the attitude you display toward the audiences and subject matter of your work.

Convention

A good place to start is with the concept of rigidity (see Kostelnick and Hassett). Rigid conventions often masquerade as rules, especially among novice writers and their teachers: never start a sentence with *and*, never end a sentence with a preposition, never use the first person in formal writing. These conventions are often taken as matters of grammar, not style. But in fact they are regularly violated by the best writers and speakers of English. Why do they persist? The short answer is that they serve the needs of some community of writers and readers. Teachers may find it useful to reserve the use of *and* as a compounding conjunction to be used between independent clauses. By prohibiting students from using it as a sentence opener, they keep the word separate from another class of words—conjunctive adverbs like *however, moreover,* and *thus*. By prohibiting students from ending on a preposition, they teach the formal use of relative pronouns, especially the troublesome *who* and *whom*: Instead of "He is the man I spoke of," you have to say, "He is the man of whom I spoke." By prohibiting first person, the teacher forces students into the variations of formal academic writing, notably the use of impersonal pronouns such as *one* and the passive voice. If the goal is to move students from a set of colloquial conventions of speech to a set of formal conventions of writing, these "rules" can work nicely.

Often teachers are unaware of these goals, and they themselves come to think of the conventions as unbreakable rules. They are simply passing on what they were taught. Conventions generally work this way. They are reinforced by habitual usage and often serve to mark social boundaries. Students who know and use the conventions of "Standard Edited English" get marked as "educated" or "advanced" by their teachers. Students who have not formed these habits get marked as "at risk" or somehow deficient. Linguists have worked for decades to get teachers to see deviation from these norms as indications of difference instead of deficiency. Students may be bringing dialectical or second-language patterns into English class that have a perfectly good logic of their own, but a logic different from that of Standard Edited English. Moreover, some scholars argue that the stylistic and rhetorical differences these students bring to academic writing may in fact invigorate their prose and lead to productive innovation (see Balester, for example).

Outside of English class, conventions also arise from habitual use and serve to create and maintain social boundaries and distinctions. The use of "sir" and "ma'am" as a form of address in the south is an interesting case, made even more interesting in places like Texas because of the large number of Spanish speakers. Southerners of the old school were taught to address their elders as "sir" and "ma'am" (a contraction of "madam"). This formality has disappeared in many places, but gets reinforced in Texas, perhaps because of the Spanish influence. "Sir" (or "señor") gets used primarily as a deferential form. We say "sir" not only to elders but to strangers and to bosses and customers as a sign of respect. If a middle-aged man buys a shirt at the local department store and a young clerk waits on him, it is conventional for the clerk to say, "Thank you, sir" at the end of the transaction. This usage says, in effect, "I am in your service and I am showing you respect as my elder." If the older man responds, "Thank YOU, sir," he confuses the relationships of age and service. Such a deviant response may communicate dissatisfaction with what he considers to be antidemocratic conventions involving age and service. Maybe he wants everybody to be equal, so he insists that if the clerk calls him sir, he's going to return the same honor. The young interlocutor may understand this message, or he may think the old fellow just made a mistake. Maybe he's a foreigner, the clerk might think, from Japan or New Jersey.

The problem of sexist and racist language is an obvious case of convention clashing with changing social norms. Until recently, the use of the masculine pronoun was considered conventional when the gender of the antecedent was unclear, as in the sentence "Every student should bring his book." As the problem of inequality between men and women became a political issue in the ongoing process of democracy, people began to question the convention and said, "Every student should bring his or her book." Now the so-called indefinite masculine is banned in most editorial styles, such as MLA. What name to give social groups also comes under scrutiny. Do you say Negro, black, or African American? Mexican, Mexican American, Hispanic, or Latino/a? Homosexual, gay, or queer? Most of these terms are embattled as the process of democratic inclusion continues in the public performance of language.

In these cases, conventions that had been invisible, seemingly part of the fabric of language, are revealed as conventions that can be opened to variation. Like the social activist, the inventive stylist creates subtle shifts in the audience's habitual sense of conventional language to put forward a special agenda. The stylistic innovator wants to open the audience's awareness to new linguistic possibilities that in turn suggest new ways of seeing the world or new perspectives of thought.

Conventions of Readability

Textbooks on style have their own conventions of advising students on how to improve their prose. The standard is usually called "readability."

When critics and editors say a writer's prose is "readable" (or "clear" or "lucid" or "user-friendly"), they can mean many different things. Back in the 1960s and 1970s, analysts tried to develop readability formulas such as the Flesch Readability Index, which is still used to determine grade-level readability in school textbooks and in some journalism. The formulas tend to be based on such easily countable (and programmable) features as sentence length and word length. These random measures rarely satisfy experts in stylistic analysis.

If you look through the best books on stylistic clarity, such as those by Richard Lanham and Joseph Williams, a few general and more variable characteristics of readable prose emerge:

- It is active.
- It flows.
- It organizes for emphasis.
- It uses familiar language.
- It is concise.

Let's consider these features one at a time on the way to both acknowledging their usefulness and questioning their status as rigid rather than flexible conventions of prose performance.

It Is Active

Active prose involves three things: it is in the active voice, it puts human beings in the subject position whenever possible, and it uses a high percentage of action verbs.

Active Voice. English sentences have two voices: active and passive. Active voice says, "I will take out the trash." Passive says, "The trash will be taken out." Active voice: "You should now enter the data." Passive: "The data should now be entered."

In active voice, the subject position is filled with the person or thing actually performing the action, the active agent: "Bob recorded the information." In passive voice, the subject position is taken by what would be an object in active voice: "The information was recorded by Bob." The active agent may even drop entirely out of the sentence: "The information was recorded."

Though passive voice is perfectly grammatical and at times very useful, research has shown that it sometimes requires readers to perform an extra step in comprehending the information. In one study, researchers watched while small business owners tried to make sense of federal tax instructions. They were told to talk aloud while they worked through the instructions. Time and again, when they came upon a sentence like "The information should now be recorded," they would say something like "OK, now I'm supposed to record the information," or "Am I supposed to do the recording myself?" The researchers concluded that a step would be saved if the instructions used the active voice ("Now you should record the information") or simply the imperative ("Now record the information") (Flower, Hayes, and Swarts, 51–68).

The passive voice is preferred in some styles, notably in scientific prose. The presence of too many active agents can be distracting in this kind of writing. If, in a lab report, you were to write, "The assistant recorded the data," the emphasis would be all wrong. It doesn't matter who records the data. The data and the act of recording are the important things. So the passive is preferred: "The data were recorded." Scientific prose is "objective" in the sense that objects are emphasized over human subjects.

Human subjects. The downside of this "objective style" is that passive voice obscures who is doing what. Even in scientific writing, the habit of writing passive sentences can create confusion. In our example below, notice how hard it is to distinguish between findings reported in the literature and the authors' own findings, even with the parenthetical references to the names of researchers:

The existence of a singularity phenomenon (SP) has been verified many times (Smith, 1984; Jones, 1988). But the exact nature of the event remains unclear. The possibility that it actually comprises two or three distinct phenomena was raised by research using electron-optical methods (Jones, 1989; Rama, 1990). With the introduction of laser-based methodology (Rama et al., 1992), the hypothesis can be reconsidered.

Our revision uses more active voice and connects agents to the actions they perform, clarifying who is responsible for each action:

> The research of Smith (1984) and Jones (1988) verified the existence of a singularity phenomenon (SP) but did not go very far in specifying its exact nature. Later researchers used electron-optical methods to show that the events observed in the first experiments may actually comprise two or three distinct phenomena (Jones, 1989; Rama, 1992). Using the laser-based methodology introduced by Rama et al. (1992), we were able to establish that the SP is in fact a single, though complex, phenomenon.

Sorting out who does what in this manner can even prevent confusion and keep the reader moving through the material.

Action verbs. Think about your experience in reading stories. Narrative moves you forward, but description may slow you down. Description favors the use of "to be" verbs (*am, are, is, was, were,* and so forth). Writers who use "to be" too often create a descriptive prose that favors nouns over verbs. "The committee's first task," you might write, "involved the determination of the proper orientation of the buildings." Notice how nouns like "determination" and "orientation" are formed from simpler action verbs, "determine" and "orient." Such words are called "nominalizations." Some writing guides call them "shun words" because of the "-tion" ending and because they should be shunned whenever possible. To revise a sentence like this one, turn the nominalizations back into verbs and find a grammatical subject for each: "The committee first determined how the buildings should be oriented," or "The committee first determined how they should orient the buildings."

It Flows

To create prose that flows, you need to write sentences that fit together in a cohesive structure. Cohesion results from overlapping old and new information in each sentence, paragraph, and section of a document (see J. Williams, chapter 3; also Kolln, chapter 1).

Remember that a sentence is composed of a subject and a predicate. The subject presents a topic, and the predicate (the part with the verb) makes a comment about the topic. In cohesive prose the topic relates to information that has already been presented, whereas the comment carries the writing forward to new information. Three possible patterns will develop:

- An overlapping, woven pattern with each subject taking up the information presented in the previous predicate.
- A pattern in which a single topic is repeated as the subject in consecutive sentences.
- A pattern that blends the first two.

If we represent each bit of information as a letter in the alphabet (A, B, C, D . . .), then the patterns will look something like this:

- A—B. B—C. C—D.
- A—B. A—C. A—D.
- A—B. B—C. B—D.

Consider a set of simple sentences that fail to follow any of these patterns. Because each subject introduces new information, the paragraph does not flow:

The sales team (A) left the St. Louis meeting with many new ideas for promoting the project (B). Wilcox (C) liked the direct mail approach (D). Customers (E) can be located by mailing lists purchased from professional organizations (F). Then we (G) can send them a brochure on the product (H).

Here's a revision that improves cohesion by creating a flow of overlapping information:

The sales team (A) left the St. Louis meeting with many new ideas for promoting our product (B). Our favorite (B) was the direct mail approach (C). Direct mailing (C) is best for companies like ours that have a good idea of who will buy the product (D). Additional customers (D) can be located by mailing lists purchased from professional organizations (E). These lists (E) will boost the number of people who receive a product brochure (F).

There is a drawback to this woven pattern: because the subject (although carried over from the previous predicate) changes with each sentence, the result can seem a bit scattered. To give their prose a tighter focus, writers will often use the second pattern listed above and repeat a single subject across consecutive sentences (J. Williams 85). Here David Quammen largely adheres to this pattern while explaining how wild dogs were first domesticated by humans:

> Wild dogs (A) were welcomed as scavengers, it seems, to the fringes of those nomad camps (B). The dogs (A) cleaned up what would otherwise stink and draw flies (C). When a camp was moved they (A) tagged along as walking garbage Disposalls (D). [They (A) were] [t]olerated at a distance (E). Eventually they (A) became familiar and permanent (F). (*Flight* 65)

Even more common is a blending of the two patterns, writers using the first to switch focus from one topic to another, and the second to keep it centered on a single one:

> Let's say you've (A) created a network television series for the 2006–2007 season (B). It's (B) beautifully calibrated to appeal to the only viewers of any value to advertisers: young people (C). It's (B) about a family of migrant lifeguards (D). They (D) travel beaches all over the world in revealing swimwear, saving lives and drinking popular beverages (E). They (D) have a soon to be famous catchphrase, which they use in the face of any adversity: "You can't stop progress" (F). (Hauck A15)

For a variation within any of these patterns, you can put the old information in an introductory phrase or clause instead of in the subject itself, as Munro does in a passage we considered earlier:

> A small screen (A) hung over his head (B). On the screen (A) a bright jagged line (C) was continually being written (D). (Munro 307)

The important thing is to begin with the old and lead toward the new.

The same is true for transitions between paragraphs, sections, chapters, and even whole documents. For example, a literature review at the beginning of an essay shows how previous research flows into the information presented in the current article.

It Organizes for Emphasis

Readability improves when you put the most general and most important information in positions of emphasis, where hurried readers will look first, such as the beginning and end of organizational units. Positions of emphasis include the following:

- The title
- The abstract or summary at the beginning and list of conclusions at the end of a document (if available)

- Any list or item set off from the rest of the text
- Headings, figure and table lists, and captions (if available)
- The first and last page of every section or chapter (in a long work)
- The first and (less frequently) the last sentence in each paragraph

The positioning in paragraphs is particularly important because all prose has paragraphs even if the other items are missing. The first sentence of each paragraph should answer the question, "What is the point of this paragraph?" (Williams 97).

This *point sentence*, often called a topic sentence, gets the most attention from busy readers, many of whom read the first sentence of a paragraph before they decide to read the rest. They are like newspaper readers, who start with the headline, then read the first sentence, and finally, if their interest holds, the whole article. Journalists caught on to this reading trend years ago and began to use the well-known "pyramid structure" in organizing news articles.

One exception to the "rule of firsts" is in the sentence itself. The most important information (the news) tends to come last in the sentence (as discussed in our treatment of flow).

It Uses Familiar Language

George Orwell once said never to use a fancy term where an ordinary word will do. The idea is to create an open style, accessible to the greatest number of readers. Even readers with a large vocabulary appreciate the simplest possible language in a style that reserves unfamiliar language for special nuances of meaning. In other words, nobody—or perhaps only the smallest percentage of your readers (such as your high school English teacher)—wants to be impressed by your command of the language; rather, they want to know what you have to say. According to the conventions of readability, your style should seem effortless to read. It should not require the reader to stop and puzzle over the meaning of a word, or even to stop too long to admire your usage.

One of the most common kinds of language that hampers readability is technical jargon. Certainly it's fine to use the technical terminology of a specialized research field to show your identity with that field. Economists, education specialists, literary critics, and physicists all have their own technical jargon. As a kind of shorthand, jargon terms are useful. They save space and time. Biologists pack more than a hundred years of evolutionary theory into the term "natural selection." Computer engineers have co-opted the term "interface" from biology to describe the combined techniques and technologies that users employ to make a computer work. Literary critics who use a term like "mimesis" allude to Aristotle and the long tradition of poetical theory rooted in classical Greece. But jargon has a self-limiting effect on your audience. Knowledgeable members of your in-group will find jargon-filled prose fluent, but others will find it an obstruction to their reading comprehension. Even people who are highly educated in another field have difficulty because they do not often use the term or use it in a different way. The key is to be aware of the possible effects of jargon on your audience, then select, define, and explain words accordingly. Also consider keeping the density of specialized language low, even in specialized discourse.

Using unexplained technical jargon outside the field in which people understand it shows disrespect for your audience. The tone you project suggests pomposity and arrogance. Worse yet is the use of merely inflated language—obscure or rarely used words. Why say "rubbish receptacle" when you mean "trash can"? Examples of pompous words substituted for simple ones include *endeavor* rather than *try*, *utilize* rather than *use*, *termination* rather than *end*, and *subsequent to* rather than *after*.

It Is Concise

The term *wordiness* can mean many things. It does not refer simply to long passages or ones with a lot of words. Sometimes you need a lot of words. The point is to make your prose economical, getting the most out of every word and phrase, never using more words than what you need to get the message across with the right tone.

Wordiness, then, refers to unnecessary words, or unnecessarily big and pompous words, or sentences that drag on pointlessly. Here are a few guidelines for reducing wordiness (based on Rawlins' treatment of economic style in *The Writer's Way*; see also Williams, *Style* 116–33).

- Cut out pretentious language. You can usually do without impressive-sounding, pseudo-academic phrases such as *fundamentally, it is important to note that . . . , the fact is that . . . ,* or *it is a commonly held assumption that. . . .*
- Reduce redundancy. Planned repetition may be highly effective in oral presentations, but it is quickly overdone in writing. Also avoid redundant pairs of words (*basic and fundamental, question and problems, hopes and desires*), redundant modifiers (*true facts, final outcome*), and redundant categories (*period of time, red in color, slimy to the touch*).

- Look for the news in every phrase, sentence, and paragraph. In a sentence such as "The project is profitable and scientifically valid," the only important words may be "profitable" and "scientifically valid." Can you work those into another sentence?
- Reduce transitional words and phrases. As long your paragraphs are well structured (moving from old to new information in a woven pattern), you can often eliminate such expressions as *moreover, furthermore, thus,* and *therefore.*

Deviation (Using an Arbitrary Norm)

Under normal conditions, the conventions of readability will serve your needs as a working writer. Even so, you should not think of these guidelines as a sure-fire formula for effective performance. A study of the best writers will show that, while they follow these guidelines a high percentage of the time, they deviate in ways that make their work unique and rhetorically engaging. They follow clear principles. The writers themselves may not be able to articulate these principles, but an observant prose analyst or stylist can usually derive good reasons for deviations. The advantage of analyzing prose to discover principles for stylistic variation is that, when you come to write yourself, you don't have to treat every decision as a new one. You can begin to theorize a number of possible moves in any given sentence based on your experience as an analyst of other people's writing.

Assuming that rhetorical style involves deviation from a norm, our first problem as prose analysts is defining the norm. One approach is to designate an arbitrary norm. Let's say, for example, that the norm follows the guidelines for readability we have developed in this chapter: the language should be active, fluent, organized for emphasis, familiar, and concise. We might also add that normal diction is constituted by the first definition of a given word in a standard dictionary. We'll notice some problems with these guidelines immediately in that even so simple a norm becomes something of a moving target. As we move from region to region, what is considered denotative and familiar will shift, for example; the same is true for historical shifts. But in general, we can use this norm to begin to pick out and discuss possible deviations.

Consider the following sample from Edward Abbey's 1971 essay "Canyonlands and Compromises":

> Like the network of new highways proposed for the canyon country, these power plants are meant not for current needs but for "anticipated" needs.

"Planning for growth," it's called. The fact that planning for growth encourages growth, even forces growth, would not be seen as a serious objection by the majority of Utah-Arizona businessmen and government planners. They believe in growth. Why? Ask any cancer cell why it believes in growth. (393)

A few of the deviations that might make the hurried reader pause and mull over the language, or at least register it subliminally, include the following:

1. The phrase "network of new highways," a metaphor. Unlike a metaphor such as "web of new highways," which connotes something natural, "network" suggests an elaborate technological system.

2. The predicate "are meant not for current needs but for 'anticipated needs,'" the syntax of which involves passive voice, inversion of positive and negative complements, and use of quotation marks. Passive voice allows the writer to put "roads" in the subject position for emphasis and provides cohesion with the previous sentence; the inversion puts "anticipated needs" at the end of the sentence so that it can be explained further in the next sentence. So both of these seeming deviations ultimately serve the goals of readability—*flow*, to be precise. The quotation marks around material not clearly taken from another source serve to distance the author from the quoted phrase, creating irony.

3. The sentence "'Planning for growth,' it's called," the syntax of which involves an inversion of the verb and complement, as well as quotation, contraction, and the substitution of the expletive "it" for a human agent in subject position. Putting the complement first makes the transition to the previous sentence; the quotation sets up the troublesome phrase to be interpreted later in the passage; the contraction creates an informality typical of the author's persona (the informal, natural man); the omission of the agent keeps the focus on the idea of "growth," which is being criticized. It also suggests (and this is an interpretive stretch) that anyone who uses the phrase is inhuman in one sense or another.

4. The phrase "cancer cell," a metaphor that identifies economic growth with the spread of cancer cells. The author urges the reader toward a new perspective by associating something usually considered positive (economic growth) with something considered bad to the point of being terrifying and life-threatening (cancer).

Thus we can use deviations from arbitrary norms—Abbey's use of irony, metaphor, and other variations—to bring stylistic characteristics to the foreground for analysis. In the following chapters, we will continue to develop a vocabulary for discussing such deviations. But even without the specialized vocabulary, you should be able to pick out deviations from the norm of readability conventions, such as Abbey's "cancer cell" metaphor and his backwards sentence, "'Planning for growing,' it's called."

Deviation (Using a Community Norm)

The problem with using arbitrary norms is that the method doesn't account for historical and cultural differences. Using the terms developed in chapter 1, we can say that with this kind of analysis, we remain within the textual arena and do not advance to the social and cultural arenas of performance. An approach more sensitive to shifts in the arena of performance involves analyzing deviations by beginning with a community norm, a style that is characteristic of a particular group of writers and readers. You can then point out deviations within the work of a subgroup or individual writer.

In the scientific community, for example, it is conventional to write impersonally, avoiding first-person references and obscuring human subjects by the use of indirect and passive sentences; nouns and strings of noun modifiers predominate over variety in the use of action verbs, adjectives, and adverbs; conciseness is greatly valued, aided by the use of technical terminology, which constitutes a kind of insider shorthand. But conciseness yields to the value of precision, so that repetition of key words and phrases is preferred if there is any chance of ambiguity; hedging and qualification are common manifestations of caution in interpreting data. Here's a typical sample from the field of environmental toxicology:

> Nonpoint source pollution can be defined as the diffuse input of pollutants that occurs in addition to inputs from undeveloped land of similar genesis. ... Agricultural nonpoint sources of pollution significantly altered water quality in 68% of the drainage basins in the United States, and in nearly 90% of the drainage basins in the north central region of the United States. ... Agricultural sources are probably the major contributors of suspended and dissolved solids, nitrogen, phosphorus and associated biochemical oxygen demand loadings in U.S. waters. (quoted in Killingsworth and Palmer 119)

Consider a slight deviation from this style, a sample from the famous 1953 paper in the journal *Nature* by James Watson and Francis Crick announcing the double-helix structure of DNA—a contribution for which they won the Nobel Prize:

> We wish to suggest a structure for the salt of deoxyribose nucleic acid (D.N.A.). This structure has novel features which are of considerable biological interest.

A structure for nucleic acid has already been proposed by Pauling and Corey1. They kindly made their manuscript available to us in advance of publication. Their model consists of three intertwined chains, with the phosphates near the fibre axis, and the bases on the outside. In our opinion, this structure is unsatisfactory for two reasons:

(1) We believe that the material which gives the X-ray diagrams is the salt, not the free acid. Without the acidic hydrogen atoms it is not clear what forces would hold the structure together, especially as the negatively charged phosphates near the axis will repel each other. (2) Some of the van der Waals distances appear to be too small.

Another three-chain structure has also been suggested by Fraser (in the press). In his model the phosphates are on the outside and the bases on the inside, linked together by hydrogen bonds. This structure as described is rather ill-defined, and for this reason we shall not comment on it.

We wish to put forward a radically different structure for the salt of deoxyribose nucleic acid. This structure has two helical chains each coiled round the same axis (see diagram). We have made the usual chemical assumptions, namely, that each chain consists of phosphate diester groups joining ß-D-deoxyribofuranose residues with 3', 5' linkages. The two chains (but not their bases) are related by a dyad perpendicular to the fibre axis. Both chains follow right- handed helices, but owing to the dyad the sequences of the atoms in the two chains run in opposite directions. . . . (Watson and Crick np)

The authors preserve many key features of scientific style, notably the technical terminology and frequent use of the passive voice. But the use of first-person plural "we" works to emphasize the originality of the discovery and to distinguish this work from that of other scientists working on the same problem. The greater frequency of action verbs adds a sense of urgency and excitement to the presentation.

Watson and Crick are unusually gifted stylists who, not surprisingly, often irritated their fellow scientists and have been criticized for egotistically trumpeting their own originality. Both wrote memoirs in later years that capitalized on their fame and showed their ability to appeal to a wider audience. Watson's book *The Double Helix* has become a classic in the genre known as science writing or scientific journalism, nonfictional accounts of scientific research and theory written for a general audience of educated readers.

Below is a paragraph from *The Double Helix* describing one of the many steps in Watson's reasoning that ultimately led to the discovery of the structure of DNA. Watson speaks forthrightly throughout the book of the emotions involved in the search, the ego conflicts, and the competitive drive behind scientific research. In the chapter that includes our sample, he writes thus of the reaction to his views by one of his colleagues: "Rosy by then was hardly able to control her temper, and her voice rose as she told me that the stupidity of my remarks would be obvious if I would stop blubbering and look at her X-ray evidence" (105). Need we say that in formal scientific writing we rarely hear of human emotions or encounter such diction as "stupidity" and "blubbering." Notice how Watson narrates with gusto, using the first-person singular, placing human beings in subject positions, and favoring active verbs. He calls people by their first names and includes details about his personal experience—the English weather, his means of transportation, his worry over his colleague's acceptance, and so on—that would all be edited out in even the most stylistically deviant scientific report:

> Afterwards, in the cold, almost unheated train compartment, I sketched on the blank edge of my newspaper what I remembered of the B pattern. Then as the train jerked toward Cambridge, I tried to decide between two- and three-chain models. As far as I could tell, the reason the King's group did not like two chains was not foolproof. It depended upon the water content of the DNA samples, a value they admitted might be in great error. Thus by the time I had cycled back to college and climbed over the back gate, I had decided to build two-chain models. Francis would have to agree. Even though he was a physicist, he knew that important biological objects come in pairs. (Watson 108)

In this kind of writing, Watson has not just deviated from the conventions of scientific style; he has decamped entirely, switching genres of discourse. Instead of a scientific report, he is writing a personal memoir. Compared to writers in that genre, his style is not especially deviant. Now he's a storyteller, writing like a novelist or an autobiographer. The audience of novels and memoirs thrives on juicy gossip, strong emotions, and plenty of vivid detail about personal experience.

Genres are discourses that follow a pattern that gets repeated over and over again, a rhetorical situation that keeps coming up, a writer addressing an audience that wants something fairly predictable to occur. A detective novel has a crime that must be solved; a tragedy has a hero who must experience a tragic fall; a how-to book gives steps toward completing a task. These conventional forms, like all conventions, involve audience expectations in matters of style and delivery. People read scientific reports to further their own research; people read scientific memoirs to gain insight into the lives of scientists and a general knowledge of important ideas. Each rhetorical situation fosters an appropriate style. For this reason, even so skilled a scientific writer and essayist as Stephen Jay Gould may seem naïve when he argues the following:

> I deeply deplore the equation of popular writing with pap and distortion for two main reasons. First, such a designation imposes a crushing professional burden on scientists (particularly young scientists without tenure) who might like to try their hand at this expansive style. Second, it denigrates the intelligence of millions of Americans eager for intellectual stimulation without patronization. If we writers assume a crushing mean of mediocrity and incomprehension, then not only do we have contempt for our neighbors, but we also extinguish the light of excellence. The "perceptive and intelligent" layperson is no myth. They exist in millions—a low percentage of Americans perhaps, but a high absolute number with influence beyond their proportion in the population. (12)

In suggesting that popular science writing and professional scientific reports need not be separated so widely as they are in the minds of most scientists, Gould has neglected the social and cultural arenas of stylistic performance. Any discussion of deviation involves locating the text in question within a particular genre and arena of performance and then designating the audience expectations within those limits. Authors use conventional styles to project identity with various social and cultural groups—or they break ranks by deviating from those styles or decamping to another style and genre.

Exercises

1. Rate the effectiveness of the following passage using the five criteria for readable prose: it is active, it flows, it organizes for emphasis, it uses familiar language, and it is concise. Be precise and point to specific words and structures:

> The committee's first task involved the determination of the proper orientation of the buildings. Landscape designs were drawn up by the committee next. There was a disagreement among several members over the placement of trees and shrubs around the perimeter of the parking lot. This nonconformity of opinion was resolved, however, in a short period of time. The topic of zoning laws was the next item of concern on the agenda to which the committee then turned its attention.

Now revise the passage, improving its readability.

2. The movie review is a well-established genre with fairly stable conventions, especially in terms of structure: there's typically a "lead" that captures readers' interests and hints toward the reviewer's overall assessment of the film, followed by a plot summary of the film (without giving the ending away!), and then a more detailed evaluation of the movie's merits. Of course there's room for structural deviation (changing up the order, for instance, or blending the plot summary with the evaluation), but most reviews have these three parts. More variable is the style in which the review is delivered, and those variations often depend on the venue in which the review is published: a review appearing in the *New Yorker*, for instance, will likely differ stylistically from one found in *Rolling Stone* or *Entertainment Weekly*.

Find two short reviews of the same movie (the *Movie Review Query Engine* at http://www.mrqe.com lists reviews from dozens of publications). First, analyze these reviews in terms of the three-part convention we outlined above. Do the reviews contain all three elements? How are they arranged? Do either or both of the writers go outside the box in terms of organization? If so, why? Then using the norm of the dictionary standard and readability guidelines from this chapter, point out how these two reviews differ stylistically. Consider the rhetorical purposes for these differences, and be sure to identify relevant textual features throughout.

3. Write your own movie review. Or if you're not a film buff, pick something else to review (a restaurant, a book, a new computer product). Whatever you pick, begin with the three-part structure we described in exercise 2 and the readability guidelines covered in this chapter as rough maps to the organization and style of your review. Then look for opportunities to deviate in terms of either structure or style. These deviations should be "motivated"—that is, they should serve some purpose. Follow your review with a short analysis in which you describe several key moments where you either adhered to conventions or departed from them.

4. Write a brief comment about convention and deviation in one or two of the quotations in your commonplace book. Be prepared to discuss your examples in class or in a small group. Here are a couple of examples from the chapter 1 exercise:

> *Quotation*: The continent is covered by an ocean of engine noise. (Wendell Berry, quoted in Finch and Elder 724)
> *Comment*: Berry uses a figure of speech that deviates from the dictionary meaning of "ocean." By definition an ocean cannot cover a continent. By

creating this "unnatural" situation and by using a natural image to describe a mechanical problem (engine noise)—comparing the size and the roar of the ocean to noise pollution—he hints ironically at how extensive and contrary to nature the noise is.

Quotation: The smell of Funk Island is the smell of death. It is probably the source of the island's name, which in various languages means "to steam," "to create a great stench," "to smoke"; it may also mean "fear." The island certainly smells ghastly. No battlefield could ever concentrate such a coalition of dead and dying. (Franklin Russell, quoted in Finch and Elder 609) *Comment*: Russell uses etymology and dictionary definitions of "funk" to describe the island, then augments his description with a deviation, a kind of negative comparison: no battlefield was ever this bad.

4

Distinction: From Voice to Footing

How to make your style more readable, how to meet your reader's expectations, how to create a clear and lucid style . . . all such how-to approaches to style fail to account for a certain something that the word *style* usually communicates to those in the know—the sense of *distinction* that style conveys, the way a writer can create an impression of self-in-language. It often goes by the name of "voice," a possibility we consider in this chapter but ultimately set aside in favor of a different metaphor from the field of performance studies. We call the revised notion "stylistic footing."

The main advantage we argue for footing over voice is that it better communicates the idea that style is always a matter of agreement (or disagreement) between an author and audience, two social entities that stand in some relationship to each other. To use terms we introduced in chapter 2, the switch from voice to footing involves a change in motive from one focused on the writer alone (distinctive self) to one that relates writer to reader (writer-reader interaction). The socialization of style implied in the concept of footing also picks up the idea from chapter 3 that conventions and deviations in language create and break the expectations of readers who alternately seek both comfort and surprise from the authors with whom they engage.

Distinction as Voice

Distinction is considered a characteristic of the best writing. It comprises the set of traits or the overall character—the deviations from a norm—by which a writer's work distinguishes that writer from others. The notion is usually applied to literary artists of high regard. We hear of Emily Dickinson's riddling elliptical style; Mark Twain's informal, colloquial style; Ernest Hemingway's telegraphic, understated style; William Faulkner's long and winding sentences. But writers of nonfiction are also praised or blamed for a luxuriant style, a hard-hitting style, a deadpan style, or an engaging style, as if style were an outgrowth of their personal character.

And that kind of distinction from the masses is just what the concept of "voice" captures. As physical voice is literally an expression of an individual body—so distinctive that, like fingerprints or DNA evidence, it can be used to identify the speaker—so style, the concept implies, is an outgrowth of the author's character, a virtual fingerprint on the body of an author's work (his or her "corpus," or body of work). "Finding your voice as a writer" is a topic of great concern in dozens of courses on writing. "You've found your voice!" is a sentence of great praise from composition and creative writing teachers alike.

But what does it mean? Too often it means little more than "I like it!" In other words, such references to voice can be a cop-out on the part of the teacher. Voice is natural ("It can't be taught"). It's something you have to find ("I can't teach it to you"). It is supposed to emerge from your hands as naturally as your spoken voice emerges from your lungs and larynx and tongue. No doubt, most distinctive styles actually do emerge without a teacher's intervention—though hardly so "naturally" as the cry of a voice at a baby's birth—but we would hope that teachers might be able to show a path to achieving distinction rather than merely saying, "Keep practicing, and I'll tell you when you get there."

But there's another possibility. "Voice" in writing sometimes refers to the actual intersection of writing and speaking, between literacy and orality. Now here's a place we can go and make a study. Focusing a student's attention on the difference between habits of speech and habits of writing, or having people read their writing aloud, can have a dramatic effect on style. A student in a class one of us taught a few years ago—call her Vicky—distinguished herself as the class clown, known for her biting wit and smart-aleck humor. The first papers she wrote for class were stilted and awkward academic exercises, as boring to read as they must have been to write. The teacher invited her to his office and asked her why there was such a difference between her dull and convoluted papers and her in-class talk. "Well I can't very well write the way I talk, can I?" she said. Out of either desperation or inspiration, the teacher said, "Try it." Her next paper was about the ways that young women pressure each other into mediocrity with their harsh judgments about appearance and ambition. When she read it to the class, it provoked something just short of awe. No one could believe the transformation in her writing. Now the words somehow embodied her personal style, the sardonic wit, the clipped ironic sentences, the parodies of her enemies, the sympathy for her damaged friends. She had found her voice by listening to herself talk in her head and writing it down.

Vicky discovered that her style improved not only in personal essays but also in technical writing—a transfer we have a hard time explaining. Perhaps it had less to do with "voice" as an expression of character and more to do with learning to "talk out" her papers before she committed herself to sentences on a page. This phenomenon was called "talk-write" in a famous study of English composition by Robert Zoellner. In a 1969 monograph published in *College English*, Zoellner observed that when students wrote awkward prose, he could often get them to improve by asking, "How would you say that?" In these conversations, they would almost invariably blurt out something better than what they had originally put on the page. He started having his students talk to each other about their topics in class and write down key sentences that they spoke. They then took this "protoscribal" material home and worked it up as written prose. Since we've been talking and listening longer than we've been reading and writing, the method makes sense. In this light, Vicky learned not so much to capture her truest character in written prose but rather to listen to her own writing as well as look at it, to capture the fluency of conversation in the black and white of writing.

According to one of the finest authorities on style, Richard Lanham, not all writing is "voiced." In his book *Analyzing Prose*, he confines voiced writing to such works as essays, novels, poems, and personal letters. By contrast, he says, some prose is "voiceless": scientific reports, technical manuals, many business memos, and bureaucratic prose of all forms. Several of Lanham's books are devoted to breathing some voice into these drier, voiceless forms of discourse.

But we must respectfully disagree with his original premise that any writing is voiceless. Bureaucratic writing may be monotone or stiffly inappropriate to most conversation, but it still has a distinctive sound. Think of Mr. Spock on *Star Trek* or any number of intelligent alien beings or robots in science fiction. What their technical, monotone voices communicate is distance and logical frigidity. Their style can seem inhuman certainly but under certain conditions could be considered comforting or calming. "Captain, a crisis ensues from the loss of power. Three alternatives present themselves, of which the first two must be considered inefficacious."

The how-to books on style imply that you can revise for readability with no loss of voice; indeed, by meeting the reader's needs for fluency and speed, you add voice to your writing. But we have our doubts. We have come to think that prose is never absolutely improved by any change. Everything comes at a cost. This outlook can be stated as a general principle, the *law of compensation*, which applies to life in general (see Ralph Waldo Emerson's essay on the topic), but especially to writing: *With every change, something is lost and something is gained.*

Consider William Faulkner's 1950 acceptance speech for the Nobel Prize in literature. Often reprinted and easy to find online, the speech is often quoted as an eloquent manifesto of the spirit of literature in the atomic age, when the continuity of humanity is threatened on a daily basis. The one question that obsesses people living under the nuclear threat is, according to Faulkner, "Will I be blown up?" The speech calls for courage in the face of possible destruction and the need for writers not to forget "the problems of the human heart in conflict." The modern writer, says Faulkner

> must teach himself that the basest of all things is to be afraid . . . , leaving no room in his workshop for anything but the old verities and truths of the heart . . .—love and honor and pity and pride and compassion and sacrifice. Until he does so, he labors under a curse. He writes not of love but of lust, of defeats in which nobody loses anything of value, and victories without hope and worst of all, without pity or compassion. His griefs grieve on no universal bones, leaving no scars. He writes not of the heart but of the glands. (np)

One of our students, following the principles that she had learned in books and courses on revising technical prose—in fact, it was Vicky, the very student who learned to write "in her own voice"—condemned Faulkner's famous speech as pompous and wordy. If we relied exclusively on the conventions of readability given in chapter 3, we could certainly join her in complaining about a number of features in this passage, the use of inactive and indirect sentences, weak cohesion, unfamiliar and inflated diction ("basest," "verities," "doomed," "curse"), redundancy ("verities and truths"), odd syntax and predication ("griefs grieve"), not to mention the sexist use of the pronoun "he" to refer to both male and female antecedents. Here is a revision that might have pleased Vicky:

> These days everybody worries about the atom bomb (or terrorism). Every day they wonder, "Will I be blown up?" This fear distracts our young writers from the problems that matter in life, such as love, honor, pity, and pride. Love gives way to lust. Pity disappears, along with compassion.

Victories come without honor. Pride is empty egotism. Without the values that these universal themes convey, writing can only fail. It will not appeal to the broadest range of humans and will be confined to mere questions of physical survival.

The revision may gain a few degrees of readability, but what have we lost? To get at this question, try reading the two passages aloud. You may hear echoes of the old south in the pace of Faulkner's sentences and in the biblical language ("sacrifice," "lust"). You may also hear elements of poetic language, such as alliteration, particularly the repetition of L sounds, what the linguists call liquids, that add a particular fluidity to this prose, or the H sounds that give a sense of breath moving in rhythm, suggesting urgency. The sounds are lost in the revision, along with Faulkner's voice. It is a voice out of history, and the history is lost too, the old-fashioned style of an old-fashioned man. Is the gain in readability worth the loss?

Notice that in the revision, we have not created "voiceless" bureaucratic prose, but we have changed voices, and in doing so we have transformed the original into a different kind of performance. The new voice sounds more modern, something like a television news commentator or pundit. Such shifts involve a concept related to the concept of voice, namely tone.

Tone is defined in rhetoric and literary criticism as *an author's attitude toward the subject matter and audience of a particular text.* Tone is conveyed by style, as in the choice of words, or diction. Every word has two kinds of meanings—denotation and connotation. The word "doomed" denotes "fated" and particularly "fated not to last." But it also summons up connotations of old prophesies and soothsayers. Connotations have to do with the word's associations in a literary and cultural tradition. To say "writing is doomed" denotes about the same thing as "writing can only fail." But "doomed" conveys something scarier and more certain, something stronger than mere failure, sort of like the difference between "sin" and "misbehavior." It is not the word of a commentator or pundit; it is the word of a prophet.

Just as much as denotations, connotations are part of a word's meaning. They offer a palate of colors to the literary artist. The color of a work, its tone, contributes to its meaning. So changing the style of a text also involves changing its meaning, at least at the level of overtone and nuance.

Sometimes we want a flat, deadpan delivery. In some disciplines, such as the social sciences, such a delivery frees the writer and reader from making the value judgments implied in words like "sin" and "broken family."

To say "unacceptable behavior" and "dysfunctional family" is a way of allowing the writer to look hard at these phenomena without imposing a moral judgment. That can be a good thing.

From Voice to Footing

But like "voice," "tone" has its limitations as an analytical tool. Both concepts suggest the spoken voice, the sound of a passage, more than its written qualities. Worse yet, both seem to render a judgment too quickly, one that glides over the specific features of language that make the style what it is. We might say that an author conveys a flat or sarcastic or serious tone. But saying that doesn't help us understand how he or she created that tone or how we, as writers, may produce similar effects in our own writing.

So let's try something different—*footing*. The term comes from everyday expressions like "getting off on the right foot," "meeting on equal footing," and "putting your best foot forward." Notice one difference right away. The concept of voice focuses on the performer, but footing always puts the performer in relation to something else—or somebody else: the audience. What it suggests is that style never is merely produced and sent abroad into the world; it is delivered, shared, negotiated between an author and an audience.

Footing is a metaphor derived from the physical act of gaining a stable placement of the feet, but when used to describe social interaction, it covers a range of behaviors—from the actual physical stance speakers take with respect to listeners, to the emotions and attitudes they express, to the social roles, languages, and dialects they adopt. Style is important in establishing particular footings and signaling changes from one footing to another—so important that we could devote an entire book to its study. Here, by way of introduction, we treat two kinds of footings: those that orient readers in physical space (also known as point of view), and those that position writer and reader in social space (which include levels of formality, the social roles writers adopt for themselves and assign to readers, and the various social languages they draw upon).

Physical Space

Writers have many resources for establishing physical footings, including definite and indefinite articles, pronouns, verb tense, and demonstrative adjectives and adverbs. Consider these two sentences:

- A car approaches the house.
- The car approaches a house.

Imagine that you are a film director. How would you film each of these sentences? Where would you place the camera? Our intuitions tell us that with the first sentence, the camera should be anchored in or near the house. With the second, it should be in or near the car. We can confirm these intuitions by drawing on concepts we introduced in previous chapters: definite and indefinite articles, and known and new information. There we said that readers expect known information to appear at the beginnings of sentences and new information at their ends. But writers have ways beyond sentence position to mark information as known or new. In these two sentences, that work is done primarily by definite and indefinite articles—the "a's" and "the's" that appear before the nouns. As noted in chapter 2, definite articles ("the") mark information as known, while indefinite articles ("a") mark it as new. As readers, we position ourselves with the former and treat new information as distant in some way—as spatially, emotionally, or intellectually apart and away from ourselves. Thus the first sentence locates readers with "the house" (known) and away from "a car" (new), while the second places them with "the car" away from (although approaching) "a house." Novelists often exploit this feature of language at the beginnings of their novels, using it to establish and adjust their readers' footing with respect to the world they are about to enter. The opening sentence from Cormac McCarthy's novel *All the Pretty Horses*, for example, creates the illusion that readers already share knowledge of the world its protagonist inhabits:

> The candleflame and the image of the candleflame caught in the pierglass twisted and righted when he entered the hall and again when he shut the door. (3)

Candleflame, image, pierglass, and door are all fronted by definite articles and thus presented as information already known to readers even though this sentence is the novel's first. The personal pronoun "he" furthers the illusion, while drawing the reader into the narrative. We typically expect a pronoun's antecedent to appear before the pronoun itself. By beginning with "he" and delaying the revelation of its antecedent, McCarthy accomplishes two goals: first, he sustains the illusion that writer and reader share knowledge of who this "he" is; second, McCarthy creates a little puzzle that propels the narrative forward, placing readers on a footing of expectancy. Readers may be willing to play this little game of "shared worlds" (Traugott and Pratt 281), but they still want to know who that "he" is. And it's this desire that, in part, keeps the reader reading.

Even when a physical footing is established, writers can draw upon the resources of style to create subtle and sometimes sudden shifts in orientation. Consider Mark Twain's "Journalism in Tennessee," a short story told in first person. The narrator (a northerner) relocates to the south and secures a position as associate editor for the *Morning Glory and Johnson County War-Whoop*. During his first day on the job, he's introduced to what Twain satirizes as the violent world of Tennessee journalism, a world where editors from rival papers not only exchange barbed words but also volleys of gunfire. Watching his new editor revise and amend an article he has just produced, the narrator writes,

> I never saw a pen scrape and scratch its way so viciously, or plow through another man's verbs and adjectives so relentlessly. While he was in the midst of his work, somebody shot at him through the open window, and marred the symmetry of my ear.
>
> "Ah," said he, "that is that scoundrel Smith, of the *Moral Volcano*—he was due yesterday." And he snatched a navy revolver from his belt and fired. Smith dropped, shot in the thigh. The shot spoiled Smith's aim, who was just taking a second chance, and he crippled a stranger. It was me. Merely a finger shot off. (31)

Imagine again that you are a movie director asked to create a meticulously faithful adaptation of these events for the screen. What stylistic clues does Twain provide to guide you?

Here's how we might begin. The first-person pronoun tells us to anchor the camera with the narrator—perhaps just over his shoulder so that viewers can watch along as the editor scrapes and scratches. Behind the editor would be a window through which viewers could see a person come into view in the distance. Because Twain uses the indefinite pronoun "somebody" to name that person, we'd have him appear slightly out of focus. This "somebody" would then lift his arm, pointing it at the window, and a puff of smoke would suddenly enshroud his hand followed quickly by the distant sound of a pistol shot. Almost simultaneous with that noise, the narrator would jerk hand to ear in response to the injury he has just suffered. We'd want all of this filmed in a single, continuous camera shot to capture the sudden shift in footings—from the "somebody" out there to the narrator's ear. We'd also want to capture the narrator's understated description of his injury ("marred the symmetry of my ear")—that is, the attitudinal footing he takes toward it—so we'd direct the actor playing him not to cry out in pain or panic, but to look mildly shocked, puzzled, and perhaps slightly annoyed. (Our model here might be the Black Knight from Monty Python's *Holy Grail* who, after having his arm lopped off, says dismissively, "It's just a flesh wound.")

We'll leave directing the remainder of this scene to your imagination. Here's the point: there is a cinematography to language. Writers can create many varied and subtle shifts in physical footing, while analysts track these shifts by attending closely to the stylistic evidence the writer provides. A good place for the analyst to start is answering the question "How would you film this?"

Social Space

Just as style can orient readers in physical space, it can also position them socially. We introduced the idea of social space in chapter 2 under stylistic motives focused on readers. Here we'll develop it a little further. Social footings come in three varieties:

1. The *social standing* between writer and reader, an analogue to physical distance that gauges position along two axes: one ranging from high to low, the other from formal (maximum distance) to familiar (minimum distance).

2. The various *social roles* taken up by writers and assigned to readers: advisor–advisee, expert–novice, urbane wit–country bumpkin, employer–employee, politician–constituent, trickster–dupe, lover–beloved, and so on.

3. The different *social languages, dialects, or registers*—that is, styles of writing or speaking characteristic of particular activities, groups, or professions.

To illustrate these three varieties, consider this letter one of us recently received from Cingular Wireless (the ellipses between paragraphs indicate omitted text):

Dear Christopher Holcomb,

We're holding a Nokia 6102i for you at our store. This is a great camera and video phone with Bluetooth® Wireless Connectivity . . . external color screen . . . Mobile Instant Messaging . . . speakerphone . . . voice dialing . . . and plenty more!

. . .

Here's the best part. This Nokia 6102i is yours for FREE when you activate on a new two-year service agreement. No hassles. No rebates. Nothing but a trip to our store to pick it up!

. . .

That's right. A FREE camera and video phone. A choice of calling plans that include Rollover and FREE Mobile to Mobile calling to 56 million people in your calling community.

What are you waiting for? Come into Cingular to pick up your Nokia 6102i or call toll-free 1-800-449-1679 today!

Sincerely,
Jace Barbin
Vice President
Cingular

The underlying footing here is that of a sales pitch tossed by big business to a potential buyer: Cingular Wireless (big business) has a phone plan it wants to sell to Christopher (potential buyer). What's interesting are the many ways this performance tries to conceal that footing and replace it with alternate ones. The salutation "Dear Christopher Holcomb" resides toward the middle of the formal-familiar spectrum. Jace Barbin (we doubt that he wrote this letter, but for convenience's sake, we'll assume he did) could have pushed it toward greater formality ("Dear Mr. Holcomb" or even "To Whom This May Concern"), or toward greater familiarity ("Hi Chris," or the unlikely "'Sup Dawg!"). For a letter's opening, it's probably best to play it safe and shoot for the middle distance. (It also happens to be easier to program into the form letter from the address file on the computer!)

Other stylistic features, however, move the letter toward a footing of familiarity: the contractions ("we're," "here's," and "that's"), the second person pronoun ("you"), exclamation points, and sentence fragments ("No hassles. No rebates. Nothing but a trip to our store to pick it up!"). Ol' Jace writes to Christopher as a friend, as someone who feels comfortable enough with his reader to use nonstandard, informal modes of address.

This manufactured familiarity paves the way for the social roles in which he casts himself and Christopher. When he writes, "We're holding a Nokia 6102i for you," he assumes the footing of someone doing Christopher a favor, as if he and the good folks at Cingular have been marshalling all of their energies on Christopher's behalf. Other stylistic variants are possible: Jace could have written, "We have a Nokia 6102i for you . . . ," or "There is a Nokia 6102i for you. . . ." By choosing "We're holding . . . ," Jace tries to ensnare Christopher in a relationship in which he is beholden to Cingular (as if Christopher had asked them to hold it for him). If Christopher takes up this footing (as recipient of a favor), then his most immediate and appropriate response is to feel obliged to Jace. But fear not! Christopher can fulfill his obligation with minimal effort: all he has to do is take "a trip to our store to pick it up!"

This letter also draws heavily on the social language of advertising (our third resource for establishing social footings). Clichés from the world of television, radio, and magazine ads abound. There's the list of product features (Bluetooth® Wireless Connectivity, external color screen, Mobile Instant Messaging, speakerphone, voice dialing) with the promise of "plenty more!" The unsubstantiated, hyperbolic claim: "This is a great camera and video phone." The clipped constructions offering absolute assurances: "No hassles. No rebates." And the ever popular, one-question-fits-all advertisements—"What are you waiting for?"—followed by the invitation to "come into . . . [blah, blah, blah] . . . today!" For readers bombarded with ads every day of their lives, these pat phrases and conventional maneuverings may place them on familiar ground. But if the first two kinds of footings try to conceal that this letter is a sales pitch, how do we account for all the advertising clichés? The answer can be summed up in one word: FREE. The word appears three times in the letter always in capital letters (the written equivalent of the shouting hawker at a state fair or a flashing neon sign), while the price of the activation fee and service agreement are never mentioned. How can it be a sales pitch when it's FREE?

This letter certainly has voice. It also has tone. But its cliché-ridden, hackneyed, and utterly predictable prose makes this letter far from distinctive. Writers achieve distinction by mastering all of the resources we've detailed above (and "plenty more!"), but they do so by fashioning them to new purposes.

In her essay "Show Dog" about Biff the boxer (a champion show dog) and his owners (the Truesdales), Susan Orlean begins on an ironic footing, adopting (while refashioning) the language of the personal ad to introduce Biff:

> If I were a bitch, I'd be in love with Biff Truesdale. Biff is perfect. He's friendly, good-looking, rich, famous, and in excellent physical condition. He almost never drools. He's not afraid of commitment. He wants children—actually, he already has children and wants a lot more. He works hard and is a consummate professional, but he also knows how to have fun. (161)

The pun on "bitch" introduces a major theme in this essay: how people in the show dog world habitually blur the boundaries between humans and canines. The pun also places Orlean and her readers on a playful, humorous footing with the expectation of more of the same to come. The next several sentences continue with the major theme and playful footing. While the pun on "bitch" invites readers to imagine Orlean as a dog (with echoes of the other meaning of "bitch"), the language of the personal ad ("He's friendly, good-looking, rich," "he's not afraid of commitment," "he wants children," and so on) invites them to imagine Biff as a human and even prospective mate. The distinctiveness in style doesn't come from the personal ad clichés themselves but from lifting them from their expected context (where they are used to manage interaction between potential romantic partners) and placing them in a fresh and unexpected one (where they are used to imagine interaction between humans and canines).

In other passages, Orlean achieves a distinctive style less by drawing on various social conventions (such as those associated with the personal ad) and more by managing her readers' physical and social footings toward the events and characters she describes. Here's the essay's climactic passage, with Biff competing for "best in show":

> The judge at Lehigh was a chesty, mustached man with watery eyes and a grave expression. He directed the group with hand signals that made him appear to be roping cattle. The Rottweiler looked good, and so did the schnauzer. I started to worry. Biff had a distracted look on his face, as if he'd forgotten something back at the house. Finally, it was his turn. He pranced to the center of the ring. The judge stroked him and then waved his hand in a circle and stepped out of the way. Several people near me began clapping. A flashbulb flared. Biff held his position for a moment, and then he and Kim bounded across the ring, his feet moving so fast that they blurred into an oily sparkle, even though he really didn't have far to go. He got a cookie when he finished the performance, and another a few minutes later, when the judge wagged his finger at him, indicating that Biff had won again. (168–69)

Orlean locates readers with herself, watching from ringside. She is aware of other spectators (the people near her clapping, and the flashbulb going off), but details that specify individuals and their actions are reserved for those in the ring. How she presents those details establishes the various social footings Orlean invites her readers to assume. The judge she keeps at a distance: we don't know his name (which would personalize him for readers), and the details she offers present him either as an imposing figure (the mustache, large chest, watery eyes, and grave expression) or as somewhat comical (like a cowboy roping cattle). Her positive appraisals of the Rottweiler's and schnauzer's performance and her reaction to them lessen the distance between Orlean and her readers while revealing her attitudinal footing towards Biff. As readers, we wonder why the Rottweiler and schnauzer looking good is a cause for worry. We supply the missing information (that Orlean wants Biff to win), and in doing so, we are invited into an implicit alliance with her, sharing her hopes for that outcome. Biff's distracted look, on the other hand, suggests that he is somehow above it all (the mark of a true champion). This look also provides Orlean an opportunity to crack a little joke and carry the human/canine theme further: that is, she imparts human motives to Biff (worrying about something he might have forgotten back at the house) to account for his expression. The passage ends with Biff winning, but note how the clause that announces this result is buried deep in the syntax of the final sentence—that is, as a participial phrase modifying a subordinate clause. The main clause "He got a cookie" puts readers in Biff's shoes (or paws?), suggesting that, for him, getting that cookie is what it's all about. The rest (the titles, the accolades, the applause) is strictly for the humans.

We began this chapter with voice and rode that metaphor as far as it would take us—which, as it turns out, wasn't that far at all. In its stead, we offered footing and showed how writers achieve a distinctive style, in part by exercising their spatial and social imaginations—by positioning themselves, their subject matters, and their readers in physical and social space. To continue this work, we need to think of other ways writers interact with subject matter and readers. And that's where we'll go in the next chapter, which takes us back to ancient Rome and the old rhetorical treatises on style.

Exercises

1. *Physical Footings.* The following passage comes from Sandra Cisneros's short novel *The House on Mango Street*. Earl lives in a basement apartment next door to the narrator (a young girl) and her sister Nenny:

> Earl works nights. His blinds are always closed during the day. Sometimes he comes out and tells us to keep quiet. The little wooden door that has wedged shut the dark for so long opens with a sigh and lets out a breath of mold and dampness, like books that have been left out in the rain. This is the only time we see Earl except for when he comes and goes to work. He has two little black dogs that go everywhere with him. They don't walk like ordinary dogs, but leap and somersault like an apostrophe and comma.
>
> At night Nenny and I can hear when Earl comes home from work. First the click and whine of the car door opening, then the scrape of concrete, the excited tinkling of dog tags, followed by the heavy jingling of keys, and

finally the moan of the wooden door as it opens and lets loose its sigh of dampness. (70–71)

Imagine that you are a movie director and your job is to create a meticulously faithful version of this passage for the screen. How would you do it? First note that this passage is narrated in the "habitual" or "recurrent" present tense: that is, the actions it depicts recur over time. So your first job is to find a visual analogue for this special use of the present tense. Then decide how you would film the actions it recounts? Where would you position the camera? How would you film actions that are heard but not exactly seen? And so on. Be sure to point to specific verbal features that guide your decisions.

2. *Social Footings.* When speakers or writers take up social footings that seem out of step with expectations, they tend to stand out—sometimes like a sore thumb. The following passage is a good illustration. It comes from Donald Barthelme's short story "The Sandman," which is actually a long letter written by the main character to his girlfriend's psychiatrist:

> Dear Dr. Hodder, I realize that it is probably wrong to write a letter to one's girl friend's shrink but there are several things going on here that I think ought to be pointed out to you. I thought of making a personal visit but the situation then, as I'm sure you understand, would be completely untenable—I would be *visiting a psychiatrist*. I also understand that in writing to you I am in a sense interfering with the process but you don't have to discuss with Susan what I have said. Please consider this an "eyes only" letter. Please think of it as personal and confidential.
>
> . . . To continue. I take exception to your remark that Susan's "openness" is a form of voyeurism. This remark interested me for a while, until I thought about it. Voyeurism I take to be an eroticized expression of curiosity whose chief phenomenological characteristic is the distance maintained between the voyeur and the object. . . . But your remark indicates, in my opinion, a radical misreading of the problem. Susan's "openness"—a willingness of the heart, if you will allow such a term—is not at all comparable to the activities of a voyeur. Susan draws near. Distance is not her thing—not by a long chalk. (185, 188–89)

Write a three-paragraph analysis of this passage using the three-part scheme we used for exploring social footings. In the first paragraph, identify and interpret stylistic features that reveal how the writer positions himself with respect to Dr. Hodder in terms of social distance (familiar to formal) and rank (low to high). In paragraph 2, find and interpret evidence revealing the *social roles* the writer assumes and assigns to his addressee, and for paragraph 3, do the same but this time focus on the *social languages* the writer uses. Throughout be especially attentive to the collisions between the social footings we would expect from someone addressing a credentialed professional and the footings this writer actually assumes.

3. Now it's your turn to apply what you've learned in this chapter and from the previous two exercises. Pick an incident from your own experiences—preferably a short one that you can cover in a paragraph or two. In your notes, sketch out a chronology of the events comprising that incident. Then (again in your notes) spend some time planning how you want to position your readers in terms of both physical space and social space. Next think about what stylistic resources you will need to accomplish these goals. Then write up the incident in earnest, and follow it with a self-analysis in which you explain several of the decisions you made toward creating the desired physical and social footings.

4. In your commonplace book, find some passages that demonstrate physical and social footing. Be ready to discuss them in class. Here's an example from the sample commonplace book in the exercise for chapter 1:

> *An example of physical footing*: Beneath the plane, the elephant mass moved like gray lava, leaving behind a ruined bog of mud and twisted trees. (Matthiessen, quoted in Finch and Elder 634)
> *Comment*: Matthiessen places the reader with him in the airplane above the elephant herd to give a sense of the way they actually affect the environment. If viewed from land, you would lose the panoramic view of the "ruined bog of mud and twisted trees" though you might gain a stronger sense of the elephant's size and strength within a smaller confine.

> *An example of social footing*: I can feel the grass underfoot collecting its bashful energy. Big Bluestem, female and green sage, snakeweed, blue gramma, ground cherry, Indian grass, wild onion, purple coneflower, and purple aster all spring to life on a prairie burned the previous year. (Louise Erdrich, quoted in Finch and Elder 1045)
> *Comment*: Erdrich takes the stance of the poet with heightened sensitivity (she can "feel the grass underfoot collecting its bashful energy") and the local expert who knows in great detail the names of the common flora and what will happen after a fire. By taking on these two roles, she invites (or commands) us to sit at her feet and listen.

5

The Rhetorical Tradition

In western learning, style has been included in the study of rhetoric for nearly three millennia. In classical rhetoric, it was one of the five canons, or divisions, of rhetoric: invention, arrangement, style, memory, and delivery. Each of these canons names a different step in the composing process and offers strategies and instructions for completing it. Invention, for instance, includes techniques for discovering something to say, while arrangement offers guidance on how to organize that something. Style comes into play, at least in theory, after the orator has generated and organized his or her subject matter. It involves adapting language to that subject matter as well as to audience and purpose. The orator then either memorizes the speech verbatim or assembles notes on the main points to cover. Finally, under the heading of delivery, the orator considers how to use voice, gesture, and even facial expression to enhance the persuasiveness of the speech. These divisions made rhetoric easier to teach because they broke a complex process of composition down into more manageable, more digestible parts. But they also risked obscuring the ultimate destination of all these steps combined. And that is performance: the orator mounting a raised platform (much like an actor taking the stage) and performing the speech in front of an audience.

So the truly skilled orator would keep that destination—that moment of performance—in mind even when inventing and arranging the substance of the speech. The same goes for style. In fact, in written rather than spoken texts, style *is* the moment of performance, the moment when what we want to say is realized through language and communicated to our readers. Classical rhetoric, with its overarching concern for performance, still has much to offer in its treatment of style. Two lasting contributions are its division of prose into three levels (low, middle, and high) and its collection of various verbal devices (the tropes and schemes). This chapter focuses on the levels, while chapters 6 and 7 will survey verbal devices.

Three Levels of Style

The three levels of style can be thought of as three different modes or registers of performance, as three ways writers can take up a stance toward their subject matter, audience, and purpose. You already have extensive (if only intuitive) knowledge of something like these levels in your spoken interactions with others, shifting and adapting your speech, behavior, and even manner of dress to different circumstances. When hanging out with friends, for instance, you probably talk, act, and dress in ways that differ drastically from those you would adopt in, say, a job interview. We can account for these differences, at least in part, by considering the different purposes and goals you bring to these situations: the different versions of you that you wish to present, and the different ways you hope to define your relationship with the people with whom you are interacting. In this chapter, we apply that same knowledge to writing, using classical rhetoric and its consideration of the three levels of style to get us started.

Roman rhetorician Cicero distinguished the three levels of style based on subject matter, form, and purpose. With the first two criteria, Cicero was following established doctrine. For instance, many rhetoricians writing before Cicero advised that certain subject matters (such as the deeds of gods, heroes, and kings) only be addressed in a high or lofty style, while more ordinary subjects (the doings of merchants and craftsmen, for instance, or private lawsuits) be presented in a low style. Form also served to distinguish these levels, particularly the frequency and kind of figurative language used. Orators who wished to speak in a low style were to avoid most kinds of figurative or ornamented language, except for the occasional metaphor, while those who aimed for the loftiest of oratorical heights were encouraged to unleash their full stylistic repertoire.

Cicero departed from this doctrine, and thus showed himself as an innovator, by associating the three levels with what he considered the three main purposes (or "offices") of rhetoric: to teach (*docere*), to entertain or amuse (*delectare*), and to move (*movere*) an audience. All rhetoric must meet all three purposes, but an individual document or speech might favor one purpose over another. In texts primarily devoted to teaching, the low style should prevail; in texts designed mainly to entertain, the middle style is favored; in texts intended to move the audience, the high style is preferred. In terms of performance, the low style involves a writer who poses as a teacher or trainer for an audience who needs to know new information. The middle style stages the writer as a storyteller, dramatist, or comedian, hoping to keep a more leisured audience engaged not only mentally but also emotionally. The high style represents an impassioned author—such as a preacher, prophet, or social reformer—with a message of great seriousness or importance to share with an audience whose attitudes or actions must change to avoid some great disaster or in some way change the world.

Low Style and the Teaching Purpose *(Docere)*

The low style, or plain style, supports teaching best because its goal is to disappear, to draw attention to the subject matter and not to the language itself. The low style opens access to the widest possible audience; as a result, it often becomes a focal point in broader social and cultural debates, particularly over religious and political issues. Protestantism, with its evangelical push to reach the masses, reacted against the high style of preaching typical of the established churches, especially in England. The "Puritan plain style" set a new standard in the sixteenth and seventeenth centuries. Democratic movements in the history of literacy, such as the development of daily newspapers, also favored the low style. And it continues to prosper with the "plain English movement" in law and government and the trend toward readability in professional writing. Indeed, the treatment of readability in chapter 3 is practically a primer for plain-style English.

Following is an example of good plain-style prose, from an essay by Sue Hubbell. The essay as a whole is not designed solely to teach; however, as a woman who lives in the country but writes mainly for city dwellers, Hubbell is definitely concerned with *docere*. She's talking about using a chain saw—a topic likely to be unfamiliar to much of her audience:

> The best chain saws are formidable and dangerous tools. My brother nearly cut off his arm with one. A neighbor who earns his living in timber just managed to kill the engine on his when he was cutting overhead and a branch snapped the saw back toward him. The chain did not stop running until it had cut through the beak of his cap. He was very solemn when I told him that I had bought my own chain saw, and he gave me a good piece of advice. "The time to worry about a chain saw," he said, "is when you stop being afraid of it."

I am cautious. I spend a lot of time sizing up a tree before I fell it. Once it is down, I clear away the surrounding brush before I start cutting it into lengths. That way I will not trip and lose my balance with the saw running. A dull chain and a poorly running saw are dangerous, so I've learned to keep mine in good shape and I sharpen the chain each time I use it. (Hubbell 202)

Like a patient teacher, Hubbell restricts herself to plain, straightforward prose in this performance:

- She uses simple sentences and complex ones that are easily processed—that is, sentences whose subordinate clauses express relations of time ("when," "until," and "before") or relations of cause and effect ("so").
- She similarly confines her use of adjectives except when she uses them as a manual writer would use a warning tag ("formidable," "dangerous," "cautious"), or as part of a colloquialism ("*good* piece of advice," "*good* shape").
- She uses few abstractions, sticking to concrete and specific nouns and action verbs.
- She uses only a few adjectives and adverbs that judge rather than describe.
- She almost totally avoids figures of speech and language that draws attention to itself.

Notice that the first paragraph of the passage uses interesting examples rather than the play of language to make the reading lively (*delectare*) while the second paragraph is so dry it might appear in a technical manual. Good plain-style writers typically vary their prose in this way, rewarding the reader with stories and charming details (like "the beak of his cap") to keep them moving forward.

In performing her role as a teacher, notice how Hubbell slows the pace of the prose with her relatively short sentences. The style suggests a patient but insistent attitude toward readers who are likely to take the question of chain saws lightly. The performance seems to say, "Hey, listen close here. This part is important."

The Middle Style and the Purpose of Entertainment *(Delectare)*

The middle style takes a few more risks. It is associated in Cicero with the purpose of *delectare*, which means to amuse or entertain. Instead of adding a story or amusing detail, as in plain style, the middle-style writer might produce a similar effect by varying stylistic features, such as figures of speech (dealt with more fully in chapters 6 and 7). To add a metaphor, analogy, or pun engages the reader's sense of creativity and play, allowing the mind a break from the straight delivery of information. We once heard an engineer talking on the relative safety of emissions from the plant where he worked. He said that he would splash the emissions on his face like aftershave without a single worry. Similarly, a spokeswoman for a nuclear facility used to say that there was less radioactivity in the steam from her plant than in a peanut butter sandwich. Besides straining credibility (the plant the engineer worked for had been cited for dioxin emissions, and the nuclear facility was under review as well), the risk is that the audience might muse over these departures from straight information giving to the point of being distracted from the next important point (though perhaps these speakers wanted to distract the audience away from the scarier realities of their work). The other risk, which also suggests the strength of a more linguistically diverse style, is that these breaks in the routine of the plain style tend to draw more attention and stick in the memory. Indeed, the aftershave and peanut butter analogies are the only things we remember from the two speeches just mentioned. To reduce the risk and capitalize on the strength in varying plain-style discourses devoted to teaching, the best method is to use the variations to emphasize key points. And that's just what the aftershave and peanut butter speeches did. In both cases, the main point was, there's nothing to worry about! Industrial products are not evil; far from it. They are, if not sweet-smelling and tasty, certainly harmless.

The following passage, from an essay by Scott Russell Sanders, is a good example of middle style. It still has something to teach—a point about human mobility—but its style also calls more attention to itself. We are invited to look *at* the language—its shape and the images it conjures—before looking *through* it:

> We are a wandering species, and have been since we reared up on our hind legs and stared at the horizon. Our impulse to wander, to pick up and move when things no longer suit us in our present place, is not an ailment brought on suddenly by industrialization, by science, or by the European hegemony over dark-skinned peoples. It would be naïve to think that Spanish horses corrupted the Plains Indians, tempting a sedentary people to rush about, or that snowmobiles corrupted the Inuit, or that Jeeps corrupted the Aborigines. It would be just as naïve to say that the automobile gave rise to our own

restlessness; on the contrary our restlessness gave rise to the automobile, as it led to the bicycle, steamboat, and clipper ship, as it led to the taming of horses, lacing of snowshoes, and carving of dugout canoes. With each invention, a means of moving farther, faster, has answered to a desire that coils in our genes. Mobility is the rule in human history, rootedness the exception. (Sanders, "Settling Down" 84)

Notice how Sanders varies diction and sentence structure more thoroughly:

- He draws attention to important words by repeating sounds—the repetition of "c" sounds ("clipper ship . . . carving of . . . canoes") and "m" sounds (moving, mobility, motion), among others.
- He makes use of striking imagery ("we reared up on our hind legs and stared at the horizon").
- He gives his sentences a more definite, more crafted shape. For example, he repeats words but in reverse order: "the automobile gave rise to our own restlessness . . . our restlessness gave rise to the automobile." He also uses parallelism to bind ideas and details together: "as it led to the bicycle, steamboat, and clipper ship, as it led to the taming of horses, lacing of snowshoes, and carving of dugout canoes." And he juxtaposes contrasting thoughts in a short, aphoristic statement: "Mobility is the rule in human history, rootedness the exception."

The cleverness of the language—how the historical and anthropological examples are woven in, for instance—makes the ideas of the passage more palatable to the reader, more delectable (as in *delectare*). In short, Sanders preserves many elements of the plain style (using mostly familiar language and relatively straightforward, active syntax, for example), thus ensuring readability and fluency, but he also draws upon elements of the high style discussed below.

Sanders' performance recalls the work of the best storytellers. The aim is to *engage* the audience, not just to pass information to them. If you want your readers to think about such a weighty topic as the foundational nature of the human species, you may need to wake up their creativity by giving them permission to play with language and ideas. The figures of speech that suggest the human kinship with the animal world, for example—"we reared up on our hind legs" (like horses or goats); "a desire coils in our genes" (like a snake)—may awaken the reader to new possibilities of thinking about what it means to be human (and animal).

The High Style and the Purpose of Moving the Audience *(Movere)*

The high style, also known as the grand style, is devoted in the Ciceronian system to the purpose of moving the audience. *Movere* means move in two senses: to stir the emotions and to motivate the audience to action. To this end, the high style increases the number of figures, varies the diction and sentence structure more widely, and attempts to engage the audience's senses, memories, and emotions at a deep level. It strives for memorability, for figures and images that strike the mind forcefully and lastingly.

Here's a sample, from an essay by Rick Bass. By Ciceronian standards, the style is fairly tame, but you should be able to feel the difference between this one and the others quoted so far:

> What happens to us when all the sacred, all the *whole* is gone—when there is no more whole? There will be only fragments of stories, fragments of culture, fragments of integrity. Even a child standing on the porch in Houston with the rain in his face can look north and know that it is all tied together, that we are the warblers, we are the zonetails, we are the underground river; that it is all holy, and that some of it should not be allowed to disappear, as has so much, and so many of us, already. ("On Willow" 219)

Notice the many elements of high style in this short passage:

- the complexity and variation of the sentences;
- the plays on words (such as *whole*, *holy*, and perhaps an implied *hole*);
- the hyperbole, or overstatement (can a "child in Houston" really "know" the things the passage claims?);
- the strategic repetitions of key words and patterns: the repeated "fragments" at the beginning of three parallel phrases that increase in order of importance and the repetition of "we are" at the beginnings of three parallel clauses. In the latter three-part structure, if the meaning of the words doesn't build, the sound certainly swells to a climax, moving from the two-syllable words ("warblers" and "zonetails") to the five syllables in "underground river."

More than story or even idea, the language seems to drive the passage, and the aim of the author is clearly to *move* the reader. Bass takes the role of the environmentalist prophet who wants readers to feel emotions strong enough to move them to action, to become performers in their own right, to see the world in a new way and act accordingly. Notice that, as we move from low to middle to high style, the demand for performance seems to shift so that the audience is urged to take more and more responsibility. The prose becomes increasingly performative, not only in the sense that the author seems to be more engaged and impassioned about the material but also in the sense that the audience is urged to greater and fuller participation.

Poetic Language and the High Style in Prose

The high style is the most poetic form of prose. Everybody has a gut sense of how poetry differs from prose, but consider what a well-known poet and poetry teacher, Kenneth Koch, has to say about two aspects of poetic language: its attention to sound and its preference for the fantastic or unusual. Poetry, Koch says, uses

> a language in which the sound of the words is raised to an importance equal to that of their meaning, and also equal to the importance of grammar and syntax. In ordinary language, the sound of a word is useful almost exclusively in order to identify it and to distinguish it from other words. In poetry its importance is much greater. Poets think of how they want something to sound as much as they think of what they want to say, and in fact it's often hard to distinguish one from the other. . . . Poetry would just as soon come to a musical, as a logical or otherwise useful conclusion. . . . Thanks to the music, emotion becomes stronger than reason. (Koch 20–23)

The point about emotion ties into Cicero's concept of *movere*. Poetic language, like the high style, stirs the emotions and engages the heart as well as the head of the audience. Repetition of important sounds and words, as we see above in Sanders and Bass, is the kind of almost musical incantation that Koch associates with poetic language.

Koch goes on to say that poetic language

> is also notable for its predilection for certain rhetorical forms such as comparison, personification, apostrophe (talking to something or someone who isn't there), and for its inclinations toward the imaginary, the wished-for, the objectively untrue. . . . [One] extraordinary characteristic of language . . . is that it is without any impediment to saying things that are not true. . . . Language is like a car able to go two hundred miles an hour but which is restricted by the traffic laws of prose to a reasonable speed. Poets are fond of accelerating. (24–26)

By attributing almost supernatural insights to the "child in Houston" in his essay, Bass pushes into the territory of "the objectively untrue," into hyperbole. By stepping up from the premise that all creatures are ecologically connected to a claim of total identification—"we are the warblers"—Bass is definitely writing "accelerating" prose.

The Limits of the Ciceronian System

Before leaving the Ciceronian classification of styles, let's complicate the picture a bit. In style, and in rhetoric as a whole, nothing is absolute. For one thing, as we've already suggested, the categories of style are not mutually exclusive; one fades into the other. What we really have is a continuum with plain style at one end and poetic style at the other. Most authors move back and forth as the occasion demands, often within the same text. At best, the continuum is merely a way of talking about the relationship of style and purpose at a given moment and from a definite interpretive perspective.

On top of that, the purpose to which each style is put can vary. Just because a style has the characteristics of the plain style, for example, the author may be doing more than teaching. The plain style usually keeps the emotional response of the audience at a fairly low level, but a skilled writer can deviate from this norm, working against the expectations of the audience.

Consider, for example, the following story of an attempted desertion during war from Ernest Hemingway's novel *A Farewell to Arms*, a passage whose style has been analyzed with great insight by Charles Kay Smith in *Styles and Structures: Alternative Approaches to College Writing*:

> "Halt," I said. [The two sergeants] kept on down the muddy road, the hedge on either side. "I order you to halt," I called. They went a little faster. I opened up my holster, took the pistol, aimed at the one who had talked the most, and fired. I missed and they started to run. I shot three times and dropped one. The other went through the hedge and was out of sight. I fired at him through the hedge as he ran across the field. The pistol clicked empty and I put in another clip. I saw it was too far to shoot at the second sergeant. He was across the field, running, his head held low. I commenced to reload the empty clip. Bonello came up.
>
> "Let me go finish him," he said. I handed him the pistol and he walked down to where the sergeant of engineers lay face down across the road. Bonello leaned over, put the pistol against the man's head and pulled the trigger. The pistol did not fire.
>
> "You have to cock it," I said. He cocked it and fired twice. He took hold of the sergeant's legs and pulled him to the side of the road so he lay beside the hedge. He came back and handed me the pistol. (quoted in Smith 7)

Hemingway's style is plain as plain can be. He avoids complex sentences; uses adverbs and adjectives only to describe, never to judge or color the action morally; favors concrete words over abstractions; and rarely uses a figure of speech. The language lacks music and avoids magic. It's the just-the-facts-ma'am approach of a lab write-up or a police report. But can it fail to stir emotion in the audience—if nothing else horror at the narrating officer's matter-of-fact description of killing two of his own comrades? If anything, the plain style heightens the emotion the way a thin black frame might highlight the wild color of a German expressionist painting.

A related limit of the Ciceronian system is that it tends to gloss over possible differences within each of its three categories: different kinds of low styles, different kinds of middle styles, and so forth, all identified by different sets of stylistic features. In modern prose, for instance, the high style would have to include, at the very least, two subtypes: the oratorical/ poetic high style (which we've covered) and the high style of the academic, technical expert, or bureaucrat. Consider this excerpt from chief weapons inspector Hans Blix, who is both a technical expert and a bureaucrat. It comes from the last quarterly report he submitted to the United Nations Security Council before retiring:

> UNMOVIC inspected a number of sites throughout Iraq based on intelligence information made available to it. In addition, other sites were inspected as a result of follow-up actions. Site inspections were aimed to investigate in detail the infrastructural signature necessary for the alleged function of such sites, e.g., the presence of suitable support services for chemical and biological weapons mobile production facilities during production runs. Inspection results and analysis of detailed forensic sampling of the facilities did not reveal evidence of any past involvement of those sites in proscribed chemical and biological weapons mobile production activities. At several of the inspected sites, sea containers with recently (United Nations-registered) imported seed-processing equipment, with some resemblance to production equipment, were present. (Blix np)

This passage falls within the high style. Its elevated, polysyllabic diction and oftentimes long and intricate sentences raise it above the low and middle styles. Yet it also displays features that distinguish it from the oratorical or poetic high style (review the passage by Bass for an example). It's full of technical jargon ("follow-up actions," "infrastructural signature," "forensic sampling"), and shows this style's predilection for acronyms—UNMOVIC (which, by the way, stands for this mouthful: United Nations Monitoring, Verification, and Inspection Commission). It also relies on passive constructions ("were inspected" and "were aimed"), weak linking verbs ("were present"), and nominalizations ("information," "action," "inspections," "production," "involvement"). Note also how it strings together prepositional phrases so that it's sometimes hard to figure out which phrase goes with what. But perhaps its most characteristic features are the compound noun phrases where Blix uses nouns to modify other nouns ("intelligence information," "support services," "sea containers"), and the extraordinarily long nouns phrases that use a combination of nouns, adjectives, and past participles as modifiers. Consider this doozy: "chemical and biological weapons mobile production facilities." And this one: "proscribed chemical and biological weapons mobile production activities."

The potential effect of the performance that Blix delivers in this passage also differs significantly from what we might expect from the oratorical or poetic high style. If we analyzed this performance using the Ciceronian notion of *movere* as our yardstick, we'd probably conclude that Blix falls way short of the mark. The cold technical language of his report tends to deaden emotion rather than stir it, and the heavy use of nouns and compound noun phrases argues for stasis rather than action. But applying *movere* to this passage would likely miss the point. Blix's task is to present a technical report to a bureaucratic body, the United Nations Security Council. The rhetorical situation thus calls for a techno-bureaucratic performance, and Blix's equally techno-bureaucratic style answers this expectation to a tee. Indeed, if Blix had presented a grandly stylized oration or submitted a poem for his final report, council members may have thought his retirement was long overdue.

Despite its limitations, the Ciceronian system has enduring value. For one thing, it reminds us that prose (whether spoken or written) is a thoroughly flexible medium. It allows us to match style to subject matter, audience, and purpose—or, reciprocally, to use style to leverage that subject matter, audience, and purpose into a new configuration. The Blix passage is a good example of the former result: his audience probably expected a report from a technical expert/bureaucrat to sound, well, technical and bureaucratic, so Blix adopted verbal forms that matched these expectations. Hubbell, Sanders, and Bass were also working within frameworks of expectations, but they used style to nudge their readers toward a new awareness of their subjects—not only increasing what they knew about those subjects, but perhaps even changing how they feel about them as well.

A related virtue of the Ciceronian system is that it offers a rough map to the performance possibilities of writing. With it, we can chart how writers stay at one level of style or move back and forth across several, ratcheting up the emotional intensity here, toning it down there, treating readers to a little *delectare* elsewhere, and so on. But as a rough map, the levels of style will only take us so far. To get at the nitty-gritty of performing prose, we need to dip back down to the level of word, phrase, and clause and survey the verbal devices that help comprise the writer's repertoire for performance: tropes, schemes, and images.

Exercises

1. The following passages focus on roughly the same subject—a hummingbird's metabolism—but they deliver two very different performances. How would you place each passage on the levels of style continuum presented in this chapter (from low to middle to high)? Justify your placement by pointing to specific stylistic features from each passage.

> The metabolism of the hummingbird is the fastest of all animals. Heart rates may reach over 1000 beats per minute. This rapid rate may not exist at all times. Scientists have observed hummingbirds go through what is called torpor, mainly at night, when heart rate and respiration rate drop significantly. This could be called a nightly hibernation, since it reduces the need for the birds to seek food at night. Where food supply is limited, torpor may also be induced during daylight hours.
>
> To sustain a high metabolism, hummingbirds rely primarily on sipping nectar from flowers, because sugar easily converts to energy. Some species may also eat small bugs, but nectar remains the main part of a hummingbird's diet. (WiseGeek)

> Hummingbirds, like all flying birds but more so, have incredible enormous immense ferocious metabolisms. To drive those metabolisms they have racecar hearts that eat oxygen at an eye-popping rate. Their hearts are built of thinner, leaner fibers than ours. Their arteries are stiffer and more taut. They have more mitochondria in their heart muscles—anything to gulp more oxygen. Their hearts are stripped to the skin for the war against gravity and inertia, the mad search for food, the insane idea of flight. The price of their ambition is a life closer to death. (Doyle 29)

2. Pick a subject with which you are thoroughly familiar—it can be anything: exercise, gardening, music, video games, tax reform legislation. Now imagine that you, as an expert on that subject, have been called to produce three short pieces of writing for three different occasions. For the first, you've been asked to teach your readers something about that subject. For

instance, if your subject is exercise, you might settle on the topic of how to stretch properly before running or how to do a sit-up correctly. For the second occasion, your job is to point out something quirky, interesting, or amusing about that same subject (to continue with our exercise example, you might focus on the recent popularity of fitness boot camps). For the third, you've been asked to pay tribute to some aspect of that subject, to sing its praises, or move your readers toward some deeper understanding and appreciation of it (for instance, an athlete or coach who inspired you).

Now write those three pieces (each should be about a paragraph long). Use our discussion of the three levels of style as a point of departure for thinking about how you want to "tune" each piece in terms of style. You can play it by the book, so to speak, and write three paragraphs that adhere closely to the stylistic conventions of each level. Or you can experiment a bit, aiming for a style that falls somewhere between low and middle or middle and high. Follow those three paragraphs with a fourth in which you identify your purpose for each and detail some of the stylistic choices you made toward achieving it.

3. Choose a quotation from your commonplace book, and comment briefly on the level of style. Here's an example from the chapter 1 exercise:

> *Example*: Mountain lions coo like pigeons, sob like women, emit a flat slight shriek, a popping bubbling growl, or mew, or yowl. (Hoagland, quoted in Finch and Elder 692)
>
> *Comment*: Hoagland's is a low style trending toward a middle style. His goal is to teach and to entertain. He's a writer of creative nonfiction but also a journalist of the old school who thinks that journalism should convey information and knowledge and not just be another medium of entertainment. His essay is teaching about mountain lions and telling exciting experiences about them. This sentence is creative, almost excessive even, in its multiplication of words for how the lion sounds. But it works to show the variety of the sounds that the creature actually makes, too.

6

Tropes

A figure of speech is a variation of the conventional meaning of a word or the conventional shape of a sentence. Over the next two chapters, we will deal with two kinds, tropes and schemes. "Trope" derives from the Greek word that means "turn," a definition picked up in our common expression "turn of phrase" and "turn of thought," not to mention "twist of plot." In discussions of style, trope refers to turning a word's meaning from its conventional sense to a new and oftentimes surprising one. "Scheme" also comes from the Greek—this time from a word meaning "shape" or "form." It refers to a change in the expected word order or arrangement of a sentence.

In the previous chapter, we introduced the levels of style and described them as different registers or modes of performance. How do the tropes and schemes fit in? They are specific moves writers can make within these registers. As such, they are like the steps a ballet dancer might perform as part of a longer routine: for instance, *pirouette* (spinning on tiptoes), *grand jeté* (jumping horizontally with legs extended backward and forward), and *chassé* (sliding with legs bent). These dance moves, like the figures, are units of performance: we can point to them, describe how they are formed, and judge whether they are executed effectively or not. There are no rigid rules about how they might be combined or incorporated into a broader performance. Like dance moves, the figures of speech are vehicles for managing interactions between performer and audience while shaping the latter's perceptions of what they see or read. They are also already in circulation and thus part of a general repertoire for performance. For this reason, they carry meanings and values that exceed an individual performer's use of them. In other words, they come with baggage—most of it positive but some negative.

In the case of the figures, one way their meaning exceeds any specific occasion of their use is that some of them have become associated with one or more of the three levels of style. For instance, as we saw last chapter, the low style typically avoids figurative language, but it may use tropes that explain or illustrate (metaphor, for example) or schemes that enhance readability (say, grammatical parallelism). The more elaborate or involved tropes and schemes are more characteristic of the middle and, especially, the high oratorical or poetic styles. In fact, they are among the main ingredients of these styles: they elevate the language by giving evidence of more carefully crafted prose. The down side is that overusing figurative language can make the prose seem ornate, overly mannered, or "overwritten."

This chapter looks carefully at four of the dozens of tropes identified by classical and Renaissance rhetoricians—what have come to be known as the four "master tropes": metaphor, metonymy, synecdoche, and irony (see Burke, *Grammar of Motives*). The chapter finishes with a brief survey of a few more exotic types. Our goal throughout is to build on your vocabulary for analyzing prose while adding to your writing repertoire. Toward this end, remember that it's not enough to simply identify a trope when analyzing the writing of others or to use them haphazardly in your own compositions ("Let's just toss in a few tropes for good measure"). As classical and Renaissance rhetoricians knew well, the tropes are thoroughly functional—they can be used to secure a variety of effects. To keep this functional perspective front and center, we'll draw on the model of performance we introduced in chapter 1, one that views written performances in terms of three arenas of action: textual, social, and cultural. Our discussion of each trope will thus begin with a description of its linguistic form and its primary function at the level of word, phrase, and clause (textual arena). We'll then explore how writers use each trope to shape their readers' understanding of, and attitudes toward, other elements of the rhetorical situation (social arena). Finally, we'll consider how each trope fits in with broader practices and meanings (cultural arena).

Metaphor

Most people study metaphor first as a technique of poetry in high school. They learn to distinguish it from the technique of simile. According to this plan, simile is a comparison that uses *like* or *as*—"My love *is like* a red, red rose," as the Scottish poet Robert Burns says—while metaphor is a comparison that omits *like* or *as*: "Love *is* a rose (but you'd better not pick it)," as the old country song says. A related term, *analogy*, is usually reserved for prose. We might say, for example, "Today let us compare the emotion of love to a rose, sometimes thorny but nevertheless beautiful and sensually pleasant."

This simple explanation of metaphor and its close relatives, while helpful in identifying the different figures of speech, doesn't take us very far. Instead of thinking of metaphor as a comparison that leaves something out, try thinking of it as an *identification*, a way of bringing together seemingly unlike things. In this sense, metaphor is a strong identification, while simile and analogy are more cautious attempts to link unlike things. Choosing one over the other thus has consequences at the level of performance, especially with regard to how a writer defines his or her relationship to subject matter and reader. Consider this series of metaphors from Martin Luther King Jr.'s "I Have a Dream" speech:

> One hundred years later, the life of the Negro is still sadly crippled by the manacles of segregation and the chains of discrimination. (King np)

There are three metaphors here. The first, "crippled," prepares the way for the other two: "manacles of segregation" and "chains of discrimination." Together they create a strong identification between slavery, on the one hand, and segregation and discrimination, on the other, suggesting that, even though one hundred years have passed since the Emancipation Proclamation (at the time of the speech), African Americans still live in a state of bondage. What if King had opted for simile instead? The result might look something like this:

> One hundred years later, the life of the Negro is still impaired by segregation and discrimination, which are like manacles and chains.

What changes? The strong identification between slavery and segregation and discrimination is weakened. As a result, the speaker seems more tentative about the comparison, hesitant to push the likeness too far. He thus invites listeners to take a similar stance, to entertain possible resemblances between slavery and current race relations but to do so from a position of relative detachment. Also lost is the emotional wallop the original series of metaphors conveys. The strong identifications in that series convey conviction which stirs passion, while the simile, buried in a relative clause at the end of the sentence, seems an afterthought.

Similes, however, are not always poor substitutes for metaphors. In some cases, they are the right tool for the job. David Quammen, for instance, uses a simile to begin his essay on the natural properties of ice:

> Antarctica is a gently domed continent squashed flat, like a dent in the roof of a Chevy, by the weight of its own ice. ("Strawberries" 197)

Quammen writes about science and nature for popular audiences, not experts. Accordingly, his prose usually modulates between the low style of teaching and the middle style of entertaining. In this sentence, his task is to describe the geological shape of Antarctica for readers unfamiliar with it. The simile works toward this goal, playing a supporting role to the main clause and helping readers visualize the continent's shape by comparing it to a more familiar object—the dented roof of a Chevy. If Quammen had opted for metaphor, that trope would have upstaged the sentence's main point:

> Antarctica is a dent in the roof of a Chevy, squashed flat by the weight of its own ice.

Or even more enigmatic:

> Antarctica is a dent in the roof of a Chevy.

Both of these alternatives, especially the second, push Quammen's prose toward the high style of poetry. They cast Quammen in the role not of entertaining teacher but of poet exploring connections between natural phenomena and human-made objects. Readers, for their part, are left to wonder at the depths of Quammen's imagination. The metaphorical alternatives also alter readers' relationship to the subject matter, inviting them to contemplate the strong identification between Antarctica and a dented car roof rather than the geographical contours of the icy continent.

The examples from King and Quammen remind us that style (even at the level of word and phrase) is a medium for social interaction, for managing relationships among writer, reader, and subject matter. Metaphors are particularly potent in this regard because they shape how people think about the world and their place in it.

In their influential study of metaphor, George Lakoff and Mark Johnson make several important points about this trope:

- Metaphors are fundamental to human thought.
- They pervade not just poetic language but all speech and writing.
- They emerge from, and structure, our physical and cultural experiences.

Take, for instance, this statement: "I'm feeling low today." You might not notice it at first, but there's a metaphor lurking in here. It's conveyed by the word "low," which uses a metaphor of the body to express a psychological state, depression or sadness. To grasp the full sense of this metaphor, think of it not as a comparison but as a ratio. Low is to the body as depressed is to the mind:

$$\frac{\text{low}}{\text{the body}} = \frac{\text{depressed}}{\text{the mind}}$$

"Depression" itself is merely a technical term for feeling low. When you are "low" or "down," your energy is lacking. You don't want to get out of bed ("get up"). You feel all your weight as the pull of gravity toward the earth. The ultimate "down" state is death. That kind of gravity leads to the grave (words which have the same etymological root, after all). No wonder then that when a patient is "really down," the psychologist worries about suicide. Also notice that, to take the full implication of the metaphor, there's no big division between mind and body, but rather a continuity. When you're sick, you feel low; depression often has a physical root in illness, for example, some chemical shift in the brain. Metaphor tends to emphasize such continuities and deemphasize borderline distinctions.

Because the metaphor in "I'm feeling low today" is rooted in how we experience our bodies, it would seem a natural, even inevitable way to express a psychological state. But Lakoff and Johnson would say that this body-rootedness is only part of the picture; metaphors are also products of culture. In our culture, we tend to associate good things with being up and bad things with being down: "You really *boosted* my spirits," "Our teacher came *down* hard on us," "He *fell* into a coma," "She's on her way to the *top*." While other cultures might associate positives things with up and negative ones with down, these metaphorical concepts might not be as central to that culture's way of thinking as it is to ours. There are, for instance, "cultures where balance and centrality plays a much more important role than" up-down orientations (Lakoff and Johnson 24).

Here are a few more metaphors that are perhaps more obviously the products of culture:

- I *spent* the day working in the yard.
- Can you *give* me a minute?
- You need to *budget* your time more carefully.

Lakoff and Johnson would say that all of these statements derive from the conceptual metaphor "time is money," a metaphor that understands time as something that can be spent, given, budgeted, wasted, saved, and so on. They explain the cultural basis of this metaphor:

> In our culture TIME IS MONEY in many ways: telephone message units, hourly wages, hotel room rates, yearly budgets, interest on loans, and paying your debt to society by "serving time." These practices are relatively new in the history of the human race, and by no means do they exist in all cultures. They have arisen in modern industrialized societies and structure our basic everyday activities in a very profound way. (8)

As the "time is money" identification suggests, some metaphors are so thoroughly engrained in our culture that it is hard to imagine alternative ways of thinking. Try, for instance, to imagine time not as money but as a plant (or organism). It may seem difficult and even counterintuitive, but it's not impossible: "The day blossoms," "The past is our roots, the future our branches," "Human history sometimes bears strange fruit." While these metaphors work conceptually, they lack the punch of "time is money" metaphors because they don't carry such a large bundle of cultural meanings and values.

All writers use conventional metaphors such as "happy is up," "sad is down," and "time is money." Given how thoroughly metaphorical our language is, writers can't avoid them. And in many instances, it makes good sense to use them because they offer writers dependable ways to manage their relationships with readers and subject matter. That is, they facilitate communication by allowing writers to tap into their readers' understanding of the world. Writers who wish to push beyond the conventional into the realm of creativity, however, look for ways to give a well-worn metaphor a new twist or search for entirely new ways for conceiving things. When King identifies segregation with manacles and discrimination with chains, he invites listeners to reconceive their present circumstances and primes them for change—that is, for realizing his dream.

Metonymy

While metaphor works by identifying dissimilar things, metonymy works by substituting one thing for a closely associated (contiguous) thing. For example, we refer to Queen Elizabeth II of England as "the crown," or the government of the United States as "Washington." The easiest (though not totally reliable) way to distinguish between metaphors and metonyms is to say that metaphors are about shared attributes between different things while metonyms are not. Slavery and discrimination are both products of racism, after all; depression of the mind and the state of being "down" (in bed or dead) are both conditions of the person. Metonyms are about habitual associations rather than shared attributes or features. The crown has nothing to do with the Queen's body or her character. The shape and character of the American government has little to do with its location in Washington; it used to be in New York, after all, though we might argue that by moving the capitol southward, the founders of the nation were trying to give it a metaphorical significance, putting the capitol closer to the geographical center of the nation, making it the heart of the nation's body. Since we haven't moved the capitol westward as the nation expanded, however, such a metaphorical meaning is lost. (With a poet's sensibility to metaphoric value, Walt Whitman thought we should move the seat of government to Denver, but after the addition of Alaska and Hawaii, we might suggest Los Angeles.)

The entry on metonymy in the *Encyclopedia of Rhetoric and Composition* gives a good list of examples from news captions, popular songs, ads, and cartoons, showing how metonyms involve the substitution of one thing for another closely associated thing:

- In "Bernstein gives up baton," a symbol (baton) is substituted for the action symbolized (conducting an orchestra).
- In "Our face cream removes the years," a cause (passing time) is substituted for an effect (wrinkles).
- In "He took a swig of courage," an effect (courage) is substituted for a cause (whiskey).
- In "Bush bombs Iraq," a controller (Bush) is substituted for the controlled (U.S. Air Force).
- In "You're never alone with a poet in your pocket," a creator (poet) is substituted for a creation (book of poetry).
- In "The plane brought back ten body bags," a container (body bags) is substituted for the contained (dead soldiers).
- In "The hired gun confessed," an object used (gun) is substituted for the user (killer). (Davis, "Metonymy" 445)

Metonyms function rhetorically by focusing readers' attention on the associated thing rather than the thing it stands for. It acts, in other words, like a spotlight in a musical or theatrical production, highlighting one performer or event while backgrounding others. In the "Bush bombs

Iraq" metonym, for instance, we know that Bush didn't literally fly the planes that dropped the bombs, but through metonymy, which allows us to substitute a controller for the controlled, we can spotlight Bush's responsibility for the action. Also like a spotlight, metonyms inevitably background information, a process writers can also use to strategic advantage. Imagine a press release stating, "The White House denied the allegations." This metonym substitutes a building (the White House) for the people who live or work there (the president, his or her advisors, staff, and so on). As a result, it backgrounds and thus obscures who actually denied the allegations.

A good way to tease out the social and even cultural dimensions of metonymy is to apply a technique we introduced earlier—that is, to alter or in some way undo the stylistic device in question. Consider the advertising slogan, "You're never alone with a poet in your pocket." Now undo the metonymy by reversing the substitution: "You're never alone with a book of poetry in your pocket." What's changed? The original, by highlighting the creator over the creation, seeks to entice you with the promise of forming a personal, even intimate relationship with the poet (he or she is in your pocket after all!). The revision still hints at this possibility, but its force is diminished considerably by replacing that person-to-person relationship with one between you and an inanimate object: the book (it's just not the same!). This metonymy also reveals something about how our culture understands and values the relationship between writers and their compositions. That is, we often see these compositions as extensions of the writer's personality, emotions, and so on, and this theory seems especially to apply to poets. Recently, literary critics have challenged such a notion, but it's still in play in the broader culture—so much so that a metonym such as this one can pass almost without notice.

Metonymy has other cultural implications. The two final examples on the list above ("body bags" and "hired gun") show how metonymy can be reductive, functioning much as a stereotype does, reducing a whole person to an object. Similar examples from common language include the reference to business people as "suits" or women as "skirts," substituting the container for the contained and reducing individual people to stereotypic states of dress. The tendency of metonymy to objectify and depersonalize people can prove all too effective in sexist and racist language.

Metonymy also often gives rise to the kinds of symbols, icons, and logos used as cultural indicators in everything from literature and psychology to advertising, sign making, and brand names. Think of the giant plastic cows placed in the parking lots of steak houses, the icon of a knife and fork used to indicate restaurants on interstate highway signs, the logo of a dinosaur to stand for a museum of natural history. In religion, the cross, an element from the story of Jesus, becomes a symbol for Christianity. In world politics, a flag symbolizes a nation.

Synecdoche

Synecdoche closely resembles metonymy. It also involves acts of substitution that spotlight certain details over others. While metonyms involve relationships with things external to, or not a necessary component of, the main subject (the crown is external to the queen; Washington is not a necessary component of the U.S. government), synecdoche involves using some internal part or necessary component to stand for the subject. If you say, "My heart is not in my writing today," you use a part of your body to represent your whole self. More than that, by using "heart" to stand for the whole self, you focus attention on emotions. Contrast this with another synecdoche, one that a coach might address to a distracted player: "Get your head in the game." Again another part of the body stands for the whole self, but this time, the word "head" spotlights the mind or intellect.

Consider a famous poetic example that shows in greater detail how the trope functions. In the poem "I Heard a Fly Buzz When I Died," Emily Dickinson imagines a persona on her deathbed, looking around the room and seeing in her dying moment a fly buzzing at the window pane. Just before she sees this odd symbol of stirring life (a metonym), she looks up and sees her family and friends crying over her in the traditional nineteenth-century death watch. She says, "The Eyes around—had wrung them dry" (Dickinson 223). She means that the people have wept till they can weep no more; they've wrung themselves dry. By referring to people as "eyes," using a part to stand for the whole, she focuses on the part of the body that we look into to determine how others feel. The poet's wordplay hints at the old saying that the eyes are the windows of the soul. The family and friends look into the eyes of the dying one to see if she still has life in her while she watches them watching her to understand her own state. The synecdoche draws our attention to the act of watching and the means of watching—the eyes.

Some would say synecdoche is a subspecies of metonymy, but it is useful to maintain a slight distinction in function. Synecdoche (like metaphor) involves a deeper organic or structural relationship between the paired terms, so that it can create a more powerful rhetorical effect—negative as well as positive. To call a man a "dick" or a woman a "cunt" or a "piece of ass" (synecdoche) will likely produce a stronger emotional reaction than to call them "suits" or "skirts" (metonymy). In addition to the rhetorical difference, the conceptual difference can be strong as well. Consider the way you might represent your relationship to the place you live. If you think synecdochally, you might see yourself as part of the land whose minerals you eat and whose water you drink. But if you think metonymically, you might think of your land primarily as a unit of value that could be reduced to money. Money always works metonymically. It has an arbitrary (or artificially assigned) relationship to the things it is associated with—land, food, goods, whatever.

Though ancient theorists of rhetoric considered a wide range of relationships under the heading of synecdoche, we want to focus on only one: the relationship of the part to the whole. You are using a synecdoche when you tell your neighbors that you will "lend a hand" in helping with their garden. Of course you will use your whole body, not just your hand, but you focus on the most active part. When the person on the shore says, "There are ten sails coming this way," there are really ten complete boats, but the trope focuses on the visible part of the boats.

Other good examples appear in the entry on synecdoche in the *Encyclopedia of Rhetoric and Composition*:

- We don't have wheels (a car).
- New blood (bodies) in Congress inspires hope.
- This is where the rubber (tires) meets the road.
- There's a compound fracture in the emergency room and a heart attack in Room 4 (patients with these maladies). (Davis, "Synecdoche" 712)

The main function of synecdoche in these examples is to focus the attention, and in doing so it may serve a variety of interactional or social purposes. According to T. R. Johnson, synecdoche is often a characteristic of "'hipster' slang and political slogans" (116). It thus offers speakers and writers a way to signal insider knowledge or show membership to some group. Substituting "wheels" for "car," for instance, not only spotlights those parts of a car most associated with motion, with getting from point A to point B, but also signals a speaker's or writer's "coolness" (at least it did in the distant past). A more recent example comes from the language of hip hop: "kickin' rhymes" where one part of a rap (the words that rhyme) stands for the lyrics (or even the song) as a whole. The same is true of nursery rhymes. Because rhyming is such a central feature in both rap and Mother Goose, it comes to stand for poetry as a whole (which also includes other features such as figures of speech, meter, and imagery). Or the focusing power of synecdoche may serve more practical ends. With the fourth example above ("There's a compound fracture in the emergency room and a heart attack in Room 4"), we can imagine it being spoken by a nurse to a doctor. The substitution of a patient's maladies for the patient offers an economical way for the nurse to communicate the most important information to the physician on duty.

Like metaphor and metonymy, synecdoche describes patterns of thinking our culture uses to organize and understand the world beyond the level of word and phrase. For instance, whenever we pick out some element of a set to stand for the whole, we have acted synecdochally. The rhetorical use of examples involve synecdoches that work at the conceptual level. Say you are writing a paper on problems in education, and for an example, you choose a story about a bad teacher you had in high school. Your example serves as a conceptual synecdoche, representing problems in education as a whole. Other instances of synecdochal thinking abound. Kenneth Burke notes that all forms of political representation are synecdoches, "where some part of the social body (either traditionally established, or elected, or coming into authority by revolution) is held to be 'representative' of the society as a whole" (*Grammar of Motives* 508). Even units within a government may serve as synecdoches. Think of Clinton's administration and then later Bush's where each president's cabinet was said to "look like America" as a whole. Pictures and video clips sometimes also function synecdochally: a photograph of an American flag waving over the rubble at ground zero, or a clip of Bush stumbling over a popular saying ("Fool me once, shame on . . . shame on you. Fool me . . . you can't get fooled again"). Even a single event may serve a representative function for some larger occurrence: the toppling of Saddam's statue in a Baghdad square or, conversely, the abuses at Abu Ghraib.

Irony

The most complex and difficult of the four master tropes is irony. Novices to rhetorical analysis and literary criticism generally find it to be one of the hardest concepts to comprehend and put to use, while budding (and even accomplished) writers often miss important opportunities for irony in their own prose. But the practice of irony is so common and so crucial in much of modern rhetoric that it should not be neglected.

Irony is a trope that involves inversions and reversals. It turns standard meanings and expectations upside down. It often involves saying one thing and meaning another. In the infamous essay "A Modest Proposal," for example, the eighteenth-century satirist Jonathan Swift says that the rich people of England should eat the poor children of Ireland. What he really means is that the rich should care for the poor instead of figuratively "devouring" them with their policies of neglect and exploitation.

Like the other master tropes, irony works at the level of individual phrases and at the larger level of whole discourses. It might even serve to define a persona that a speaker or writer projects through language. In Greek drama, for instance, irony was embodied in a stock character, the *eiron*, who dissimulated ignorance in order to deflate the pretensions of other characters. Modern descendants of this character type would surely include such ironists as Jon Stewart of *The Daily Show* and Stephen Colbert of *The Colbert Report*, the latter operating almost exclusively in an ironic mode.

Unlike the other tropes, however, irony depends almost completely on contextual cues, such as the delivery of the speaker (tone, gesture, expression, and so on) and what we know about that speaker, the subject matter, and the circumstances in general. Delivery, speaker, and subject matter are the contextual elements that the Roman rhetorician Quintilian singles out as crucial in identifying irony: "For if any one of these three is out of keeping with the words, it at once becomes clear that the intention of the speaker is other than what he actually says" (333). We have added "the circumstances in general," although this element may be implicit in Quintilian's reference to the subject matter.

When any of these elements are at odds with the literal meaning of a statement, we are probably in the presence of irony. Imagine a teacher saying to a class, "You've studied so hard!" The statement by itself means something positive. But if delivered with a cutting tone, roll of the eyes, or some other vocal or facial cue, the remark may appear ironic. Even if it is delivered straight, students may register an ironic intent by other contextual cues. Perhaps this teacher has a reputation for being stern and never praising students. His or her doing so now may be enough to tip students off that the remark is not a literal one. Or imagine that the remark is not necessarily at odds with the reputation of the teacher, but is delivered while the teacher is handing back a set of very bad papers. This coincidence would be enough for most students to recognize the irony.

At the level of the phrase, irony often appears as sarcasm. But in context, irony always has a moral force. By saying "You've studied so hard," the teacher is not merely complaining that the students did poorly on the papers, but is also pointing the way to what they should have done (study harder).

More important than acknowledging the moral force in understanding irony, however, is the need to realize its dependence on context. A transcript of the teacher's statement to the students would not reveal the irony. You would need a tape to hear the tone of voice, or you would need insider knowledge of the grade book to know what was really intended.

Tone and insider perspective—these are the crucial elements of irony. Tone is usually defined as an author's attitude toward subject matter (the failed tests) and audience (the students). Ironic tone is conveyed by setting up a condition of unequal knowledge. Before they look at their papers, the students may think the remark is complimentary, but after they peek at their grades, they realize the irony. The "before" condition stands in contrast to the "after" condition because in the process they have gained new knowledge that allows them to realize the irony. Irony generally contrasts a naïve position with a position of greater wisdom. In this case, the rapid shift from "before" to "after" does not allow the students to adjust to the new state of knowledge and thus will likely offend them. That's the way sarcasm usually works (and that's why using it too often is a notorious avenue to bad evaluations from angry students).

One way to get a handle on the rhetoric of irony is to use the approach of the triple persona. The approach is based on our ordinary understanding of pronoun grammar. Rhetorical irony involves creating an inner circle of a first and second persona—"I" and "you." The idea is to bring "I" and "you" into alignment—to create a plural first persona, a "we"—and then to designate a third persona, "them." "We" stand against "them," the oppressors or their accomplices, the outsiders, those who are not "in the know."

The example of the episode with the student papers turns out to be a weak one in this sense, but it still works. The "I" (teacher) and "you" (students) become a "we" position occupied by the teacher and the students in their knowledgeable ("after") state. The "they" position is occupied by the students in their naïve ("before") state. This kind of irony is sometimes called "dramatic irony" because it emerges in the unfolding of dramatic events. A change must occur before the irony can be revealed. In this case, the change probably doesn't occur, and the students reject the "we" position.

Swift's "Modest Proposal" offers a better example. As we begin to read, the "I" of the discourse appears to us as a social reformer. We may take the "you" position as the addressee for a while, but as the proposal becomes more and more preposterous, we begin to pull away, and as we do, we perceive that the author is winking at us. The first persona "I" of the essay is not the author at all but an invention of the author, an absurd mask. Likewise the "you" is not the intended audience (the reader) but the very people whose values the author is attacking, the neglectful and exploitive rich. As we pull away, we join the author in an inner circle of knowledge, a "we." The "I" of the proposer and the "you" that stands for the oppressors become together the "they" against which we take our stand with the author.

How do we know the author is winking when we can't see him? The short answer is we grasp irony by insights into context and tone. If we know something about Jonathan Swift's political leanings, we can quickly grasp his intent. Even if we don't, however, we can pick up his tone by the way he manipulates values. When the "I" of the essay suggests cannibalism as a solution to the problem of hunger and poverty, he violates not only the rules of logic but the root values of human life even as he promotes the entrepreneurial spirit and the values of hard work and ingenuity. Some values always take priority over others. Swift's irony allows the undeniable value of every human life to take priority over the lesser values promoted by his persona, the proposer. The audience is left to reflect on the way that the values of hard work and productivity often mask exploitive attitudes even when they are not taken to the extremes of "A Modest Proposal." The hope is that the "we" of the essay endures as a political "we" in public life.

Irony can thus exist in a single statement ("You've studied so hard") or run continuously throughout a larger piece ("A Modest Proposal"). In our culture, the trope has expanded to encompass a general stance toward the world, pervading such seemingly disparate arenas as philosophical thought, cocktail party chatter, and television commercials (for instance, the Geico gecko and caveman). It defines a position detached from, and skeptical of, accepted cultural truths, values, and institutions. The Geico gecko, for instance, often talks about (and thus exposes) the techniques advertisers use to persuade consumers to buy their products (the power of the celebrity spokesperson, for instance), while using some of those same techniques to sell Geico insurance. The commercial thus places viewers in a position of detachment from the tricks and gimmicks of the television ad, but do viewers register the further irony that they are being subjected to some of those very same tricks and gimmicks? And if they do, does this additional layer of irony increase the ad's appeal?

Irony gained special attention in the aftermath of the 9/11 attacks. In the wake of those events, editorialists and commentators declared the death of irony, the impossibility of remaining aloof or noncommittal about the attacks, of being ironic toward your country or toward the terrorists. (We note that *The Daily Show with Jon Stewart* suspended its broadcast for over a week and that comedian Bill Maher was booted from ABC after offering an alternative perspective on the terrorists, one that emerged from an ironic sensibility.) All of these responses imply something important about how irony functions. It's a trope of dynamism, involving closing and opening of distances, recruiting a "you" into the circle of "we" in opposition to a "they." When everybody is already a "we" or a "they" and it seems no one is likely to budge from those positions, there's little room for irony: there are no *you*'s to recruit from either side. As time passed after 9/11, however, irony began slowly to return to its former cultural prominence, owing in part to questions over and opposition to the war in Iraq. Its return is probably a good thing. For irony continually questions, continually offers fresh and alternative perspectives on issues. It is, in short, a trope well befitting a democracy.

A Miscellany of Tropes

Metaphor, metonymy, synecdoche, and irony are only four of the dozens of tropes (and hundreds of figures) identified by classical and Renaissance rhetoricians. Let's close this chapter by looking at a few additional types that are relatively common. Throughout, it is important to remember that the tropes (like the figures in general) are moves or distinct actions that writers perform when writing (like the ballet dancer who executes a pirouette or *grand jeté* during a longer routine). Moreover, writers use them not just to gussy up their prose but to secure various rhetorical and social ends that themselves might have broader cultural implications (including their long history of use in Western rhetoric and literature).

Puns are tropes that play on words that sound alike but differ in meaning. They come in at least three major varieties. The first occurs when a single word conveys several possible meanings simultaneously: "Don't Mess with Texas" (slogan from an antilitter campaign), "If I were a bitch, I'd be in love with Biff Truesdale" (Biff is a showdog; Orlean, "Show Dog" 161). A second variety involves replacing a word with another that resembles it in sound: "The Pint of No Return" (alleged title of a country song), "A good pun is its own reword," "Horsemen of the Esophagus" (the title of an article by Jason Fagone). A final variety occurs when a word is repeated but in two different senses: "You won't catch a case of the blues when you drink a case of the blues" (faux advertisement for Bluefish Beer).

The rhetorical and social uses that puns serve include making others laugh (or groan) while displaying a writer's wit (or lack thereof). They've also crept into the writings of some academics in the humanities where they reveal different nuances of meaning associated with a concept (Wales 385), or if used gratuitously and ostentatiously, merely seek to advertise the academic's nimble mind. As you have probably picked up, there is some controversy over how puns should be valued—if at all. In one of the earliest English dictionaries, Samuel Johnson defined "pun" as "the lowest form of humor." Sigmund Freud considered puns among the easiest and cheapest jokes to come by. Yet puns thrive in both low and high cultural media: the titles of country music songs, on the one hand, and the urbane prose of the *New Yorker* magazine, on the other; the bawdy humor (pun intended) of Shakespeare, and the banter of Edwardian comedy. However they are valued, puns secure their effects by enlisting readers' dexterity of mind: if a pun seems forced or involves overt sexual innuendo, it risks insulting readers' intelligence (and their sensibilities); if it is too oblique or allusive, it risks passing right under their notice.

Another trope, *onomatopoeia*, occurs when the sound of a word imitates what it names: clank, bang, tinkle, buzz, cackle, splat! Here there is a more or less direct link between the sound of the word and the thing to which it refers, although different cultures and regions may vary in how they designate particular instances of onomatopoeia (in English, for instance, a dog says, "woof-woof"; in Chinese it says, "wang-wang"). Other words may not directly imitate the things they name but merely suggest them: slither, flicker, streak. Such words are approximate onomatopoeias, and, used alone or in combination with other words, they can create patterns of sound suggestive of the meanings they express. To take a familiar example—Heimel's "a sinuous long-haired girl snaked" (149), the repeated "s" sounds suggest a hissing snake. We might also note a sound similarity between "sinuous," on the one hand, and "sin" and even "sinister," on the other. Here the sound resemblance is not between the word and the thing it names but between one word and several others. The resulting similarity suggests the girl possesses a menacing or threatening quality.

Hyperbole involves deliberate overstatement or exaggeration. Speakers and writers often use it to show just how strongly they feel about something. Hyperbole can also generate humor. In either case, hyperbole works by creating a disjunction between a thing, person, or event, on the one hand, and a statement that describes that thing, person, or event, on the other:

- I will love you till the end of time. (Countless pop songs)
- I cannot fathom how [John Cusack] isn't the number-one box-office star in America, because every straight girl that I know would sell her soul to share a milkshake with that motherfucker. (Klosterman 2)
- I'm as busy as a one-legged man in an ass-kicking contest. (Folk expression: actually a fusion of hyperbole and simile)

Usually, a hyperbolic statement supplies its own clues that it is not meant to be taken literally (are there really ass-kicking contests out there, and if so, would a one-legged man enter one?). But in some instances, a speaker or writer may intentionally blur the line between hyperbole and fact—that is, to try to pass off a hyperbolic statement as a factual one. This practice is a common feature of advertising, and it's becoming increasingly common in political discourse, especially when a politician is talking about an opponent (we also wonder if it is creeping into news media, which are supposedly only to present the "facts").

Hyperbole's complement is *litotes*, or deliberate understatement. Like hyperbole, litotes creates a disjunction between a statement and the thing, person, or event to which it refers (that is, a disjunction between form and content). But in this case, the statement doesn't exceed its referent as it does in hyperbole; instead, it falls short of it. Strictly speaking, litotes asserts something by denying its opposite, usually through the adverbs "no" or "not": "She's no friend of mine," or "He's not the smartest guy in the world." But litotes can include any form of understatement. One of its most famous instances is Mercutio's description of his death wound in *Romeo and Juliet*: "No, 'tis not so deep as a well, nor so wide as a church door; but 'tis enough, 'twill serve" (III.i.101).

Both hyperbole and litotes may be generalized into personas that a performer might take on. In ancient and Renaissance drama, hyperbole was embodied by a stock character, the braggart soldier who struts the stage boasting of his exploits and hyping his personal merits. Today, we might think of the car or mattress salesmen from low-budget television commercials: "Hurry! Hurry! Hurry! Don't miss the deal of the century!" Litotes may also sum up a persona. The British, for instance, are noted for understatement, as if it were part of their national ethos. The United States, for its part, may be a country of hyperbole, but there are pockets of understatement. In our experience, a certain brand of Texan seems fond of that trope. If you say to that Texan, "Wow! It's hot here," he's likely to respond, "Yup. It's a bit warm"; say, "Holy smokes! It's cold," and he'll say, "Maybe a tad cool." The trope projects the persona of someone who is not easily ruffled in the face of extreme circumstances—something like cowboy cool. The stance is put to new uses by the ecological activist Rick Bass. Environmentalists are known for hyperbole, but this Texas native finds litotes well suited to his purpose in an essay on the reintroduction of wolves in North America. Notice how his "just a tad" litotes sets up the shock of the numbers he presents just after:

In the absence of bison, there was the bison's replacement: cattle. The wolves preyed upon these new intruders, without question, but ranchers and the government overreacted just a *tad*. Until very recently, the score stood at Cows, 92,200,000; Wolves, 0 (Bass, *Ninemile* 1116, his italics).

Another trope, *anthimeria* occurs when a writer substitutes one part of speech for another—usually a noun for a verb. We have already seen an example of this trope in Heimel's sentence: "Through the crowd a sinuous long-haired girl snaked." Here Heimel takes a noun, "snake," and uses it as a verb. In the following, Malachy McCourt turns the noun "typhoon" into a participle: "A whirling, swirling mass of bods went typhooning toward the door, knocking over tables, bar stools, hysterical women, dinners, pictures on the walls, and all else in its path" (67). Other examples of nouns turned in to verbs: "I found his email address by googling him," "Beer me," "Pimp My Snack" (Web site offering recipes for monstrous versions of your favorite snack foods). Sometimes an adjective may serve as verb, as in "It weirds me out." Speakers or writers who use anthimeria may be showing verbal mastery, an ability to play with our language system, blurring its fundamental categories and turning them to fresh purposes. Anthimeria, however, is not always about verbal play. It's often a characteristic of jargon-filled prose (nominalizations, after all, are a form of anthimeria whereby verbs are turned into nouns). Academics and bureaucrats often use it to puff up their prose in an effort to puff up themselves and the ideas they are advancing: "This committee is *tasked* with the job of *unearthing* how *focus* groups *impact environment contamination studies*."

Antonomasia, which literally means "different name," occurs when a writer uses either a descriptive phrase in place of a proper name or uses the name of well-known person (or character) as a generic label for someone else. Bernard Cornwell uses the first kind in the opening of his retelling of the Arthur legend, introducing the fabled king with a series of antonomasias: "These are the tales of Arthur, the Warlord, the King that Never Was, the Enemy of God and, may the living Christ and Bishop Sansum forgive me, the best man I ever knew" (3). Other examples of this type applied to modern personages include: "The Comeback Kid" for President Bill Clinton, "America's Mayor" for Rudy Giuliani, and "The Queen of Soul" for Aretha Franklin. The second type of antonomasia involves applying the name of a well-known person to someone else to highlight an attribute associated with that name. For instance, Chuck Klosterman refers to John Cusack as "the neo-Elvis" to emphasize Cusack's popularity with female moviegoers (2).

Periphrasis occurs when a single word is replaced by several others to form a longer phrase that names the same thing: for instance, "briny deep" for "ocean," or "the manly art" for boxing. Periphrasis is a Greek term meaning "around speech," and it's ultimately from this term that we get "circumlocution." The term's literal meaning is helpful as we consider how writers use this trope. It's often used in euphemisms to speak "around," and thus spare readers from, any distasteful associations the more direct, single-word variant might trigger: "little girl's room" for "toilet," or "passed on to greener pastures" for "died." Writers also use periphrasis to elevate their prose, to raise it from the informality of the low and middle styles to the formality of the high one, as in the following examples—the first a case of the oratorical high style, the second from the technical high style (see chapter 5):

- And those who hope that the Negro needed to *blow off steam* and will now be content will have a *rude awakening* if the nation re-turns to business as usual. And there will be neither *rest nor tran-quility* in America until the Negro is granted his citizenship rights. The *whirlwinds of revolt* will continue to *shake the foundations* of our nation until the *bright day of justice* emerges. (King, "I Have a Dream" np)
- CSIRO has patented a process using ultrasound to *remediate contaminated soils* and create waste that can be disposed of safer, cheaper and quicker than *current alternatives*. (CSIRO np)

Periphrasis can also lend prose a poetic or even archaic flavor. As Katie Wales notes, periphrasis is at work in the "kennings" of Old English poetry ("swan road" for "sea," or "heath stepper" for "deer"); it's also characteristic of eighteenth-century verse ("finny tribe" for "fish," or "fleecy care" for "sheep") (346). More recently, Bill Bryson uses periphrasis when writing about the death of Australian prime minister Harold Holt who drowned off Cheviot Beach in 1967 while still in office. Although the area was known for its dangerous riptides and despite warnings from his friends, Holt took the plunge, swam out through the surf, and was never seen again (his body wasn't even recovered). After recounting this story, Bryson refers to Holt's "drowning" through this somewhat mischievous periphrasis: "the Swim That Needs No Towel" (*In a Sunburned Country* 141).

The four master tropes and those covered in our "miscellany" introduce you to some of the ways words can be "turned" from their conventional meanings. We've presented the tropes as moves within a writer's more general repertoire of performance. As such, these set pieces of language are not merely ornamental; rather, they help writers orchestrate their interactions with readers. More generally, they catalogue some of the ways we think about and conceptualize our experiences in the world. The next chapter continues this work by considering the other group of figures of speech: the schemes.

Summary of Tropes in Chapter 6

Name	Brief Definition	Brief Example
Metaphor	Identification of two unlike things	the manacles of segregation and the chains of discrimination
Metonymy	Substituting a thing with a closely associated or contiguous thing	The White House denied the allegations.
Synecdoche	Substituting a part for a whole, genus for species, species for genus	All hands on deck.
Irony	Saying one thing and meaning another	You've studied so hard.
Pun	Play on words that sound alike but differ in meaning	A good pun is its own reword.
Onomato-poeia	A word's sound imitates what it means	clank, bang, splat!
Hyperbole	Intentional overstatement	busy as a one-legged man in an ass-kicking contest
Litotes	Intentional understatement	just a tad
Anthimeria	Substituting one part of speech for another	Beer me!
Antonomasia	Substituting a descriptive word or phrase for a proper noun, or using a proper noun as a generic label	the comeback kid What's up, Romeo?
Periphrasis	Replacing a single word with a longer multiword description	the swim that needs no towel

Exercises

1. Identify the tropes in the following passages (there may be more than one trope in each one). Then select one passage and write an analysis of its performative dimensions using the three arenas of action (textual, social, and cultural) as a framework for your interpretation.

a. The hand that rocks the cradle rules the world. (Proverb)

b. Precisely what my parents were warring over I'm not sure, but it seems clear to me now that in the intricate territorial maneuvers that for years defined their marriage, cooking was my mother's principal weapon. Proof of her superiority. My father might not feel tenderness, but he would have to admire her. My mother cooked with a vengeance in those years, or perhaps I should say she cooked for revenge. In her hands cuisine became a martial art. (Levy 122)

c. Whether or not bowling beats balloting in the eyes of most Americans, bowling teams illustrate yet another vanishing form of social capital. (Putnam 205)

d. Pray to their spirits. Ask them to bless us:
    our ancient sisters' trails
    the roads were laid across and kill them:
    night-shining eyes
    The dead by the side of the road.

                           (Snyder 8)

2. Making the tropes part of your writing repertoire requires commitment and practice. To these ends, T. R. Johnson outlines a semester-long activity that your instructor may want to adopt. After introducing his students to the figures (both tropes and schemes), Johnson requires his students to use at least two of these verbal devices in all their short writing assignments and at least eight in their longer papers (38). Use the footnote function in your word processor to point out where you have used a trope, to identify what kind of trope it is, and to explain (briefly) why you have used it. Combined with other in-class exercises and discussions of the figures, these requirements are meant to encourage you to write with a "greater degree of inward reflection" and heightened sense of the pleasures of prose (Johnson 40).

3. Identify tropes in a sample from your commonplace book and comment briefly on how it works in the three arenas. Here's an example from the chapter 1 exercise:

> *Quotation*: . . . my faithful Land Rover . . . gave a hellish clang and, dragging its guts over the stone, lurched to a halt. (Peter Matthiessen, quoted in Finch and Elder 637)
>
> *Comment*: In the textual arena, the sentence progresses from an appropriately mechanical description of the damaged car—"clang" (using the trope of onomatopoeia)—to a metaphor that personifies, or at least animates, the machine—"dragging its guts over the stone." The metaphor also works within the social arena by urging the reader to "feel the pain" of the car (or more properly, the pain of the author projected onto the car). Culturally, it draws upon the common tendency of Americans to personify or animate their vehicles, hearkening back to the days of horsemanship among cowboys, farmers, and the cavalry.

7

Schemes

Like the tropes, the schemes are moves within a writer's repertoire of performance. They are units of verbal behavior that we can point to, analyze, evaluate, and (ultimately) incorporate into our own writing. However, unlike the tropes, which involve "turning" a word from its conventional meaning to an unusual one, the schemes name various patterns of words—that is, how words are arranged within a sentence or across several sentences. Borrowing a common distinction from linguistics, we can say that tropes correspond to semantics (word meaning), while schemes correspond to syntax (word order) (Fahnestock 11). To use another analogy, the schemes are like the plaster molds that a special effects artist might use to fashion a mask or figurine: they are the shapes that writers often use to cast their sentences.

But the analogy is not perfect. The schemes are not empty vessels devoid of meaning and function. While giving language a discernible shape, the schemes also shape the realities to which language refers, organizing it and structuring it in particular ways over others. Consider these stylistic variants and imagine they are alternatives for describing the same incident:

- The whispers grew to shouts, and the shouts became hurled stones. (Teague 54)
- They whispered. They shouted. They hurled stones.

Both variants use schemes (we'll learn their names below), but each depicts a slightly different reality. The first, with its repetition of "shouts," suggests a tightly linked sequence of events with each action building progressively into the next (the verbs "grew" and "became" further this suggestion). The second variant merely lists these actions without providing any explicit temporal or causal connections between them (although the fact that they are ordered in the way they are suggests a chronology). Its strict parallelism emphasizes equivalency among the actions over sequence; as a result, it opens up the possibility that these actions were happening simultaneously.

In addition to structuring reality, the schemes help writers organize and orchestrate their relationships with readers. As vehicles for social interaction, they can

- Signal the level of formality (high, middle, low) as well local shifts across these levels;
- Control the emotional intensity of prose—cranking it up here, ratcheting it down there;
- Showcase the writer's wit and command over his or her medium;
- Enlist readers into collaborative relationships, inviting them to desire the completion of a pattern once they get its gist. (Burke, *Rhetoric of Motives* 58–59)

Rhetoricians from antiquity and the Renaissance catalogued dozens upon dozens of schemes. Their goal was to be exhaustive, to classify every conceivable pattern into which language could fall. In this chapter, we focus on several representative schemes from four major groups: schemes of balance, schemes of omission, schemes of unusual word order, and schemes of repetition. This categorization (which borrows from Corbett and Hickey) offers a convenient way to organize these devices, although we'll see that some schemes could fit comfortably into more than one group. Our goal is not simply to name, define, and illustrate each of these schemes, which would be to stop at the level of mere stylistic description. The real payoff of learning the schemes comes with pushing further and asking, "What can these verbal devices do? How do they structure the realities or experiences they are used to express? How do they affect interactions between writer and reader?" Answers to these questions will ultimately depend on the immediate context, but for each scheme, there are usually general or conventional functions that it might serve. We identify and discuss these functions so that both writers and analysts can apply this knowledge when writing original compositions or interpreting stylistic choices in the works of others.

Schemes of Balance

Schemes of balance create relationships between words and ideas through structural similarity. In some cases, similarity in structure reinforces or echoes similarities in meaning. In other cases, structural similarity serves as a foil to throw opposite or antithetical ideas into sharper relief. Perhaps the most common scheme of balance is *parallelism*, or placing grammatically equivalent items in coordinated pairs or coordinated series of words, phrases, or clauses:

- All it takes is a dollar and a dream. (Florida Lotto slogan)
- We are more often arrested, convicted, and mobbed. (Du Bois 18)
- You make faces associated with pain, with tears, with orgasm, with the sort of exertion that would call others to your immediate aid. (Grief 63)
- He hurls people against lockers; he spits, pours, and sprays; he has a projectile relationship with food. (Denby 94)

Parallelism is both a grammatical rule and a rhetorical device. In grammar, it requires that items connected by coordinating and correlative conjunctions be grammatically equivalent. If we rewrote the Lotto slogan as "All it takes is a dollar and to dream," we would violate parallelism because the two items linked by the conjunction are no longer grammatically equivalent: "dream" is a noun; "to dream" is an infinitive. As a rhetorical device, parallelism often uses similarity in structure to reinforce or suggest similarities in meaning. The grammatical equivalency between "a dollar" and "a dream" (plus the alliterating "d" sounds that bring this pair even closer together) suggest that these two items are complete in themselves, sufficient to fulfill whatever desire we may have. In the following, Jon Krakauer uses a parallel series of coordinated pairs to help explain how Bullhead City, Arizona, is a "community in the oxymoronic, late twentieth-century idiom":

> Bullhead's distinguishing civic feature is the Mohave Valley Highway, four lanes of asphalt lined with gas stations and fast-food franchises, chiropractors and video shops, auto-parts outlets and tourist traps. (39)

The parallelism here works on two levels. First, the parallel series as a whole creates a stylistic context in which these seemingly disparate businesses can exist side by side. It thus makes more believable that this potentially confusing collection of shops can share the same civic space. Second, the parallelism within each item of the series sharpens the contrasts between each set of paired items: the syntactic proximity of, say, "chiropractors" and "video shops" creates a collision in the minds of readers and thus preserves the notion that Bullhead City is, in some way, an oxymoron.

Parallelism also facilitates communication by making writing easier to read. Sentences are sequences of both words and functions (Rice 207). In the sentence from Grief, for instance, there is a sequence of words— "You" + "make" + "faces" + "associated" (and so on)—and a sequence of functions—subject + verb + direct object + modifier + modifier + modifier + modifier. "When sentences become a continuous sequence of both *new* words and *new* functions, particularly for extended periods, reading begins to creak and strain. Hence, writers frequently lighten their readers' task by using parallelism or a series—structural repetition" (Rice 207, emphasis added). In Grief's sentence, there are twenty-three words but only four functions: subject, verb, direct object, and modifier. While processing the parallel series at the end of this sentence, readers must process the new words appearing in each item of the series ("pain," for instance, and "tears"), but because each item is grammatically equivalent, they do not have to process a new function each time.

In the following passage, Mark Singer illustrates how a writer can use parallelism to organize a vast amount of information and present it in an accessible and highly readable form (note that this is a single sentence):

Among the nonfiction movies that [filmmaker] Erroll Morris at one time or another has been eager to make but has temporarily abandoned for lack of investor enthusiasm are *Ablaze!* (or *Fire From Heaven*), an examination of the phenomenon of spontaneous human combustion; *Whatever Happened to Einstein's Brain?* (portions of the cerebellum and the cerebral cortex are thought to be in the possession of a doctor in North Carolina, other parts are floating around here and there); *Road*, the story of one man's attempt to build across northern Minnesota an interstate highway that no one else wanted; *Insanity Inside Out*, based on the book of the same title, by Kenneth Donaldson, a man who, in his forties, was wrongly committed by his parents to a mental hospital and got stuck there for fifteen years; *Weirdo*, about the breeding of a giant chicken; *The Wizard of Wendover*, about Robert K. Golka and his laser-induced fireball experiments in Utah; and a perusal of Yap, a south Pacific island where stone money is the traditional currency. (261)

Singer packs a lot of information in this one sentence, but parallelism keeps the reader on track. Each item begins with the title of the project or brief description ("a perusal of Yap") followed by some form of modification: either an appositive or elaborating sentence or adjectival phrases. The structural similarity allows Singer to keep introducing one new word after another while limiting the number of new functions readers must process.

Another scheme of balance is *isocolon*. It's a special case of parallelism using phrases and clauses that are not only grammatically parallel but also equal in length. The Grief sentence would be an example if it weren't for the final item in the series: because of its length, it breaks the pattern of two words per item. Grief does use isocolon later in his essay: "Our hidden flesh becomes our public front." Here the verb "becomes" serves as a pivot point or fulcrum balancing the two noun phrases, both of which are grammatically parallel (personal pronoun + adjective + noun) and equal in length (three words). Singer also uses isocolon in this description of Erroll Morris: "Photographs make him appear either darkly handsome or dolefully goofy" (266). In this case, the coordinating conjunction "or" serves as the pivot point balancing "darkly handsome" against "dolefully goofy." Remove one of the adverbs and the scheme goes askew: "Photographs make him appear either darkly handsome or goofy." Without the second adverb to preserve balance, the second adjective suggests a finality that tips the scale in its favor, as in "darkly handsome or [just plain] goofy." In the original, the balanced phrases suggest that Morris is just as likely to appear one way as the other.

Too much isocolon pushes prose towards poetry (Corbett 464). In some cases, this may be a writer's goal. More often, writers avoid sounding overly poetic by using what we might call approximate isocolon—two or more phrases or clauses that are roughly parallel and almost equal in length. Grief uses an approximate isocolon in a comparison between the exercise equipment of a modern gym and the machinery of an early twentieth-century factory: "We willingly submit our legs to the mangle, and put our stiffening arms to the press" (62). The two verb phrases stop short of an exact isocolon: the modifier in the second phrase ("stiffening") breaks the pattern established in the first; as a consequence, the second verb phrase is one word longer than the first.

A third scheme of balance is *antithesis*, or setting contrasting words, phrases, clauses, or ideas side by side. A strict definition of this scheme would require the contrasting items to be expressed in parallel structure to perfect the balance between them:

It was the best of times, it was the worst of times, it was the age of wisdom, it was the age of foolishness, it was an epoch of belief, it was an epoch of incredulity, it was the season of Light, it was the season of Darkness, it was the spring of hope, it was the winter of despair, we had everything before us, we had nothing before us, we were all going direct to Heaven, we were all going direct the other way . . . (Dickens 5)

Here are seven antitheses in a row each with a set of two contrasting words: "best" versus "worst," and "wisdom" versus "foolishness," and so forth. All seven are exactly parallel. This similarity in structure not only preserves balance but also creates a uniform backdrop that throws the contrasting words into shaper relief: "An antithesis is designed to deliver a contrast, and the ability to perceive a contrast, according to a commonplace in psychology, is enhanced by a uniform background" (Fahnestock 50). The repeated words and phrases ("it was," "of times," "the age of," and so on) seem to dissolve into such a background, while the pairs of contrasting words ("best" and "worst," and "wisdom" and "foolishness") seem almost to lift off the page.

A looser definition of antithesis relaxes the requirement for exact parallelism: there only needs to be a juxtaposition of contrasting words or ideas:

- In them, the constraints of celibacy have somehow been transformed into an openness that attracts people of all ages, all social classes. (Norris 130)
- It's bad enough to have to cope, privately, with one's body falling apart; there's something grotesque about having to display that disintegration on a public stage. (Perillo 140)

In the following sentence, Ian Frazer delivers a double antithesis that mixes strict antithesis with a more relaxed, less rigidly parallel version:

Among the cruelest tricks life plays is the way it puts the complicated part at the end, when the brain is declining into simplicity, and the simple part at the beginning, when the brain is fresh and has memory power to spare. (56)

This contrast between the mental capacities of age and youth presents two sets of contrasting phrases and clauses. The first item in each set is exactly parallel,

- the complicated part at the end
- the simple part at the beginning

while the second items are approximately parallel:

- when the brain is declining into simplicity
- when the brain is fresh and has memory power to spare.

As with isocolon, prose writers often stop short of exact parallelism to avoid seeming overly mannered or overtly artful.

Antithesis serves a variety of functions. One is to display the talents of the writer—his or her command over the medium. The visibility of this display is directly proportional to the exactness of the scheme: the stricter the parallelism, the showier the scheme. Here's a dandy example followed by a statelier one:

- A brain of feathers, and a heart of lead. (Pope 14)
- We observe today not a victory of party but a celebration of freedom, symbolizing an end as well as a beginning, signifying renewal as well as change. (Kennedy 11)

One reason antithesis enhances a writer's reputation for wit is that it often produces a memorable expression. When Neil Armstrong stepped onto the moon, he delivered this antithesis:

That's one small step for man; one giant leap for mankind.

It's difficult to repeat this antithesis without remembering who said it. Advertisers have capitalized on this effect of the scheme and frequently use it in their product slogans:

- Live in your world, play in ours. (Sony Playstation)
- Melts in your mouth, not in your hands. (M&Ms candies)
- You've got questions, we've got answers. (Radio Shack)

These antitheses do double duty: not only are they easy to remember, but the wit displayed in their formulation reflects favorably on the products they are meant to sell and the companies that produce them.

Antithesis may also suggest equipoise and stability. David Quammen uses antithesis to describe the "equilibrium line" on a glacier, a line marking the location where the amount of ice added through precipitation and the amount subtracted through melting "cancel each other out":

Nothing is lost, over the course of time, and nothing is gained. (Quammen, "Strawberries" 200)

This antithesis not only sums up what an "equilibrium line" is but dramatizes, through its balance and parallelism, its natural properties.

In some cases, antithesis may force terms into opposition that are not actually opposed (Fahnestock 69). Or it may misleadingly divide an issues into sets of either/or propositions, ignoring all the shades of grey in between.

- If you're not part of the solution, you're part of the problem.
- Either you're with us, or you're against us.

These are common phrases used by writers and speakers who are convinced they have *the* answer to some predicament. Both are absolutist in their logic and seek to drive a wedge between opposing camps or solutions, ruling out the possibility of achieving some middle ground or compromise.

Schemes of Omission

The schemes in this group include verbal devices that leave out words, phrases, and clauses that readers might normally expect to be included or that readers can easily recover from the immediate context. These schemes help writers secure economy of expression (and thus enhance the readability of a text), but they can serve other functions as well: they can highlight new or important information; mimic the sound, rhythm, and pace of spoken discourse; and enlist readers in collaborative or even collusive relationships with writers. Rhetoricians have catalogued a number of schemes that involve omissions. Here we focus on two: ellipsis and asyndeton.

Ellipsis occurs when a word or group of words are omitted but easily recoverable form the context. A basic form of this scheme involves omitting a shared grammatical subject in successive verb phrases, as in this example from Tim O'Brien's *The Things They Carried*: "The girl went up on her toes and made a slow turn and danced through the smoke" (136). O'Brien could have repeated the grammatical subject ("the girl") before the second and third verb or chosen to use the pronoun "she." The first option would sound strangely emphatic (insert "the girl" before each verb and read it aloud), while the second option (although less emphatic than the first) would still distract readers' attentions from the actions the girl performs which seem the principal focus and point of the sentence. Other basic forms of ellipsis allow writers to avoid repeating words not only to achieve greater economy of expression but also to impart greater emphasis on what is stated:

- Sister Jeremy will appear as a warrior on horseback, Father Robert as a wise old woman tending a fire. (Norris 131)

- I thought of myself and my life as a kind of giant sculpture I worked on patiently day by day, chipping away here, adding there, forever remodeling with a view to perfection. No longer. (Schwartz 138–39)

In the first example, "will appear" is elided in the second clause, as is the conjunction "and" between the two clauses. Both omissions are easily recovered from the context, but by leaving them out, Norris places greater emphasis on what she leaves in. As Dona Hickey says, ellipsis invites readers to "supply what isn't there by stressing heavily what is" (34). In the second example, the ellipsis appears in the second sentence which Schwartz could have written as, "I no longer think of my life in this way." The effect is similar to the one created in the first example, but Schwartz adds an even heavier stress to her ellipsis by punctuating it as its own sentence.

Writers can use ellipsis for more subtle effects. John Edgar Wideman uses it when recounting his experience reading about Emmett Till's death in *Jet* magazine and his struggle to look at the included photo of the deceased and savagely beaten Till: "Turning away from his eyeless stare, I blinded myself. Denied myself denying him" (25). The omissions appear in the second sentence, but they are supplied by the context: "[I] denied myself [by] denying him." Why the ellipsis rather than the more explicit version? For one, the elliptical version has a rhythmic grace that approaches poetry. More important, the ellipsis fuses together the two acts of denial, suggesting that, for Wideman, they are profoundly merged—perhaps simultaneous or indistinguishable in his mind.

Our second scheme of omission, *asyndeton*, is a special case of ellipsis. In Greek, it literally mean "no connections" (*a-syndeton*), and it names a scheme by which writers omit conjunctions and other connectives between words, phrases, and clauses. Perhaps the most famous instance of this scheme is Julius Caesar's tightly worded account of his triumph over Pharnaces: *veni, vidi, vici,* or "I came, I saw, I conquered." In a series such as this, we might expect a conjunction before the final clause: "I came, I saw, and I conquered." But the addition would dampen if not destroy the effect. In the original, it seems as if Caesar wants to suggest that his conquest was just as easy to achieve as his coming and seeing. Add the final conjunction and the coming and seeing seem mere preliminaries to the real climactic event—the conquest. Remove it and all three actions are of equal magnitude.

Asyndeton serves other functions as well. When it is used in a series of words, phrases, or clauses, it suggest the series is somehow incomplete, that there is more the writer could have included (Rice 217). To put it somewhat differently: in a conventional series, writers place an "and" before the final item. That "and" signals the end of the series: "Here it is folks—the last item." Omit that conjunction and you create the impression that the series could continue:

- Like most people who knit, I have bags of yarn stashed in my closet for future projects. The bags are a record of the cities where I've wandered into yarn stores: Madison, Portland, Cambridge, New Orleans, Evanston, Washington, D.C. (Mori 234)
- There was a store in downtown Manhattan I used to visit, near where the banana boats came in, that sold pythons, tiger cubs, pangolins, parrots, ocelots, leopards—what couldn't you buy? (Hoagland 317)

Asyndeton can also create ironic juxtapositions that invite readers into collaborative relationships with writers: because there are no explicit connections between phrases and clauses, readers must supply them to reconstruct the writer's intent:

I cried the first time I saw Bambi's mother die. I was twenty-nine. (Simpson 134).

Asyndeton can also quicken the pace of prose, especially when it is used between clauses and sentences. Just such an effect is created at the beginning of Jerome K. Jerome's *Three Men in a Boat*. After confessing his inability to read about some disease or illness without being convinced that he's got it in "its most virulent form," the novel's hypochondriac narrator recounts how he once read through a medical treatise and, by its end, was sure he was suffering from every malady it listed (except for "housemaid's knee"):

Then I wondered how long I had to live. I tried to examine myself. I felt my pulse. I could not at first feel any pulse at all. Then, all of a sudden, it seemed to start off. I pulled out my watch and timed it. I made it a hundred and forty-seven to the minute. I tried to feel my heart. I could not feel my heart. It had stopped beating. (5)

Apart from the temporal connectives "Then" and "Then, all of a sudden," asyndeton pervades this passage. It serves wonderfully to capture the narrator's panicked response to discovering he has (or *thinks* he has) nearly every ailment in the book.

Asyndeton's counterpart is *polysyndeton* ("many connectives"), or employing a greater number of conjunctions (usually the conjunction "and") than conventionally used. Because the defining characteristic of this scheme is the use of multiple conjunctions, it could be grouped among the schemes of repetition. We treat it here because stylists often pair it with asyndeton—and for good reason: it often serves functions complementary to those served by asyndeton. For instance, if asyndeton can quicken the pace of prose, polysyndeton can slow it down. The insertion of conjunctions between a coordinated series of words, phrases, or clauses inevitably lengthens that series, adding an extra (and usually unstressed) beat between each item. Joseph Mitchell creates just such an effect while describing his fascination with the Hudson River, particularly on Sundays "when there are lulls [on the river] that sometimes last as long as half an hour" and the river "becomes as hushed and dark and secret and remote and unreal as a river in a dream" (37). Each "and" creates its own rhythmic lull, little lapses in the sentence's movement that lengthen this series of adjectives while mirroring the lapses in activity on the river. Remove them and the effect is lost: the river "becomes as hushed, dark, secret, remote, and unreal as a river in a dream." Gone are the rhythmic dips and undulations that, in addition to slowing readers down, suggest the motion of the river's waves.

Readers expect "and" to link items that are grammatically equivalent (noun with noun, phrase with phrase, and so on), and this is especially the case in a polysyndetonic series of words, phrases, or clauses. Writers can play on that expectation and undermine it to create subtle surprises for readers, as Mitchell does when describing his sighting of a large sturgeon:

> It rose twice, and cleared the water both times, and I plainly saw its bristly snout and its shiny little eyes and its white belly and its glistening, greenish-yellow, bony plated, crocodilian back and sides, and it was a spooky sight. (37)

Again a passage rich in polysyndeton, but here it links items at different grammatical levels and thus causes sudden shifts in perspective. We can better see these shifts by diagramming the sentence, highlighting the different levels of connections:

	It	rose twice	
	and	cleared the water both times,	
and	I	plainly saw	its bristly snout
		and	its shiny little eyes
		and	its white belly

    and   its glistening,
                 greenish-yellow,
                 bony plated,
                 crocodilian   back
                        and   sides,

and it   was a spooky sight.

Mitchell presents this sentence as a collection of nested coordinate series. The structures aligned on the left of the diagram reside at the highest grammatical level (the clause), while those on the right occupy the lowest (the word). This sentence, of course, begins at the level of the clause, then moves in to coordinate verb phrases ("rose twice and cleared the water"), then back out to coordinate clauses ("It rose . . . and I plainly saw . . ."), then in again to a series of noun phrases ("its bristly snout and its shiny little eyes [and so on]"), all the way down to coordinate words within one of the noun phrases ("back and sides"). Following this descent to ever decreasing levels of grammatical structure, the reader, by the sentence's end, is suddenly thrown back out to the highest grammatical level—the level of the clause: "it was a spooky sight." In this sentence, Mitchell not only makes use of polysyndeton, but toys with the scheme, sensing its internal trajectories, harnessing them, and shaping them to his own purposes.

Schemes of Unusual Word Order

We'll touch lightly on this group of schemes because we have already treated its salient characteristics through one of our featured examples in this book: "Through the crowd a sinuous long-haired girl snaked." Schemes in this group offer writers ways for gaining and then directing a reader's attention. Departures from conventional or usual word order are, by themselves, invitation enough for readers to pause and wonder what's going on. Once that attention is secured, these schemes then highlight information through syntactic inversion or insertion.

Syntactic inversions rhetoricians call *anastrophe*. The "snaked" sentence is a good example. Heimel inverts the conventional word order of subject-verb-adverbial adjunct by placing the adverbial phrase up front. Other patterns of inversion are possible. In the following, David Quammen not only places the adverbial up front but also reverses the usual word order between subject and verb: "In response comes a wooden silence" (*Flight* 70). Here again we have the adverbial first ("In response"), but instead of moving from subject to verb, Quammen places the verb ("comes") before the subject ("a wooden silence"). Charles Simic illustrates still another possibility: "Without histrionics life is boring" (87). A more conventional arrangement would place the modifier ("without histrionics") either after the subject ("Life without histrionics is boring") or after the predicate adjective ("Life is boring without histrionics").

Once inversions such as these invite readers to linger, they then direct readers' attentions within the scheme itself. To put it somewhat differently, writers use anastrophe to highlight important words (or words they want to emphasize) by moving them to positions of stress: either the beginning of the sentence or, even more emphatic, its end. Compare the original sentence from Quammen with one of our variations: "In response comes a wooden silence" and "In response a wooden silence comes." In the original, "a wooden silence" appears in the final slot of the sentence; it is thus marked as the new and important information. In our variation, that role is played by the verb "comes." What's the difference in meaning? In the original, "wooden silence" receives the emphasis; in our variation, that such a silence "comes" is the sentence's primary news.

When you compose your own anastrophes or analyze those of other writers, attention to context is crucial. In some cases, the demands of the immediate context (especially the expectation for information to flow from known to new) may prompt the inversion in the first place. As we saw in earlier discussions, the inversion in Heimel's "snaked" sentence works so well not only because it allows her to shift the verb "snaked" to the end of the sentence but because it frontloads "Through the crowd" and thus preserves the flow of information from known to new (that is, we already know Heimel is in a crowded bar; what we don't know is that a "sinuous long-haired girl" is about to snake through it). Similar considerations seem to influence the use of inversion in the sentence from Simic: "Without histrionics life is boring." In the original essay "Dinner at Uncle Boris's," this sentence appears immediately after Simic portrays his uncle as either liking or engaging in theatrical behaviors. The word "histrionic" sums up these behaviors nicely (in its context, it's known information); for this reason, it serves as a natural transition to the assertion that follows it: "life is boring."

A second scheme of unusual word order is *parenthesis*, or inserting a word, phrase, or clause into a sentence. Parentheses interrupt a sentence and often function as editorial or conversational asides that comment on the sentences in which they appear. They are little moments within a text when writers break frame, as it were, and speak in a voice that differs from the main or dominant voice in a text. In the following, Geeka Kothari uses parenthesis to comment on the accuracy of her own account of getting sick while visiting relatives in India:

When I throw up later that day (or is it the next morning, when a stomachache wakes me from a deep sleep?), I cry over the frustration of being singled out, not from the pain my mother assumes I'm feeling as she holds my hair back from my face. (94)

The parenthesis here splits the narrator's voice in two: there's the voice of a confident narrator relating the events of her illness; and, within the parenthesis, there's a second voice, one that comments on the sentence in which it appears, questioning the accuracy of the details it offers.

When speaking, we signal conversational or editorial asides in a variety of ways: lowering the voice, altering its tone, contracting or raising the eyebrows, tilting the head, raising hand to mouth as if whispering. Once we finish delivering the aside, we resume our normal speaking voice (and posture). In writing, where these audible or gestural cues are absent, writers signal parentheses typographically—that is, with various kinds of marks on the page: parentheses, commas, or hyphens. A few more examples:

- The experiences are novel, I grant you, and entertaining, too, after a fashion, but they are not judiciously distributed. (Twain 34)
- Morris found his way to Dr. George Arndt, a Gienologist and author of a study—a catalogue of Ed Gein jokes, basically—titled *Community Reaction to a Horrifying Event.* (Singer 268)
- The most widely loved (and profitable) faces in the modern world tend to be exceptionally basic and abstract cartoons: Mickey Mouse, the Simpsons, Tintin, and, simplest of all—barely more than a circle, two dots, and a horizontal line—Charlie Brown. (Franzen 46)

Each of these parentheses signal subtle, momentary changes in alignment between the writer and the assertion in the framing sentence, and (in most cases) between writer and reader. In the sentence from Twain, for instance, the narrator uses the first parenthesis, "I grant you," to concede the point to his addressee (another character in the story) that the "experiences are [in fact] novel," and uses the second, "after a fashion," to allow that they are also "entertaining," although this second parenthesis also seems to hint that the narrator harbors some reservations about the degree to which they are entertaining. Both parentheses are also displays of politeness to the other character, while to the reader they may be taken as ironic. In the sentence from Singer, the parenthesis undercuts the assertion in the framing sentence, redefining the "study" as a collection of jokes. The parenthesis presents this redefinition as insider information, and thus brings writer and reader closer together: they both belong with those in the know.

Schemes of Repetition

Rhetoricians have identified many schemes that involve some form of repetition. Here we focus on a select few that illustrate the different ways repetition can be used as a patterning device. Two of these schemes, anaphora and epistrophe, combine the power of repeating key words with the additional "oomph" given to placing those words in positions of emphasis—that is, the beginnings and ends of phrases and clauses (Fahnestock 158). Another scheme of repetition, antimetabole, involves repeating words but in reverse order ("Eat to live, not live to eat"). Finally, climax uses the repetition of key words or grammatical structures to build series organized by a pattern of increasing or decreasing importance.

Anaphora, or repeating a word or group of words at the beginnings of successive phrases or clauses, is one of the most commonly used schemes. It is a staple of formal oratory, and speakers and writers faced with solemn, important, or momentous circumstances often use this scheme to rise to the occasion, to match the dignity of the situation with dignified forms of address. In his first address to Congress after 9/11, President Bush began his speech with anaphor, declaring there is no need to deliver a report on the state of the Union because we have seen it in the actions of the American people:

> *We have seen* it in the courage of passengers who rushed terrorists to save others on the ground. . . . *We have seen* [it] in the endurance of rescuers working past exhaustion. . . . *We have seen* the unfurling of flags, the lighting of candles . . . *We have seen* the decency of a loving and giving people.

Standing before a nation deeply shaken by recent events, Bush offers comfort and encouragement not only in the sentiments expressed but also in the form of their expression—that is, through anaphora. This scheme is one of formal oratory's most familiar and widely used devices. Bush's listener may not know its technical name, but they know its sound. And it is the familiarity of its sound (in addition to the sentiments it expresses) that seeks to reassure listeners. The anaphor also elevates the discourse, lends it an air of traditional formality, as Bush tries to sound the right notes in his address.

Anaphora is also at home in more colloquial or conversational writing when writers need a vehicle for conveying some strong emotion. Cynthia

Heimel uses it in the following to express her anger over, and frustrations with, people who engage in passive-aggressive behavior:

> *Passive-aggressive* means that you figure out a way to do really nasty things and then if anybody calls you on it you can say, "Who, me? Why I was only . . ." *Passive-aggressive* means that your behavior causes other people to make the moves toward their own destruction, while you just sit back, smoke a joint, and watch. *Passive-aggressive* is sneaky, wimpy hatred. (147)

The repetition of "Passive-aggressive" at the beginning of these sentences allows Heimel to ratchet the emotional intensity up a notch. The repetition not only serves as a vehicle for defining passive-aggressive behavior but also reveals how Heimel feels about it. But even though she uses the same scheme as Bush, this passage is not high oratory. Heimel's subject matter (modern dating rituals), colloquial diction and idioms ("nasty things," "calls you on it," and so on), and use of the second-person pronoun "you" keep the style firmly anchored at the level of informal discourse. Anaphora itself is no stranger to such discourse. It's probably already part of your own expressive repertoire. Have you ever been in an impassioned and intense conversation and made use of such phrases as this: "How many times do I have to [and so on]. . . . How many times . . . . How many times . . . ?" So while anaphora is a defining feature of formal and ceremonial writing and speaking, it is (like many of the other figures) highly mobile, migrating from one level of style to another, or one register to another, or one genre to another. How it combines with other stylistic features, subject matter, and occasions ultimately determines at what level of style a piece of discourse resides.

Anaphora's complement is *epistrophe*, or repeating the same word or group of words at the ends of successive phrases or clauses. Because the ends of phrases and sentences are "already positions of stress," epistrophe is doubly emphatic (Fahnestock 158):

- There is an amazing democracy about death. It is not aristocracy for some *people*, but a democracy for all of the *people*. (King, "Eulogy" 97)
- Until just a few years ago Guam had six endemic species of bird— *endemic* meaning they were found nowhere else in the world. Today the bridled white eye is *extinct*. The Guam broad-bill is *extinct*. The rufous-fronted fantail is almost certainly *extinct*. And the other three species are not much better off. (Quammen, *Flight* 108)

Like anaphora, epistrophe is a staple of high oratory and formal writing. Speakers and writers use it (together with the other schemes) to accommodate their styles to formal occasions or important or solemn subject matters, or to define that occasion as one that is worthy of such accommodation. They may use the schemes throughout a speech or composition to sustain a high degree of formality, as Martin Luther King does in his eulogy for four girls slain in the bombing of a Birmingham church. Or they might use them sparingly in an otherwise informal piece of writing to create temporary shifts or modulations across levels of style. The epistrophe from David Quammen is a good example of this second possibility. It appears in an essay that is largely pitched at an informal level. What this epistophe does is to create a little moment of formality within the informality of the essay as a whole, a slight shift in tone to signal to readers a more grave or serious stance towards the extinction of birds on Guam. The Quammen passage illustrates another function all the schemes may serve, and that is to encode or echo thematic content at the level of style. Because of his subject matter in this passage, epistrophe is a particularly appropriate scheme to use because its repetition of the same word at the ends of successive sentences captures well the finality of extinction.

Another scheme of repetition, *antimetabole*, occurs when words are repeated but in reverse order: "One should eat to live, not live to eat." This scheme often goes by the name "chiasmus," after the crossing pattern involved (*chi* is Greek for the letter "X"). Strictly speaking, however, chiasmus is a more general version of antimetabole and refers not to a reversal of the same words but to a reversal of grammatical structures: "By day the frolic, the dance by night" (S. Johnson, "Vanity" 20). Here individual words are not repeated in reverse order, but grammatical structures are: prepositional phrase + noun + noun + prepositional phrase. In most contexts, either label will serve; in fact, many use "chiasmus" to refer to what is actually an antimetabole. Lanham identifies several of this scheme's general functions (*Analyzing Prose* 121–23). It may work like a form of "verbal judo," a device by which writers can use an "opponent's power to overcome him" (122): A "scholar remarked of another's theory: 'Cannon entertains that theory because that theory entertains Cannon'" (Lanham 122). It can also be used to express relations of reciprocity or interchangeability: "Do unto others as you would have them do unto you"; "I made art a philosophy and philosophy an art" (Wilde 912). In other instances, it may work like antithesis and express two mutually exclusive options or possibilities: "Either the United States will destroy ignorance, or ignorance will destroy the United States" (Du Bois 19). Whatever function it serves, antimetabole offers writers and speakers a way to package an expression in a highly economical and memorable form. Perhaps this accounts for its frequent use in adages and advertising slogans:

- When the going gets tough, the tough get going.
- You can take the girl out of Texas, but you can't take Texas out of the girl.
- Sustocal may not add years to your life, but it will add life to your years.

Our last scheme of repetition, *climax*, serves as a fitting conclusion to this chapter because it often combines with other schemes (particularly parallelisms, isocolon, and anaphora) to achieve its effects. It comes in two varieties: strict and more loosely conceived. The strict version meets two criteria: first, it includes a parallel series that moves forward step by step according to some pattern of organization (usually a pattern of increasing or decreasing importance); second, the last word in each item is repeated at the beginning of the next. The example from the movie trailer to *The Gladiator* meets both criteria: "The general who became a slave, the slave who became a gladiator, the gladiator who defied an empire." The less strict version of climax names any series that simply increases or decreases:

- It is, after all, what produces our leprechauns, our fairy rings, all our beguiling fakery. (Wilson 283)
- But, in a larger sense, we can not dedicate—we can not conse-crate—we can not hallow—this ground. (Lincoln 405)
- This was a time when townspeople in nearby Anniston clubbed riders and burned the buses of Freedom Riders. This was a time of horrors, in Birmingham, in the backwoods of Mississippi. This was a time when the whole damn world seemed on fire. (Rick Bragg, *All Over but the Shoutin'* 66)

With its swelling momentum, climax almost invariably ratchets up the emotional intensity of prose. Rick Bragg, for instance, combines climax with anaphora, leading his readers from incidents of brutality in a small town in Alabama, to horrors visited upon a larger geographical region, to global conflagration. So deeply ingrained in our stylistic capacities is the trajectory of this scheme—this pattern of increasing or decreasing importance—that writers often use it to organize seemingly disparate and unrelated items. Describing a speech former New York City mayor

Rudy Giuliani delivered at a "Get Motivated" business seminar in Des Moines, Iowa, Hanna Rosin inserts a somewhat surprising series capper in this climax:

> For a few moments the business seminar has taken on shades of something deeper, more meaningful—a great political speech, church, Oprah. (40)

When we think of things "deeper, more meaningful," a political speech might come to mind, as would church going, but Oprah? Well, yes and no. The climax here presents an alternate reality, a reality that we might not share but still recognize as possibly real for others, a reality in which the power of Oprah as a cultural phenomena transcends that of even politics and religion.

We began this chapter stressing the importance of not only being able to identify several schemes but examining how they function in their immediate and broader contexts. Of these two goals, the second is far more important. Applying the correct label to these devices comes easily enough through practice. The real accomplishment, from the standpoint of stylistic analysis, is being able to explain how they operate: how they present a writer in a particular way; how they highlight certain bits of information and downplay others; how they help writers manage relationships between themselves, their subject matters, and their readers; how they structure and organize the information they convey and encode, reinforce, or even work against thematic content. As writers, you can apply this knowledge of both the schemes and their general functions in your own written performances. In fact, the schemes were first gathered and collected in the context of performance, as available moves orators could make during their public speeches. Today's orators and writers continue to make use of the schemes, although they may not be as conscious of the fact as orators from ancient Rome and Greece.

Summary of Schemes in Chapter 7

Category or Name	Brief Definition	Brief Example
Schemes of Balance		
Parallelism	Grammatically equivalent items (words, phrases, or clauses) in coordinated pairs or series	All it takes is a dollar and a dream.

| Isocolon | Parallel items equal in length or number of terms | Our hidden flesh becomes our public front. |
| Antithesis | Contrasting items set side by side | It was the best of times, it was the worst of times. . . . |

Schemes of Omission		
Ellipsis	Items omitted but easily recovered from context	Sister Jeremy will appear as a warrior on horseback, Father Robert as a wise old woman tending a fire.
Asyndeton	"No connections": Ellipsis that omits connecting words	I came, I saw, I conquered.
Polysyndeton	"Many connections": An "anti-ellipsis" that adds more connecting words than usual	The river becomes as hushed and dark and secret and remote and unreal as a river in a dream.

Schemes of Unusual Word Order		
Anastrophe	Inverted order	In response comes a wooden silence.
Parenthesis	Item that interrupts the normal flow of a sentence	The experiences are novel, I grant you, and entertaining. . . .

Schemes of Repetition		
Anaphora	Repeating items at the beginning of a series of sentences (or phrases or clauses)	Passive-aggressive means that you figure out a way to do really nasty things. . . . Passive-aggressive means that your behavior causes other people to make the moves toward their own destruction. . . . Passive aggressive is sneaky, wimpy hatred.
Epistrophe	Repeating items at the ends of sentences (or phrases or clauses)	It is not an aristocracy for some people, but a democracy for all people.
Antimetabole	Items repeated in reverse order	One should eat to live, not live to eat.
Climax	Items in a series that increase or decrease in strength or suggest a narrative or progressive change	The general who became a slave, the slave who became a gladiator, the gladiator who defied an empire.

Exercises

1. Identify the schemes in the following passages (there may be more than one scheme in each one). Then select one passage and write an analysis of its performative dimensions: how it imitates or structures reality, and how it orchestrates relationships between writer and reader.
   a. Intellectual gain can be imaginative loss. (Burroughs 39)
   b. The best of men are but men at best. (Proverb)
   c. They flew upside down, and straightened out; they did barrel

rolls, and straightened out; they drilled through dives and spins, and landed gently on a far runway. (Dillard, "The Stunt Pilot" 181)

d. You can brick up your heart as stout and tight and hard and cold and impregnable as you possibly can and down it comes in an instant, felled by a woman's second glance, a child's apple breath, the shatter of glass in the road, the words "I have something to tell you," a cat with a broken spine dragging itself into the forest to die, the brush of your mother's papery ancient hand in the thicket of your hair, the memory of your father's voice early in the morning echoing from the kitchen where he is making pancakes for his children. (Doyle 196)

e. As a child in Hampton, New Hampshire, I knew husbands who cheated on their wives. Openly. My father. I knew men and women who beat their children. We all knew them. We all knew men who were too lazy to bring in a paycheck or clean the leaves out of their yards, women who spent the day on the couch crying while the kids ran loose in the neighborhood. We knew who drank at the Meadowbrook after work each day and drove home to burn SpaghettiOs on the stove for the children. We even knew a witch. We called her Goody Welsh, as if her magic had kept her alive since the Salem days. (Hall 49–50)

2. As with the tropes, making the schemes part of your writing repertoire takes commitment and practice. Following Johnson's advice again, we suggest that, for the rest of the semester, you make a conscious effort to use two schemes in your short writing assignments and eight of them in longer assignments. Again, use footnotes to identify where you have used a scheme, what scheme you used, and why.

3. Comment briefly on the schemes in an example or two from your commonplace book. Here's an example from the nature writing commonplaces:

Quotation: To enjoy a thing exclusively is commonly to exclude yourself from the true enjoyment. (Thoreau 187)
Comment: The sentence uses parallelism "To enjoy . . . exclusively is . . . to exclude . . . enjoyment" to emphasize the contrasting meanings of the similar words "exclude" and "exclusive." The contrast is reinforced by antimetabole, in which the similar terms are repeated in reverse order. "Exclusive" enjoyment suggests a good thing—something special, something limited to just you. But "to exclude" others is a bad thing for the democratic Thoreau.

It ultimately means to reduce your own enjoyment. Things are best enjoyed in company, he suggests. The balance of the parallelism hints at the ideal of democracy—the equivalence of people mirrored by the equivalence of form—while the contrast of antimetabole mirrors the distinction between democracy and the more exclusive social ideals of aristocracy or elitism.

8

Images

The late E. B. White, undoubtedly one of the great stylists in modern American literature, wrote successfully for the toughest audiences. He caught the notoriously wandersome attention of children and held it for generations in such classics as *Charlotte's Web*. He not only met but set the standards by which the personal essay is judged by sophisticated readers of such publications as the *New Yorker*. In one widely anthologized essay, "Once More to the Lake," his prose fairly glimmers, sliding with seeming effortlessness from plain to grand style within the space of a single paragraph, the one that ends the essay, leaving the reader with a chilly finish for the nostalgic performance:

> When the others went swimming my son said he was going in too. He pulled his dripping trunks from the line where they had hung all through the shower, and wrung them out. Languidly, and with no thought of going in, I watched him, his hard little body, skinny and bare, saw him wince slightly as he pulled up around his vitals the small, soggy, icy garment. As he buckled the swollen belt suddenly my groin felt the chill of death. (White 385)

If you want the secrets of how he accomplished such wonders of prose performance—how he connects the familiar old chill in the crotch of the swimsuit to the hug of mortality and the passing of the generations—don't expect to find them in another of White's perennially best-selling books, *The Elements of Style*, which he built up from the class notes of his old English teacher, William Strunk. "Strunk and White," as the book has come affectionately to be known, never gets past the barest conventions of how to write English prose. If, as the ancients said, style is the dress of thought, *The Elements of Style* only gives us underwear. We don't get much farther in any of the dozens of other imitators or new and improved books on style that vie to replace Strunk and White in the hearts and libraries of writers and teachers. They all give advice on grammar and important hints for how to achieve readability. But they rarely go beyond this baseline of good writing and hint at how we might achieve magically evocative prose. One recent book seems to promise something larger and stronger with its witty title, *The Elephants of Style*, but it too sticks mainly to rules for punctuation, usage, and sentence grammar, and steers clear of the hugely vibrant, complexly evolved, thinking, breathing, stomping, charging, trumpeting, ear-flapping effects of language.

This chapter takes a modest step toward a fuller understanding of evocative prose with a discussion of imagery, a technique that White puts to good use in "Once More to the Lake." The image of the boy pulling on the cold swimming trunks, along with White's compact interpretation of the image, somehow gathers the whole wistful tone of the essay up into a single sweep of prose. The study of imagery has a long history, extending from the ancient rhetoricians who spoke of vividness—of putting a scene before the eyes of the reader—to modern literary critics such as I. A. Richards who developed a full-blown theory of the image.

The easy definition of the image as a "word picture" is a bit of a paradox or an oxymoron. A word is a word, and a picture is something different, right? But the very weakness of the definition opens the way into the mysteries of imagery.

More than a Word Picture

What we seem to have here is another case of style trying to overcome the disabilities of writing. We've already seen one such disability in chapter 4: Writing cannot speak. Style tries to overcome this disability by imitating the spoken word—hence "conversational" or "colloquial" style. And because the voice is so closely allied with individual identity, we use the metaphor of voice to describe a deeply personal or comfortable style. "The author really has a voice," we say, or "You've really discovered your voice." If the conversational style tries to overcome the disability, the metaphor of the virtual voice may well be an attempt to ignore it.

Another disability is that writing cannot paint, draw, or otherwise display pictures. Common sense tells us as much—in the cliché that a picture is worth a thousand words. The meaning of the cliché depends upon the fact that pictures differ from writing. Above all, they seem to have a faster, more dynamic impact. Style can compensate for this disability, you would think, through the use of "word pictures," or images.

What we usually call an image is not merely a description. Look at the example of the boy pulling on the swim trunks in White's essay. The image creates a picture in the mind, an illustration; it stimulates the *imagination*. We might see something like a Norman Rockwell painting of the wincing boy and the father standing by, thus connecting the essay with an illustrator of roughly the same historical period. This image is the kind of thing, in fact, that artists pick up when they illustrate essays like this one or similar writings. Notice how White doesn't give the artist much to work with in the way of descriptive details. We see the boy's "hard little body, skinny and bare," but we don't know his hair color, skin shade, height relative to the father, and so on. The lack of detail may appeal to the illustrator, a license to be more creative. The same with the reader: White invites us to fill in the details as we watch along with him. Perhaps we substitute a mental image of a younger brother or cousin and thus create a point of identification. We participate in the creative process by filling in the details, virtually illustrating the essay. How often have you heard someone say about a film version of a familiar novel, "That's not the way I saw the character in my mind"? The film, like the reader's mind before it, does not merely illustrate the character; it interprets the character. And that's usually the case with writing. As description trends toward imagery, it moves toward interpretation. Scenes become symbols. Stories take on allegorical significance.

The case of Junior's swimming trunks takes us even deeper into the theory of the image. Its ability to evoke—to call forth memories and pictures from the mind of the reader—is not only visual. It also involves the sense of touch. Anyone who has ever pulled on wet or cold clothes will *feel* the chill of the boy's wet swimsuit upon reading the words. In this way, White gets close to the reader, gets "under your skin." As we have seen with the tropes (chapter 6), the image makes a connection between words and the experience of the body. Images enter by way of the senses, not only vision but touch, smell, taste, and sound.

Images, then, are the techniques by which the author interprets things and creates interpretive opportunities for the reader. The technique also attempts to activate the senses of the reader, ultimately connecting thoughts and ideas to the experience of the body through references to sight, sound, touch, smell, and taste.

Getting in Touch with the Reader

In the experience of reading, sound and touch, after vision, seem to have the most power, depending of course upon the experience and predilections of the reader as well as the abilities or disabilities. Readers without the sense of sight or hearing or smell will be affected differently from those with a full capacity. Among readers with a full range of aural ability, the sense of hearing becomes engaged by a kind of inner ear even in silent reading—an effect called subvocalization. Our vocal chords actually move even when we read to ourselves, so no reading is ever absolutely silent. To some extent we always "hear" (and feel) the writer speaking to us. The writer can enhance the aural experience of the reader by using alliteration and other repetitions of sounds or by imitating speech in such a way as to encourage the reader to hear the words. Indeed, some readers find dialect writing—as in Mark Twain's novels and "local color" stories like the Uncle Remus tales by Joel Chandler Harris—to be irritating because it requires too much participation. You have to work out the sound of the characters' speech or read aloud to make sense of the meaning.

The sense of touch is activated to some degree by the act of holding the book or paper. (You might wonder how that changes with reading on a computer screen.) Notice how the poet Walt Whitman plays upon the fact that the reader holds the book to create a sense of intimacy in his poem "So Long":

Camerado, this is no book,
Who touches this touches a man,
(Is it night? Are we here together alone?)
It is I you hold and who holds you,
I spring from the pages into your arms—decease calls me forth.

O how your fingers drowse me,
Your breath falls around me like dew, your pulse lulls the tympans of my ears,
I feel immerged from head to foot,
Delicious, enough.

(Whitman 611)

The reader lovingly holding a book of poems thus appears metaphorically as a lover holding the body of the poet. Along with evoking the sense of touch, Whitman uses onomatopoeia to awaken the sense of hearing, the repetition of the *s* and *th* sounds in stressed syllables mimicking the sound of whispering close to a person's ear.

The sense of touch can be evoked along with the other senses by direct or indirect references to the body. Notice how Whitman mentions the arms, fingers, eardrums, pulse, head, and foot. We find another good example in Annie Dillard's brilliant essay "Living like Weasels." She relates the tale of a man who shot an eagle and found a weasel's skull clamped to its neck: "The supposition is that the eagle had pounced on the weasel and the weasel swiveled and bit as instinct taught him, tooth to neck, and nearly won" (Dillard 95). In this extraordinary story, Dillard seems to be merely describing the two animals, eagle and weasel, but the imagery suggests much more. She repeatedly calls attention to parts of the anatomy that people share with other mammals and with birds: throat, tooth, neck, breast, and bones. She never goes so far as to personify the animals, make them human with the use of metaphors. Instead, the images invoke (literally "call to") the body of the reader, hinting at the connection that, as it turns out, she will make explicit later. Invocation of the body leads to the evocation (literally "calling forth") of a response, a feeling.

Dillard's next step is to tell of a personal encounter with a weasel. As a witness, she invites the reader to look upon the creature with her, to identify with her perspective. To set the experience up, she uses quite a bit of descriptive detail, laying the scene out visually for the reader. She mentions a fallen tree, for example, that "makes a dry, upholstered bench at the upper, marshy end of the pond" (96). The metaphorically transformed tree becomes a piece of furniture, a kind of sofa, so that the city-bred or indoor-oriented reader will have a stronger point of identification. The image seems to say, "Have a seat out here with me." She also repeats the word *body* again and again, as in "a shallow blue body of water and a deep blue body of sky" (96). What seems like a nice description is also an evocative image, an effort to bring the reader's physical being into play.

Now that she has you sitting with her on the tree-bench, she's ready to narrate the encounter. As her eyes follow the movement of a yellow bird, she tells us, "I swiveled around—and the next instant, inexplicably, I was looking down at a weasel, who was looking up at me." The action verbs "caught my eye" and "swiveled" set her body into motion (96). On hearing the word "swivel," the attentive reader, now identifying with this guide into the woods, may even feel the muscles around the rib cage activate. You don't actually swivel, but something may happen in that bodily place. The difference between activating and engaging muscles is a distinction known to students of martial arts and other sports. The muscle prepares for action but does not yet move. The tension is something palpable when the eyes are already engaged. You can really feel it watching movies or spectator sports. For this reason, it can be dangerous, for example, to watch football or soccer on TV while using the treadmill at the gym if you are intently following the moves of a football player cutting this way and that on a long run. You might find yourself stumbling in a sympathetic turn or cut. In writing, powerful imagery—imagery that engages the body—similarly invites the reader into the arena of performance.

Dillard's emphasis on the body continues as she shifts from description of the weasel sighting to communicating her excitement through hyperbole (rhetorical overstatement) and a kind of transcendentalist humor, in which she becomes mystically one with the weasel or falls into a lover's (or enemy's) gaze. "Our eyes locked, and someone threw away the key," she says; then:

> Our look was as if two lovers, or deadly enemies, met unexpectedly on an overgrown path when each had been thinking of something else: a clearing blow to the gut. It was also a bright blow to the brain, or a sudden beating of brains, with all the charge and intimate grate of rubbed balloons. It emptied our lungs. It felled the forest, moved the fields, and drained the pond; the world dismantled and tumbled into that black hole of eyes. If you and I looked at each other that way, our skulls would split and drop to our shoulders. (96–97)

She creates humor with "Our eyes locked, and someone threw away the key" by playing with a cliché, or what Orwell calls a "dying metaphor"—the idea of locking eyes. Dillard brings the metaphor back to life and adds a tactile element by introducing another cliché, "threw away the key." The look of the two creatures is so strong that all else seems to disappear. In this sense, as the prose hyperbolically tells us, the look "felled the forest, moved the fields, and drained the pond." She seems to get caught up in her own metaphor of the gaze's power when she turns her attention to what might happen if two humans looked at each other in that way—"our skulls would split and drop to our shoulders"—and in that moment, a shift to human-to-human thought, the weasel disappears, as in the blink of an eye (to use yet another cliché). The references to the body and to bodily movement—the gut, lungs, skull, brain—right down to the final separation, "the yank of separation, the careening splashdown into real life and the urgent current of instinct" (97)—create a kinetic richness and energy by summoning the emotions and sympathetic movements of the reader at the level of actual physical life.

By communicating with this sensual richness—or rather by communicating this bodily engagement and intensity through her imagery—Dillard prepares us for the final brainy allegory of the essay. Having activated our senses with her imagery, she has paved the way for interpretation. She wants us to live like weasels. Circling back to the image of the weasel skull attached the eagle, she urges the reader to "grasp your one necessity and not let it go, to dangle from it limp wherever it takes you" (98). The writing itself, with all senses engaged and alert, has its own likeness to the weasel. It won't let the experience go but strains all the significance and every possible lesson out of it, the way a person hangs on to a precious memory and turns it over and over again in the mind, musing on its meaning from new perspectives at every turn.

Images as Narrative

Besides encouraging audience participation and interpretation and engaging multiple senses, thereby connecting not only the mind but the body of the reader to the text, imagery also engages the reader's narrative sense. We can see each image as an embedded part of a story or as a compacted or potential narrative that may be expanded by the writer or left for the reader to unpack and thus again participate in the creative process of reading and thinking and feeling with the author. The narrative potential of imagery suggests two distinct and equally powerful functions within a text:

1. Images can be expanded to become the focal point of brief vignettes;
2. They can be compacted and enumerated as lists, each item of which can imply further iterations of the overall story, other stories embedded in the images but left implied and untold.

Both functions play a role in Dillard's "Living like Weasels," though the first is by far more important. The best example of function 1 is the anecdote of the dead eagle with the weasel skull affixed to its neck. In addition to giving focus to its own vignette—a complete little story centered around the tenacious jawlock of the tiny but ferocious mammal—the central image ultimately gives unity to the essay as a whole, which in the end urges the reader to live like a weasel, "to grasp your one necessity and not let it go, to dangle from it limp wherever it takes you" and so on (98). Dillard also offers a shorter vignette that functions similarly (and in fact sets up the yet more extraordinary story of the eagle):

One naturalist refused to kill a weasel who was socketed into his hand deeply as a rattlesnake. The man could in no way pry the tiny weasel off, and he had to walk half a mile to water, the weasel dangling from his palm, and soak him off like a stubborn label. (95)

The essay also uses brief catalogues of images that imply stories left untold (function 2): "The water lilies have blossomed and spread to a green horizontal plane that is terra firma to plodding blackbirds, and tremulous ceiling to black leeches, cray fish, and carp" (96). On another day, in another essay, the story of these creatures might be unpacked, but today their narrative energy remains potential as the weasel comes to the spotlight.

As another example of an image-rich text that makes more varied use of the narrative functions of imagery, consider a personal essay entitled "Birdwatcher," recently published by one of the authors of this book (Killingsworth). The main difference between this essay and Dillard's "Living like Weasels" is that she focuses on a single animal while "Birdwatcher" celebrates the profusion of experience that greets the person who stays interested in birds over time. So in addition to a single central story, which tells of one man's lifelong experience of bird-watching and his changes in attitude through the years, the essay contains a number of brief vignettes (function 1), each unified around a central striking image that creates a surge of special emotion in the bird-watcher, as in the following examples (all written in the present tense, in a further effort to intensify the emotion of the story):

- I'm at Hilton Head some time in the mid-seventies, standing by a black-water lagoon near a golf course at dusk. I've ridden my bike over from the new house, just kind of looking around. Movement catches my eye on the other side of the lagoon, the water rippling near a ragged gray tree stump. Was there a big turtle in the water or an alligator? I'm watching intently now, and then the entire stump takes wing and rises slowly out of the water.

  It was a great blue heron feeding on the edge of the lagoon. It had frozen under my gaze.
- At home one late evening in Texas, I'm taking dry clothes off the line strung across the deck in the back yard. Working under an outdoor light, I unpin a pair of cotton briefs and start to fold them when I notice a peculiar, almost familiar weight in the crotch. As I pause in wonder, a Carolina wren flies out of the open place where the leg would go.

It had been hanging in that low sling, perfectly suited to its size and shape, taking a little rest. I stand there laughing with the empty shorts, dry and light now, wavering in a warm breeze.

- It's dusk and I'm with my family up in the tower of the San Jacinto Monument in southeast Texas. Among the water and golden grasses in the surrounding marsh turning pink, a group of shore birds feeding in shallow water, snowy egrets I assume, reflect the sunset.

  Then the sun falls behind a cloud on the horizon, and the landscape goes gray and white like an old movie—except for the birds, which magically retain the pink. I drop a quarter in the scope the state provides and get a better look.

  They are roseate spoonbills. I'd never seen them before in nature, but knew their names and their image from Audubon's watercolor. (Killingsworth, "Birdwatcher" 602–3)

Many other stories are compacted even further, forming lists of images whose full story remains unpacked (function 2). Notice how, in the following examples, the images form into lists of birds, and each item in the list implies a story that fits the pattern of the larger story, a pattern that in experience gets repeated again and again but that, in the telling, readers can fill in for themselves. In the first example, the images stretch out a bit into mini-vignettes, while in the second two they become progressively shorter until by the third they are condensed into a short, simple list of bird names (although the names of the birds themselves have an imagistic effect, since they contain descriptive terms like "downy," "hooded," "warbler," "yellow-billed," and "hermit"):

1. I began to trace the flights and staggers of the marsh and shore and woodland birds—the pelicans cruising in squadrons low across the surf, the little plovers skittering along the beach in numbers I would never see in later years, the gray-brown osprey sweeping into the water with its eagle's talons and bringing out a fish so big it could barely fly back to feed its nested young, and the pileated woodpecker breaking the still air of the pine woods with a wild cry before taking my breath away in a flight across a clearing with its big black and white wings and bright red crest. (Killingsworth, "Birdwatcher" 597)

2. The western tanager with its striking red-orange face and canary yellow body, the stately western grebe, the flickers with shafts of

red instead of yellow, the burrowing owls, prairie and peregrine falcons, the whimsical roadrunner, the sociable snow geese, and the retiring cactus wren—we marked them all down. (599)

3. I saw downy woodpeckers, hooded warblers, yellow-billed cuckoos, solitary vireos, and the hermit thrush, as I sat on that porch—until the woods gave way to first one new house, then another; the woods thinned and all but disappeared. (598)

Lists may seem a natural outgrowth in an essay on bird-watching. Birders are notorious for keeping lists, often with dates and notes about the sighting of any particular bird, the raw materials of narrative. But lists have a strong attraction among writers and readers of all narratives. Not quite reduced to data, the items in a list tug at the imagination of the reader and suggest the wealth of experience from which the overall story is drawn. In classical times, listing was one of the schemes, *enumeratio*, and became the foundation of the so-called enumerative style. In recent years, books made wholly of lists have been published, including the bestseller *The Book of Lists* by Amy and Irving Wallace. In popular culture, personal playlists or disks of song selections are shared among friends to enact a special theme (birthday songs, freedom songs, songs for the gym) or to trigger mutual memories (our college favorites, best party tunes)—a practice immortalized in the novel *High Fidelity* by Nick Hornby. A well-known teacher and scholar in English composition (Geoffrey Sirc) has his students produce playlists and then write essays about their projects. He is well aware of how items in a list contain the seeds of larger stories and ideas and can thus be expanded into anecdotes and full essays.

As a final note on learning to use images in their narrative functions, we can use this occasion to answer a question that students often raise: Are authors really as aware of their style at the time of writing or revising as analysts are when they go looking for tropes and schemes and images? Of course, the level of awareness varies from author to author and occasion to occasion, but in the case of the narratively charged imagery in "Birdwatcher," we can say for sure that the techniques were modeled on the poems of Walt Whitman, whom Killingsworth has studied for nearly as long as he has been watching birds. In pioneering free verse poetry, Whitman made the enumerative style a central part of his experiments, using lists of images to suggest the great diversity of urban life and the values of democracy, in which everyone deserves mention even if his or her whole story cannot be told. Here's a sample from "Song of Myself":

The little one sleeps in its cradle,
I lift the gauze and look a long time, and silently brush away flies with
  my hand.

The youngster and the red-faced girl turn aside up the bushy hill, I
  peeringly view
        them from the top.

The suicide sprawls on the bloody floor of the bedroom,
I witness the corpse with its dabbled hair, I note where the pistol has
  fallen.

The blab of the pave, tires of carts, sluff of boot-soles, talk of the
  promenaders,
The heavy omnibus, the driver with his interrogating thumb, the clank
  of the shod
        horses on the granite floor,
The snow-sleighs, clinking, shouted jokes, pelts of snow-balls,
The hurrahs for popular favorites, the fury of rous'd mobs,
The flap of the curtain'd litter, a sick man inside borne to the hospital,
The meeting of enemies, the sudden oath, the blows and fall,
The excited crowd, the policeman with his star quickly working his
  passage to the
        centre of the crowd,
The impassive stones that receive and return so many echoes,
What groans of over-fed or half-starv'd who fall sunstruck or in fits,
What exclamations of women taken suddenly who hurry home and give
  birth to babes,
What living and buried speech is always vibrating here, what howls
  restrain'd by decorum,
Arrests of criminals, slights, adulterous offers made, acceptances,
  rejections with convex lips,
I mind them or the show or resonance of them—I come and I depart.
                                        (Whitman 195)

Throughout the poem, the images expand and contract, creating a kind of
narrative rhythm that moves the reader along. Not all critics have admired
the technique. The lists have been dismissed as mere "catalogues" of impressions. The poem as a whole with its multiple anecdotes of everyday life and
stories of the street in mid-nineteenth-century New York has been called

"journalistic" and "prosaic" (indeed Whitman worked as a city journalist at the time he wrote the poem). Still, "Song of Myself" has managed to survive on most critics' playlists of the greatest and most influential poems in American literature. It is certainly worth the attention of any student interested in the way image intertwines with narrative. (For more on Whitman's enumerations, see Killingsworth, *Cambridge*.)

Image and Interpretation

Once you begin to think about the narrative potential of images, every isolated image and every list seems to be bursting with narrative potential. But most images that grow beyond listed or embedded items to full vignettes do not just advance the plot or tell more of the story. Usually the author adds expository or interpretive material so that the narrative is thickened with explanation or argument. Here are a few sentences from examples we've given so far that perform this thickening function by offering explanations or briefly sizing up the situation described:

- My groin felt the chill of death. (White 385)
- This tree is excellent. (Dillard, "Living like Weasels" 96)
- This was only last week, and already I don't remember what shattered the enchantment. (Dillard, "Living like Weasels" 97)
- [The wren] had been hanging in that low sling, perfectly suited to its size and shape, taking a little rest. (Killingsworth, "Birdwatcher" 603)
- I'd never seen them before in nature, but knew their names and their image from Audubon's watercolor. (Killingsworth, "Birdwatcher" 603)
- What living and buried speech is always vibrating here, what howls restrain'd by decorum. (Whitman 195)

To take a yet thicker example, notice how, in the following passage from an essay by the Korean American novelist Chang-Rae Lee, a short list of Korean foods—stewed meat, sushi, and radish kimchi—vividly contrasts with a list of the insipid dining hall American foods Lee has had to endure at school ("pork parmigiana and chicken patties and wax beans"). His mother brings his favorite foods from home when she comes to visit him at school. In an expanded vignette, Lee features an especially pungent food, kimchi (the one likely to be considered especially Korean and exotic by most American readers), and explains its peculiar attraction:

She pulled out her old metal cooler and dragged it between the beds [of her hotel room]. She lifted the top and began unpacking plastic containers, and I thought she would never stop. One after the other they came out, each with a dish that traveled well—a salted stewed meat, rolls of Korean-style sushi. I opened a container of radish kimchi and suddenly the room bloomed with its odor, and I reveled in the very peculiar sensation (which perhaps only true kimchi lovers know) of simultaneously drooling and gagging as I breathed it all in. For the next few minutes they watched me eat. I'm not certain that I was even hungry. But after weeks of pork parmigiana and chicken patties and wax beans, I suddenly realized that I had lost all the savor in my life. . . . I ate and ate, so much and so fast that I actually went to the bathroom and vomited. I came out dizzy and sated with the phantom warmth of my binge. (Lee 252)

The simultaneous "drooling and gagging" may be, as he says, something that only "true kimchi lovers" can appreciate, but Lee shares with outsiders this almost confessional insight about the powerful attraction of culturally specific experiences, an insight augmented with the intensity of body-conscious imagery.

Just as interpretive sentences can add substance and thought to image-centered vignettes, a well-placed vignette can also advance the cause in paragraphs devoted mainly to interpretation, as in this paragraph from Joan Didion's "Marrying Absurd." The vignette contained in the parentheses performs the function usually known as "giving an example" but with more imagistic verve and vividness than a teacher who says "Give me more specific examples" might reasonably expect:

But what strikes one most about the Strip chapels, with their wishing wells and stained-glass paper windows and their artificial bouvardia, is that so much of their business is by no means a matter of simple convenience, of late-night liaisons between show girls and baby Crosbys. Of course, there is some of that. (One night about eleven o'clock in Las Vegas I watched a bride in an orange minidress and masses of flame-colored hair stumble from a Strip chapel on the arm of her bridegroom, who looked the part of the expendable nephew in movies like Miami Syndicate. "I gotta get the kids," the bride whimpered. "I gotta pick up the sitter and get to the midnight show." "What you gotta get," the bridegroom said, opening the door of a Cadillac Coupe de Ville and watching her crumble into the seat, "is sober.") But Las Vegas seems to offer something other than "convenience"; it is also merchandizing "niceness," the facsimile of proper ritual, to children who do not know how else to find it, how to make the arrangements, how to do it "right." (Didion 91)

To convey the peculiar combination of convenience and "niceness" of Las Vegas wedding chapels, Didion has only to put slogans copied from the neon advertisements before the eyes of the reader in a dizzying enumeration of services:

> Our Photos Best Anywhere, Your Wedding on A Phonograph Record, Candlelight with Your Ceremony, Honeymoon Accommodations, Free Transportation with Your Motel to Courthouse to Chapel and Return to Motel, Religious or Civil Ceremonies, Dressing Rooms, Flowers, Rings, Announcements, Witnesses Available, and Ample Parking. (Didion 91)

In giving these examples, Didion combines visuals and language in one blow—neon signs are experienced verbally and visually. But perhaps the more important point is that in such lists, the author makes her case by alternately expanding and contracting stories and by alternating between single well-chosen images and lists that work much like the data in a scientific report. To rely too heavily on the single image would be to risk overrating it as evidence. But to overdo the lists would risk boring the reader and creating incoherence. The essayist must seek a balanced performance in making her case.

The Power of the Image

In sum, images perform a variety of functions within a prose performance. They can

- engage the senses of the reader (not just sight, but also hearing, smell, touch, and taste) and promote participation at the level of the body,
- advance the plot, shift the tone, or intensify the action in narrative prose,
- provide the central focal point of short bursts of narrative, or vignettes, within all kinds of prose,
- serve as implied narratives or potential narratives embedded within full stories or contained in lists,
- advance interpretive work by adding vividness to examples and illustrations.

One final point deserves mention. The tendency among young writers and many teachers of writing is to aim for more and more specific detail in developing descriptive imagery. The more realistic or "photographic" a picture is, after all, the more effectively it describes the scene it portrays and brings that scene before the mind of the reader. Description in writing can certainly aim for this kind of vividness, but written imagery also creates different effects by being incomplete or compacted in detail. This minimalist approach to imagery engages the reader's mind in the interpretive acts of filling out the picture or completing the story. By awakening the body and the mind, the most effective imagery leaves the reader virtually vibrating with the experience of reading.

Exercises

1. Analyze the imagery in the following passages. List the principal images in each and identify which senses each image activates (sight, sound, touch, smell, and taste), remembering that a single image can activate more than one sense. Then select one image from each passage and describe how it interprets one of the main ideas or actions the writer conveys. The first passage you'll recall from one of the exercises at the end of the previous chapter. There we asked you to analyze its use of schemes; here you'll focus on its imagery.

    a. You can brick up your heart as stout and tight and hard and cold and impregnable as you possibly can and down it comes in an instant, felled by a woman's second glance, a child's apple breath, the shatter of glass in the road, the words "I have something to tell you," a cat with a broken spine dragging itself into the forest to die, the brush of your mother's papery ancient hand in the thicket of your hair, the memory of your father's voice early in the morning echoing from the kitchen where he is making pancakes for his children. (Doyle 196)

The second passage comes from an essay recounting how a man named Werner wakes in the middle of the night to the sound of screaming and the smell of smoke and gradually comes to realize that his apartment building is on fire.

    b. It was a familiar scent, but distant—campfires in his past, in the Oregon woods. Boiled coffee, damp socks, Werner rooted to a stump, bow across his lap. Deer, someone had told him, needed two senses to pinpoint danger, some combination of sight, sound, smell; otherwise they just stood there, waiting. . . . Werner bounded naked to the front door, flipped the locks, flung it open, and a wall of smoke hit him in the face. He slammed it shut, turned, and squinted into the apartment. . . . He stepped back into the bedroom and a dry, papery gray cloud consumed him. He dropped to his hands and knees and put his cheek to the floor. With this nearsighted, close-up view, he could see smoke curling up through the floorboards, black specks inside tendrils like a flock of birds banking and moving together. Dark geese rising into the Oregon sky. (Beard 3)

2. You'll remember that an image can function as a vignette, an implied or highly condensed narrative, embedded in a sample of prose. Chose an image from one of the passages above and tap its narrative potential by expanding it into a full-blown anecdote. As you do so, generate and embed your own images in the story you are crafting in order to activate your readers' senses and nudge them toward particular interpretations. To focus your efforts, it might help to quote the image (or part of the image) you are expanding and use it as the title of your anecdote—for instance, "A Child's Apple Breath" or "Making Pancakes for His Children."

3. Comment briefly on the imagery in one of the examples from your commonplace book, as in the following example:

Example: Picked up by the scruff of the neck, [the bear cubs] splayed their paws like kittens and screamed like baby bears. The cry of a baby bear is muted, like a human infant's heard from her crib down the hall. (John McPhee, quoted in Finch and Elder 685)

Comment: The reference to the body—the scruff of the neck—and the relation of the familiar (kitten splaying its paws, infant crying down the hall)—to the unfamiliar (baby bears screaming) are the images by which McPhee brings his readers into relation with his material. The humor of the passage comes when, in the middle of a string of comparisons (it's like this, it's like that), he says that the bear cubs "screamed like baby bears." An analogy of something to itself? That brings the distance back: baby bears' screaming is like nothing you've ever heard. It is the movement between closeness and distance that gives the passage its interest, its drama, and its humor.

9

Rituals of Language

Rituals are patterns of behavior that recur either at fixed intervals (weekly forms of worship, birthday parties, presidential inaugurations) or under certain circumstances (weddings, funerals, ship christenings). Some rituals are highly formal (a royal coronation, for instance); others are so ordinary, so woven into the fabric of our daily lives, that we hardly notice them (waving good-bye, reading the morning paper, kissing our beloved good night). Still others fall somewhere in between (Sunday dinners, homecoming dances, tailgating). Rituals serve a range of purposes: from revealing some spiritual truth or meaning, to reaffirming the bonds among members of a community, to imposing a sense of order or structure to some event or process, including how you might organize your day. But one thing they have in common is that they all involve, to some degree, performance. Think, for instance, how many different ways a person can "perform" waving good-bye.

We typically think of rituals as actions—as things we *do*. If language plays a role at all, it's often as a set piece within a broader ritual occasion (a prayer, song, vow, oath, or curse). But language itself is full of rituals—fixed sayings or habitual patterns of words or meaning that serve as mini-performances within the broader flow of writing. To be more precise, a ritual of language is any sequence of words or grammatical structures

- that is widely shared in a group or culture,
- that carries meanings beyond what the words express,
- and that serves a variety of interactional purposes between writer and reader.

The figures of speech that we covered in chapters 6 and 7 meet all of these criteria and would thus fall within the category of rituals of language. Examine almost any presidential address, for instance, and you'll find instances of anaphora and antithesis. These schemes are little rituals that make up and help define the more general ritual of a presidential address. Beyond the schemes and tropes, there are other verbal rituals that, while they may use figures of speech to secure their effects, fall outside their official precincts. The remainder of this chapter introduces you to a hand-ful of these devices: proverbs, epigrams, rituals of three, short sentences, cumulative and periodic sentences, and verbal allusions.

Proverbs

Of all the rituals of language that we'll cover in this chapter, proverbs are the most overtly ritualistic. They consist of fixed sequences of words and structures that do not originate with the person who utters or writes them. Instead, they belong to a culture in general or to traditions within that culture. Although not a figure of speech itself, a proverb is often cast in the form of some trope or scheme to create a tightly worded and highly memorable saying: "No news is good news" (alliteration, epistrophe, and isocolon); "One hand washes the other" (synecdoche and ellipsis); "The squeaky wheel gets the grease" (metaphor, onomatopoeia, and assonance); "Do as I say, not as I do" (antimetabole).

Like rituals that recur under certain circumstances, proverbs are re-peated when similar situations present themselves. In an exceptionally good analysis of proverbs in "Literature as Equipment for Living" Ken-neth Burke argues, "Proverbs are *strategies* for dealing with *situations*. In so far as situations are typical and recurrent in a given social structure, people develop names for them and strategies for handling them" (original emphasis, 296–97).

Imagine, for instance, that a friend of yours is pining for a beloved who is on a long trip or who has taken a job in another state (both com-mon enough occurrences in our highly mobile society). To console your friend, you resort to the following proverb: "Absence makes the heart grow fonder." The proverb helps make sense of the situation while offering your friend a strategy for dealing with it—that is, to hang tight and nourish the hope that the separation will only strengthen the relationship. If you were feeling mean-spirited that day, you could have chosen an alternate proverb: "Out of sight, out of mind." Or if you wanted to enlist your friend for a night on the town, you could have said, "When the cat's away [wink, wink], the mice will play."

From antiquity through the Renaissance, proverbs wielded a cultural authority that rivaled arguments based on logic and reason. Orators and writers would fill their notebooks with lists of proverbs and other pithy sayings so they could draw upon them and use them to score points against an opponent in debate. By the seventeenth and eighteenth centuries, however, the cultural authority of proverbs began to wane, and writers often shunned them as trite and hackneyed, as too general in scope, too didactic, and too easy to come by to capture the complexities of real life. Our best writers today continue to avoid them for similar reasons, although proverbs still seem to have a healthy life in pulp fiction and on the editorial pages of our local papers.

They sometimes even find their way into presidential addresses. A few years ago, President George W. Bush had planned to use the following proverb in one of his stump speeches: "Fool me once, shame on you; fool me twice, shame on me." The hope, it seems, was to use a folksy, down-to-earth saying to project the image of a folksy, down-to-earth guy. But when it came time to deliver this proverb in his speech, Bush forgot it in mid-utterance: "Fool me once. . . . shame on . . . shame on you. . . . If fooled . . . can't get fooled again." If you watch the video clip of this incident on the Internet (it's easy enough to find), you can see him try to cover over and compensate for this verbal slip by drawing on other resources of performance: after his verbal stutter-step, he places his hand on the podium as if about to make an important point, leans into the microphone, and races through the last few words as if these were the ones he meant to utter all along. Although the Bush proverb is a negative example, it does illustrate how, in oral communication, style should work in concert with other resources of performance. In written communication, where those other resources are unavailable, style is performance.

When accomplished writers do use proverbs, they usually do so in one of two ways. First, they attribute them to characters in dialogue, especially in fictional works, although writers of nonfiction may also quote proverbs uttered by the people they write about. Presumably, these writers have notebooks full of conversations with their subjects or recordings of interviews. From this plethora of material, they may seize upon a proverb used by one of their subjects to suggest something about that subject's character. In *Ava's Man*, a memoir about life along the Georgia-Alabama state line, Rick Bragg writes of his grandmother and her unflappability:

> I think about how the sudden summer thunderstorms would rattle the window glass and make cups jump off their saucers, and how, unimpressed, the old woman would just take a dip of snuff and mumble, "Ol' devil's beatin' his wife." (6)

Later in the same memoir, Bragg features another proverb, one his brother Sam spoke after the two had spent a day on the lake fishing. Bragg had caught six bass, while his brother (the more skilled fisherman) had caught none:

> [Sam] dismissed the whole afternoon with a grunt. "Ricky," he said, "I was fishin' for the big fish."
> Then he stared up at a perfect blue sky, a sky without a cloud.
> "And everybody knows," he said, "the big fish won't bite on a bluebird day." (18)

The second way accomplished stylists use proverbs is to alter them in some way, to refashion them to some new purpose, or to borrow just a hint of a proverb's diction and cadence. In *Moby Dick*, Herman Melville not only refashions the familiar proverb "The calm before the storm" but recasts it as an antimetabole: "The mingled, mingling threads of life are woven by warp and woof—calms crossed by storms, a storm for every calm" (565). Dorothy Parker takes the same proverb and reworks it to yet another purpose: "I have a need for wilder, crueler waves; / They sicken of the calm who knew the storm" (141). In some instances, a writer may skim off a pattern of sound associated with a particular proverb. We saw an example in an earlier chapter with a quote from Suzanne Britt: "Give them a coffee break, and they'll jog around the block. Supply them with a quiet evening at home, and they'll fix the screen door and lick S&H green stamps." Here there's a distant echo of the proverb "Give them an inch, and they'll take a mile."

From Epigram to Blog Entry

A close cousin to the proverb is the epigram. Originally a short verse form with a satiric twist at its end, the epigram now refers to any pithy or witty saying. A chief difference between proverbs and epigrams is that proverbs are traditional sayings whose origins are unknown, while epigrams are frequently identified with their authors, particularly as evidence of their wit. For this reason, the epigram helped propel many writers to fame and thus served as little stylistic stages upon which they built their reputations. For some writers, their epigrams have come to all but eclipse their other literary achievements. Oscar Wilde, for instance, was a novelist, dramatist, and poet of the late nineteenth century, but today we remember him chiefly through his epigrams: "I can resist anything but temptation" (388); "Experience is the name everyone gives to their mistakes" (663); "We live in an age when unnecessary things are our only necessities" (79). These epigrams illustrate several of the form's hallmarks: paradoxical statement, play on words, and disparate ideas yoked together in compressed and balanced structures.

In modern prose, the epigram has largely gone the way of the proverb—that is, it's not as common as it once was. The reason for its rarity may be that it strikes modern readers as too artificial and contrived. Even so, epigrams still pop up from time to time, although their authors may try to avoid the charge of artificiality by muting their effects in some way. In his essay "Adagio, ma non troppo," Lewis H. Lapham uses epigrams to eulogize his recently departed mentor Otto Friedrich. One of the attributes Lapham praises is Otto's erudition—his refined sensibilities when it comes to writing, music, gardening, and so forth. The epigram, with its associations to wit and urbanity, seems an ideal vehicle for celebrating this quality, but note how Lapham dilutes the punch or pithiness of his epigrams by extending the sentences in which they appear (the epigrams are highlighted with italics):

- *He [Otto] was as suspicious of metaphors as he was of politicians,* and because he was a better writer than all but a few (a very few) of the more famous authors whose work he ushered into the light of print, I seldom quarreled with his judgment.
- An historian in the amateur tradition of Henry Adams and Bernard DeVoto, Otto wrote his books on an old manual typewriter, ignored the apparatus of academic scholarship, and *approached the study of history in the same spirit that he approached Mozart's piano concertos.* (Lapham 9; emphasis added)

If Lapham had ended the first sentence right after "politicians," the result would have been a perfectly good, stand-alone epigram, one that joins disparate ideas (metaphors and politicians) and achieves syntactic balance and compression ("suspicious" is elided in "as he was of politicians"). By carrying the sentence forward, however, he avoids the sense of finality, of being rounded off, that would have come with punctuating the epigram as its own sentence. Lapham creates a similar dampening effect in the second example where the epigram appears as part of a larger structure—that is, in a series of parallel clauses.

The epigram (or something like it) may be making a comeback in a new prose venue—the Weblog or, more simply, the blog. When seasoned bloggers talk about what they do, they often focus on issues of style, saying that blog entries should be pithy. Surveying the short history of blogs, Rebecca Blood writes, "the format of the typical weblog, providing only a very short space in which to write an entry, encourages pithiness on the part of the writer" ("Weblog" 8–9). Elsewhere, Blood expands on this observation and attributes the pithiness of blog entries to more than just limits in space: many of these entries contain links to other Web sites; if written in a pithy and entertaining style, these entries serve as a kind of advertisement for the link they introduce, an invitation for the reader to click through (Hack the Planet). We can add one more reason behind these calls for pithiness: the blog entry is an arena, albeit a tiny one, for showcasing the wit and verbal talents of its writer. Here are a few examples from two popular blogs:

- The didgeridoos and didgeridont's for playing one of Australia's most pun-prone instruments. (http://forums.fark.com/cgi/fark/comments.pl?IDLink=1563679)
- Mr. Nobody is worth exploring. (http://www.metafilter.com/mefi/32532)
- An architect, falling apart. (http://www.metafilter.com/mefi/33367)

All three of these entries contain links to other websites: the first to a news article about didgeridoos, a woodwind instrument native to Australia; the second to a Web site (no longer available) called "Mr. Nobody"; and the third to an eBay listing of a chronically unemployed architect auctioning off his diploma. More important, all three use rituals of language (puns and word play) that have come to be valued on blogs, rituals for both drawing attention to the links they supply and displaying the verbal talents of the entry's writer. If the blog allows for readers' comments (which these do), then a writer can receive almost immediate feedback from his or her audience. In response to the didgeridoo entry, one reader wrote, "Very clever, indeed." Another reader responded by joining in with this ritualistic use of language—that is, by offering a rejoinder that comes even closer to the original form of an epigram as a short, witty poem:

Best's a vocal track that's limber
For wringing timbres from the timber.

Rituals of Three

In the 1970s as part of its Saturday morning television lineup, ABC ran a series of short educational cartoons called *Schoolhouse Rock!* One of our favorites was "Three Is a Magic Number," which celebrated the virtues of three while teaching viewers some of its multiples ("Three, six, nine—twelve, fifteen, eighteen . . ."). Lurking behind the title of this animated short is a phenomenon long noted by anthropologists: the prominent role three plays in ritual, myth, and folklore in western cultures—so prominent, in fact, that doing things in threes has come to permeate just about every aspect of our everyday lives. Alan Dundes has catalogued some of the diverse areas in which patterns of three play a leading role:

- Folklore (three wishes, three little pigs, three blind mice).
- Games and spectacles (tick-tack-toe, three strikes and you're out, three-ring circus).
- Product sizes and appliance settings (small, medium, and large; low, medium, and high).
- Eating rituals and food (three meals per day; coffee, tea, or milk; rare, medium, and well-done).
- Common or well-known sayings ("Beg, borrow, or steal"; "Lock, stock, and barrel"; "Ready, willing, and able"). (Dundes 404–09)

Dundes even wonders if some "supposedly objective analytical categories" devised by scientists and academics are products of our culture's preference for patterns of three: solid, liquid, and gas; thesis, antithesis, and synthesis; id, ego, and superego (418). In one instance, at least, the direction of influence has gone the other way—that is, not from cultural practice to science, but from science to cultural practice. Here we are thinking of the technique of triangulation. With this technique, astronomers can calculate the distance of celestial bodies from the Earth, while navigators can use it to determine the position of their vessels. Today, scholars from a variety of fields talk about "triangulating" data—that is, confirming some observed phenomenon by finding at least three instances of it, or looking at a single phenomenon from three methodological perspectives. On the whole, three implies stability, completeness, and reliability.

Patterns of three permeate all genres of discourse. We've already seen their influence on common or well-known sayings. But they also appear in other kinds of compositions:

- Most jokes fall into three parts with three leading characters: "A priest, rabbi, and penguin walk into a bar. . . ."

- Stories typically divide into a beginning, middle, and end.
- The five-paragraph essay, so familiar from high school and freshman English, is a ritual of three sandwiched between an introduction and conclusion.

Patterns of three at the level of word, phrase, and clause are so common in prose that rhetoricians devised a name to identify them: tricolon. Technically a scheme, tricolon is defined as any series with three parts. Such a definition, however, is too general for our purposes and ignores the various principles that typically organize three-part series. To put it differently, tricolon is a general response to a variety of situations, so to understand some of its different applications let's catalogue a few of the ways writers use it.

When writers want to offer a well-rounded description of a person, thing, or event, they often use rituals of three:

- [Colin Duffy] is four feet eight inches high, weighs seventy-five pounds, and appears to be mostly leg and shoulder blade. (Orlean, "American Man" 99)
- We are all of us exiles from a landscape of streams and hills and forests. We come from a climate of cold dark winters, a few weeks of exuberant spring, and abundant snow and rain. (Jackson 241)
- The guy broke in, held her at knife point, and made off with three hundred dollars in cash. (Sedaris 62)

The first two passages are examples of stylistic triangulation. They present their subjects (Colin, the landscape, and the climate) in terms of three different attributes or features, and in doing so, they impart a fullness to the description, creating the impression of seeing each subject in three dimensions. The passage from Sedaris also comes with a sense of completeness, but here it's not so much about "triangulating" as it is about matching our expectation that events and processes have three parts: a beginning, middle, and end. Sedaris's tricolon answers that expectation, and as a result, it offers readers a well-rounded account of the robbery.

Another form of stylistic triangulation occurs when writers use patterns of three to present a representative sample of some phenomenon or class:

- He kept scraps of wood in a cardboard box—the ends of two-by-fours, slabs of shelving and plywood, odd pieces of molding—and everything in it was fair game. (Sanders, "Inheritance" 134)

- Many of us had suspended the connections to the world we had established back home—the part-time job in the library, the graduate program, the circle of supportive friends—and we resented the loss. (Gordon 121)
- I barely knew who I was, only who I pretended to be: a pony express rider, a space alien, an unrecognized genius, all of us flailing around in the white water of a desperation to escape. (Grealy 175)

The first example offers a representative list of scraps of wood; the second, social and work connections; the third, pretend identities. If these writers had only listed two samples of each, the lists would seem to have fallen short by one item; it would seem an inadequate sampling of the thing or class it was meant to represent. Adding a fourth item to each list would probably do no harm, but as a colleague recently remarked, "With four, you don't get much more."

In addition to presenting well-rounded descriptions and representative samples, writers use patterns of three to signal the end of a section or composition:

- The buzzer sounded. The gears kicked in. The day started. (Komunyakaa 90)
- Eventually the game petered out. Traffic died down on 61st Street. The neighborhood went to sleep. (Staples 181)
- This house is quiet. The city is quiet. Even the cops are catching forty winks in their patrol car on the corner. (Simic 143)

Even though the first passage ends with the word "started," this parallel series of three sentences appears at the end of an anecdote embedded in Komunyakkaa's essay. Like the other two passages quoted above, this three-part structure functions like a cadence in music, marking a boundary between sections in a larger piece or even signaling the conclusion of the piece as a whole.

Sometimes one pattern of three will prompt another. In other words, if a sentence includes two parallel series and the first one includes three items, writers often use three more in the second to complete the symmetry:

- [W]e jerked up, down, or away at the last second, so we left our hearts, stomachs, and lungs behind. (Dillard, "The Stunt Pilot" 185)
- I wanted everything I did to express what I considered my essential nature: casual, relaxed, and intuitively creative, rather than formal, precise, and meticulous. (Mori 238)

- In Vietnam and Cambodia and amid the famines of Africa, I was there too, helping the lost and injured and sad. (Grealy 177)

These writers could have included only two items in the first series or only two in the second. In prose, you can do pretty much whatever you want. But by doing so, these writers would have denied their readers the satisfaction that comes from appreciating symmetry, the satisfaction in recognizing one series of three balanced by another.

Short Sentences

A short sentence is one of the most powerful devices in a writer's repertoire. When a writer wants to drive a point home, to cast it in an emphatic and memorable form, then a short sentence is often the right tool for the job—provided that it is well constructed, strategically placed, and sparingly used.

Simply composing a short sentence does much towards ensuring a forceful delivery. As Hickey explains, "The most powerful positions in a sentence are the first and last words. The closer these come together, the more forceful the message is" (33). Consider these famous examples:

- History is bunk. (Henry Ford)
- Jesus wept. (John 11:35)
- War is hell. (William Tecumseh Sherman)

To enhance a short sentence's effectiveness, writers can draw on other stylistic resources: selecting monosyllabic words over polysyllabic ones, alliterating consonants, inverting conventional word order, and other devices designed to attract readers' attention.

As a ritual of language, short sentences appear in predictable locations: typically at the beginning or end of a paragraph, or sometimes in the middle to pivot from one topic to the next. When they appear at the beginnings of paragraphs, they often anticipate other, more specific information:

> Water is everywhere. A potato is 80 percent water, a cow 74 percent, a bacterium 75 percent. A tomato, at 95 percent, is little *but* water. Even humans are 65 percent water, making us more liquid than solid by a margin of almost two to one. Water is strange stuff. It is formless and transparent, and yet we long to be beside it. It has no taste and yet we love the taste of it. We will travel great distances and pay small fortunes to see it in sunshine. And even though we know it is dangerous and drowns tens of thousands of people every year, we can't wait to frolic in it. (Bryson, *A Short History* 270)

This paragraph contains two strategically placed short sentences: "Water is everywhere" and "Water is strange stuff." The first sets up the three sentences that follow it, sentences that elaborate on and provide specific examples of water's ubiquity. The second short sentence serves as a transition. It moves the reader from the pervasiveness of water to human's paradoxical relationship with it. Like the first short sentence, the second also anticipates the sentences that follow it, sentences that elaborate on the strangeness of water and human's interaction with it. Both sentences also facilitate memory. Readers may not recall every detail that Bryson presents, but they are likely to remember the paragraph's two main points because those points are expressed through short, emphatic sentences.

When a writer places a short sentence at the end of a paragraph, that sentence typically sums up or comments on the information that precedes it. Here's another example from Bryson:

> A bolt of lightning travels at 270,000 miles an hour and can heat the air around it to a decidedly crisp 50,000 degrees Fahrenheit, several times hotter than the surface of the sun. At any moment 1,800 thunderstorms are in progress around the globe—some 40,000 a day. Day and night across the planet every second about a hundred lightning bolts hit the ground. The sky is a lively place. (*A Short History* 260)

The final sentence sums up the facts about lightning listed in the preceding sentences. It is also a little moment of social interaction between Bryson and his readers. When Bryson calls the sky a "lively place," he uses understatement (litotes), evoking an image of human sociability (lively) to characterize the high level of electrical activity in the Earth's atmosphere. He thus invites readers to share his wry, yet appreciative, perspective on this wonder of nature.

Short sentences, if they are to retain their potential for emphasizing information, should be used sparingly. As Hickey explains, short sentences "emphasize ideas," but if "every idea is emphasized, nothing is" (35–36). A paragraph full of short sentences is like a road sign that points in every direction. As the old adage says, such a sign actually points in no direction. A short sentence is thus more effective, more powerful, when surrounded by longer ones. Its contrast to its surroundings makes it stand out more.

Too many short sentences can also deaden prose rhythm. As many stylists have warned, stringing together too many sentences of equal or similar length creates a monotonous, mind-numbing rhythm. A monotonous rhythm can, in turn, weaken reader interest (we have all had professors who bore us not so much with the subject of their lectures as with their droning and tedious delivery). To sustain reader involvement, vary sentence length. Gary Provost offers similar advice while dramatizing it in action:

> This sentence has five words. Here are five more words. Five-word sentences are fine. But several together become monotonous. Listen to what is happening. The writing is getting boring. The sound of it drones. It's like a stuck record. The ear demands some variety. Now listen. I vary the sentence length, and I create music. Music. The writing sings. It has a pleasant rhythm, a lilt, a harmony. I use short sentences. And I use sentences of medium length. And sometimes, when I am certain the reader is rested, I will engage him with a sentence of considerable length, a sentence that burns with energy and builds with all the impetus of a crescendo, the roll of drums, the crash of cymbals—sounds that say listen to this, it is important. (60–61)

Readers experience prose in time. For this reason, it's important to note how writers (including yourself) orchestrate their readers' experiences from one moment to the next—not only how they stage information (moving from old to new, for instance, or from general to specific), but also how and by what means they deliver it. The sentence is a versatile instrument. Play it like a virtuoso.

Cumulative and Periodic Sentences

Besides classifying sentences by length (short, medium, and long), rhetoricians also classify them according to where the main clause appears: either at the beginning of a sentence or near its end. Sentences that begin with the main clause are called "cumulative" or "running" sentences. The main point of the sentence comes first followed by modifying phrases and clauses:

- A shark swims past me in a kelp forest that sways back and forth with the current. (Terry Williams 211)
- I happen to love essays that take a small notion and find the universe inside it. (Orlean, introduction xvi)
- Otto wrote books in the way that other people wander off into forests, chasing his intellectual enthusiasms as if they were obscure butterflies or rare mushrooms—books about roses and Eduard Manet's Olympia, extended essays about Scarlatti, the Albigensian Crusade, the siege of Monte Cassino and the fires of Auschwitz, books about Berlin in the 1920s and Hollywood in the 1940s, biographies of Glenn Gould and Helmuth von Moltke. (Lapham 9–11)

Cumulative sentences are the more usual sort and conform to our expectations about how a sentence typically develops: grammatical subject, then verb, then objects or complements, adjuncts, modifiers, and so on. Cumulative sentences are like all those little informal, barely visible rituals that fill our everyday lives: the pattern is so common that we barely notice it. As a result, cumulative sentences often create the impression "of utter spontaneity, as though the mind [of the writer] were spinning itself out naturally, portraying itself in the very process of thinking" (Fakundiny 727). The exception would be the cumulative sentence that seems consciously elongated for effect, as in the Lapham sentence above. There we sense that something special is going on, that the meandering syntax is mirroring the action it describes.

Sentences that end with the main clause or at least delay its appearance or completion are called "periodic" sentences. As readers, we don't feel that the sentence completes itself—delivers its main point—until at or near its end:

- At length, toward noon, upon the final dismissal of the ship's riggers, and after the Pequod had been hauled out from the wharf, and after the ever-thoughtful Charity had come off in a whaleboat, with her last gift—a nightcap for Stubb, the second mate, her brother-in-law, and a spare Bible for the steward—after all this, the two captains, Peleg and Bildad, issued from the cabin. (Melville 135)
- Fred Fulton, who lived next door to the Flavels in a nearby beach community, heard Florence Flavel shouting for help. (Trillin 80)
- On the northern margin of the Alaska Range, just before the hulking ramparts of Mt. McKinley and its satellites surrender to the low Kantishna plain, a series of lesser ridges, known as the Outer Range, sprawls across the flats like a rumpled blanket on an unmade bed. (Krakauer 9)

Periodic sentences create tension and suspense. The Melville sentence achieves this effect by piling modifying phrases and clauses in front of the main clause. The sentence from Trillin does so by inserting a long relative clause between grammatical subject and verb. Krakauer combines both techniques, frontloading his sentence with a modifying phrase and clause and inserting an adjectival phrase ("known as the Outer Range") between subject and verb.

Periodic sentences are like mini-dramas. The frontloaded or inserted elements create tension that is then resolved either by the arrival of the main clause or by its completion. Writers can heighten the suspense by front-loading or inserting more modifying phrases and clauses (the Lapham sentence is a good example). Reciprocally, they can reduce the suspense by limiting the amount of material frontloaded or inserted:

- On the school playground, basketball players carried on after dark. (Staples 181)
- If Colin Duffy and I were to get married, we would have matching superhero notebooks. (Orlean, "The American Man" 99)

We might call these two sentences weakly periodic. The main clause is delayed in each, but the goal here seems less about creating suspense and more about establishing the setting ("On the playground") or a precondition ("If Colin Duffy and I were to get married") before delivering the main action.

As a ritual of language, periodic sentences are characteristic of the oratorical high style. They are a mode of verbal behavior that suggests formality or emotional intensity. Martin Luther King combines both effects in what is possibly the most famous periodic sentence in the history of American rhetoric:

> But when you have seen vicious mobs lynch your mothers and fathers at will and drown your sisters and brothers at whim; when you have seen hate-filled policemen curse, kick and even kill your black brothers and sisters; when you see the vast majority of your twenty million Negro brothers smothering in an airtight cage of poverty in the midst of an affluent society; when you suddenly find your tongue twisted and your speech stammering as you seek to explain to your six-year-old daughter why she can't go to the public amusement park that has just been advertised on television, and see tears welling up in her eyes when she is told that Funtown is closed to colored children, and see ominous clouds of inferiority beginning to form in her little mental sky, and see her beginning to distort her personality by developing an unconscious bitterness toward white people; when you have to concoct an answer for a five-year-old son who is asking: "Daddy, why do white people treat colored people so mean?"; when you take a cross-county drive and find it necessary to sleep night after night in the uncomfortable corners of your automobile because no motel will accept you; when you are humiliated day in and day out by nagging signs reading "white" and "colored"; when your first name becomes "nigger," your middle name becomes "boy" (however old you are) and your last name becomes "John," and your wife and mother are never given the respected title "Mrs."; when you are

harried by day and haunted by night by the fact that you are a Negro, living constantly at tiptoe stance, never quite knowing what to expect next, and are plagued with inner fears and outer resentments; when you are forever fighting a degenerating sense of "nobodiness"—then you will understand why we find it difficult to wait. (King, "Letter" 220–21)

As Lydia Fakundiny observes about this sentence, reading it aloud "will take your breath away—literally" (726). And that seems precisely the point. Its suspended syntax—ten subordinate clauses' worth—dramatizes King's exasperation with segregation and racism. By delaying and delaying and delaying the delivery of its main clause, this sentence compels readers to experience, if only in small measure, the magnitude of King's frustrations.

Sampling Other Voices

In the early 1990s, *Saturday Night Live* premiered what would become one of its most beloved recurrent sketches, "Wayne's World." The sketch featured Wayne Campbell and his sidekick Garth, sitting on a couch in Wayne's parents' basement while broadcasting a show for cable access. The sketch was so popular that it led to two feature-length films and, more important for our purposes, to a new set of expressions that found their way into the everyday conversations of "Wayne's World" fans: for instance, "Excellent," "Party on," and *"Schwing!"* At the time, it wasn't uncommon to hear friends incorporating these expressions into their daily banter, riffing off them, and infusing their conversations with the humor they carried over from the original sketch and films. We call this process of quoting another voice or discourse *sampling*, a term we borrow from hip hop and rap, which means to lift a piece (or "sample") from one song and use it in another. You may be familiar with a related and very similar device: literary allusion where one writer refers (either directly or indirectly) to the work of another writer. We prefer the term sampling. Not only does it have a current cultural resonance, but it is also more comprehensive: it includes references both to other specific texts and to various cultural repertoires in general.

Sampling occurs all the time in prose. We've already seen examples of it in a passage we quoted earlier from Susan Orlean's "Show Dog," where she samples the language of the personal ad to introduce Biff the boxer:

Biff is perfect. He's friendly, good-looking, rich, famous, and in excellent physical condition. He almost never drools. He's not afraid of commitment. He wants children—actually, he already has children and wants a lot more. He works hard and is a consummate professional, but he also knows how to have fun. (161)

Later in the same essay, Orlean samples the language of the high-fashion model and the languages of diet and exercise:

> Biff has to watch his weight. Usually, he is as skinny as Kate Moss, but he can put on three pounds in an instant. The holidays can be tough. He takes time off at Christmas and spends it at home, in Attleboro, Massachusetts, where there's a lot of food around and no pressure and no schedule and it's easy to eat all day. The extra weight goes to his neck. Luckily, Biff likes working out. He runs for fifteen or twenty minutes twice a day, either outside or on his Jog-Master. When he's feeling heavy, he runs longer, and skips snacks, until he's back down to his ideal weight of seventy-five pounds. (161)

The sampling here works towards humorous ends, as Orlean creates an amusing collision between language usually reserved for humans and the behavior of Biff the dog.

Writers can also take up a reverential or even celebratory footing toward the voices they sample. In both of his memoirs about the South, Rick Bragg frequently samples expressions and sayings that circled around him as he was growing up. The effect is atmospheric, infusing his prose with the voices of northeastern Alabama (the verbal samplings appear in italics):

- Poor people in the South do not make many historical registers unless we *knock some rich man off his horse*. (*All Over but the Shoutin'* xvi)
- Everyone with a *lick of sense* knew Bobby would *cut you as soon as look at you*. (*All Over but the Shoutin'* 57)
- What kind of man was this . . . who is so beloved, so missed, that the mere mention of his death would make them cry forty-two years after he was *preached into the sky*? (*Ava's Man* 9)
- There was plenty of work then, so *they ate good, real good*. There were no *one-egg days*, but *two- and three-egg days*. (*Ava's Man* 69)

The following is an especially complex example of sampling. It comes from John Edgar Wideman's "Whose War: The Color of Terror," an essay that criticizes both the U.S.-led invasion of Afghanistan after the 9/11 attacks and the rhetoric President Bush used towards mobilizing it:

> I'm sorry. I'm an American of African descent, and I can't applaud my president for *doing unto foreign others what he's inflicted on me and mine*. Even if he calls it *ole-time religion*. Even if he tells me all good Americans *have nothing to fear but fear itself* and promises he's *gonna ride over there and kick fear's ass real good*, so I don't need to worry about anything, just

let him handle it his way, *relax and enjoy the show* on TV, pay attention to each breath I take and be careful whose letters I open and listen up for the *high alerts from the high-alert guy* and *gwan and do something nice for a Muslim neighbor this week.* (34)

Here Wideman samples from a range of voices and discourses: the New Testament, an African-American spiritual, Franklin D. Roosevelt's first inaugural address, cowboy lingo, 1950s cinema advertising, weather forecasts, and more cowboy lingo. Although very diverse, all of these voices share the characteristic of either wielding some kind of power in our culture or having some sort of persuasive appeal—even the cowboyisms come with a certain swagger. But Wideman is not interested in appropriating or tapping that power or appeal. Instead, the sheer density of the sampling and the sudden shifts from one seemingly disparate voice to another create a feeling of saturation. These features also suggest that no matter what voices of authority or power the president invokes to make his case for war, Wideman is not going to buy it.

We have barely scratched the surface when it comes to classifying rituals of language. They are everywhere. Indeed, if you sense that a pattern of words or structures comes from somewhere else or has been used or said before, then you are likely in the presence of one. Being aware of such patterns, like being aware of the steps and protocols of any ritual, will help you successfully navigate the complexities of style as a medium for performance and social interaction, whether you are analyzing the writings of others or composing your own.

Exercises

1. Identify the rituals of language in the following paragraph from an article about the Internet's possible effects on the human brain. Look for sequences of words that you've seen or heard before (like the "I swear" from Heimel's fantasy essay) and sentence structures and patterns of meaning that have become conventionalized through repeated uses (for instance, rituals of three, short sentences, schemes, tropes, and so on):

> Over the past few years I've had an uncomfortable sense that someone, or something, has been tinkering with my brain, remapping the neural circuitry, reprogramming the memory. My mind isn't going—so far as I can tell—but it's changing. I'm not thinking the way I used to think. I can feel it most strongly when I'm reading. Immersing myself in a book or a lengthy article used to be easy. My mind would get caught up in the narrative or the

turns of the argument, and I'd spend hours strolling through long stretches of prose. That's rarely the case anymore. Now my concentration starts to drift after two or three pages. I get fidgety, lose the thread, begin looking for something else to do. I feel as if I'm always dragging my wayward brain back to the text. The deep reading that used to come naturally has become a struggle. (Carr 57)

Select three of the rituals that you identified and write a short analysis of each, explaining how that ritual might convey meanings beyond what the words literally express and shape interactions between writer and reader.

2. Pick a proverb that interests you (your library should have several dictionaries of proverbs, and there are many online collections). Identify any tropes, schemes, or images it uses, and then describe how it might work as a strategy for handling or summing up a situation. Now using the sentences we quoted in this chapter by Melville and Parker as models, rework the proverb and describe how these alterations in its form change how a writer might apply it.

3. Try to locate a ritual of language in an example from your commonplace book, and write a brief comment on it, as in the following:

> *Example*: To enjoy a thing exclusively is commonly to exclude yourself from the true enjoyment. (Thoreau, quoted in Finch and Elder 187)
> *Comment*: Like his mentor Ralph Waldo Emerson, Thoreau was famous for using epigrams, or sentences of his own that sound like proverbs or old sayings. By doing so, he was able to infuse his writing with greater cultural weight or authority—or what's sometimes called sententiousness.

10

Style and Culture

The previous chapter showed how one cultural category—ritual—can enhance our understanding of prose style. By way of conclusion, this chapter moves in the opposite direction, exploring how our vocabulary for prose analysis can reach beyond language and illuminate cultural forms other than speech and writing. Accordingly, it will revisit key concepts covered in previous chapters, showing how they might serve as a vocabulary for analyzing cultural practices and objects in general.

The first step toward understanding the relationship between style and culture is to realize that the two concepts are thoroughly interdependent. Every style of speaking and writing has effects on matters other than language—music, dress, technology, architecture, and so on. And every culture uses styles of speaking and writing to establish its own identity and carry on its day-to-day concerns. A culture can be national (American culture), regional (Southern culture), ethnic (the Jewish culture), religious (Mormon culture), or something much smaller, as when we speak of a particular university (institutional culture) or youth group (gaming culture). Every culture uses style to maintain its identity in a wide range of objects and practices, artifacts and behaviors. Styles of speaking and writing do not operate independently of these forms but work in concert with them. Indeed, the first time you ever heard the word *style*, it probably referred not to language but to the different ways of singing a song or swinging a tennis racquet, or the latest fashions from Paris or New York.

In this chapter, we will briefly consider how such key concepts as convention and deviation apply to other cultural forms as well as to language. And we will show how even such esoteric-seeming notions as troping, scheming, and imaging have broader applications. Finally, we will reinforce a key lesson: style involves the performance of identity within specific cultural contexts. We use style to say who we are in relation to others.

Cultural Grammars and Styles

Let's start with clothing. Clothes have something like a grammar, the rules by which people are required to get dressed each morning. In the United States, you are supposed to wear a top and a bottom, such as pants and a shirt, and at least some minimal covering of the feet—shoes or sandals. Gender restrictions (as with pronouns) enter pretty quickly. Women can substitute a skirt for the pants or a dress for both the pants and shirt, but men cannot, at least not conventionally.

Beyond these basic outer coverings, everything is a matter of style—even underwear. It is normally a part of one's clothing—"implied" or "understood" like the "you" in imperative verbs. It is certainly conventional to wear some kind of underwear, and it would seem to be foundational, a part of the grammar, but because it is not open for public view, underwear becomes an issue of style. It can be plain, fancy, or even absent.

Different places and groups have different conventions for attire. At the corporate office, more items of clothing may be required—not only shirts and pants or skirts, but also suit jackets, neckties (for men), socks (for men) and stockings (for women), and certain bodily preparations as well: make-up (for women), shaved faces (for men), and various hair dressings. Dark colors are usually preferred, especially for men. Style enters the picture when people deviate even slightly from these conventions. Men might wear colorful ties with bold designs, and women might press the color limits on shirts and scarves. Such deviations are said, significantly, to be "loud," a metaphor like "voice" in writing. It suggests that bright clothes shout above the conventional muted tones of the office.

At the beach, fewer clothes are conventional. Shoes are not required. Men can leave off the shirt (especially young men with nice bodies—older, hairy, fat guys are often criticized for putting their bellies on display). Women are still usually required to wear tops, but these can be minimal (again, especially for young, conventionally attractive women). All else is a matter of style. Men can wear baggy trunks or European-style swim suits ("Speedos"); women can wear conservative one-piece suits with a modest little skirt or a skimpy string bikini. Clothes for both genders may approach the vanishing point. The skimpier they become, the more daring and self-confident the wearer will appear. Beyond the basic bathing suit, everything is a matter of style.

Like the business suit and bathing suit, all cultural artifacts—songs, cars, religious ceremonies, entertainments of all kinds, food—can be analyzed by isolating conventional standards and deviations from those conventions. Within the same culture—such as the same geographical region or the same corporate office—differences involve deviations from those conventions.

At the level of cultural difference, however, the conventions themselves change. For example, in Arabic culture, the grammar of clothing involves not shirt and pants but the long robe that covers the body and some kind of head scarf. Conventions governing color variation and robe design vary from region to region and nation to nation. The Omani culture, for example, is known for its impressive variations of the basic desert garb. In U.S. culture, Californians are said to be more informal than East Coast dwellers in their dress and more adventurous in their foods. East Coasters look to Europe for their conventions, while West Coasters may look to Asia.

The kinds of conventions and the degree of deviations and variations, in short, indicate the sorts of identities that people form, the way they achieve distinction. Stylistic variation may be an expression of one's individuality, a deviation from a cultural norm, or it may indicate an attempt to identify with another culture, a completely different set of norms.

Footing

Footing, you'll recall, describes the stance or "alignment" someone takes toward other people and toward the situations they all occupy. In face-to-face encounters, people can draw on many resources to establish a particular footing or signal a shift from one footing to another: not only language, but also bodily posture, gesture, facial expression, and vocal tone, volume, and pacing (Goffman 128–30). In writing, many of these resources are unavailable; thus, writers must depend on style to create or change footings.

We can extend our understanding of footing beyond everyday conversations and written prose to include almost any cultural form. All we need to do is ask what stance or alignment that form takes toward the situation in which it appears. A cereal box, for instance, can assume a particular footing towards potential consumers. Is its front covered in bright, neon colors designed to catch the eye of the passing shopper? Does it feature some cartoon character (a tiger, toucan, or rabbit, perhaps) holding a bowl of frosted, enticing delights? Or is the front more austere—perhaps a white or beige background with a bowl of bran fiber pressed into twig-like shapes topped with berries? The former promises fun, excitement, and sugary goodness; the latter defines its relationship to consumers more simply, less intrusively, with an implicit assurance of good health and wholesomeness.

This kind of analysis works especially with architectural structures and statuary, which are often consciously designed to establish particular footing with respect to visitors and passers-by. Take, for instance, the Vietnam Veterans Memorial. Sonja K. Foss has examined its wide appeal to various audiences, and although she doesn't explicitly use the term footing, parts of her analysis assume something very close to it. She characterizes the memorial as having a "welcoming stance" (333). Set inconspicuously between the Lincoln Memorial and Washington Monument (both towering structures, especially the latter), the Vietnam Veterans Memorial is only ten feet at its highest point, made of polished black granite (not white marble as is usually the case with war memorials), and shaped in an open "V" that cuts gracefully into the earth behind it. Its design "invites, draws us in, and almost seems to embrace us" (Foss 333). Inscribed on its surface are the names of the 58,000 Americans who died in the war. These inscriptions encourage visitors to experience the memorial at a deeply personal level, to walk up to the memorial and touch the name of a fallen loved one, to trace it onto a sheet of paper, and to leave a keepsake or memento beneath the name at the memorial's base. The memorial also "suggests respect for the elements that surround it":

> It does not appear to struggle against them. . . . The memorial is integrated and interdependent with the earth as it is engulfed by and conforms to the earth's contours. It is attuned and sensitive to the landscape around the memorial. Each arm of the memorial points to the northeast corners of the Lincoln Memorial and the Washington Monument, suggesting as well a connection between the memorial and America's earlier history. (Foss 333)

The net effect is a footing sufficiently inclusive to transcend the divisions and conflicts engendered by the war and appeal powerfully to all who visit it.

Troping and Scheming

In chapter 6, we already hinted how tropes might extend beyond language—how the logic of synecdoche, for instance, is at work whenever a part stands for a whole: a photograph for an event, a movie trailer for the movie, an indicted politician for the political party to which he or she belongs. The logic may not always be sound, yet it may chart how people process the world around them.

The other tropes capture other ways of thinking, communicating, and perceiving. Teachers often use visual metaphors, for instance, to describe complex or abstract concepts. A science teacher who uses a basketball to represent the sun and a BB to represent the Earth uses a visual metaphor to help students understand the relative size of objects in our solar system. If she places that basketball and BB 86 feet apart (the actual distance from sun to Earth to scale), she extends the metaphor to teach students something about astronomical distances. Visual and other nonverbal metonymies also abound in our culture. We mentioned a few in the tropes chapter: a cross for Christianity, or a flag for a nation. Here we might add more examples to the list. Consider how frequently young, attractive, and fun-loving people appear in advertisements. They serve as metonymies for the products they sell—that is, they impart their appeal to a product by association, implicitly promising consumers that once they buy that product, that same appeal will be imparted to them. Smells and sounds may also work metonymically. The smell of a chicken roasting may remind someone of home. With this kind of phenomenon in mind, real estate agents sometimes urge customers to bake brownies (another genre of "comfort food") before showing a house to prospective buyers. For an example of how sounds metonymize, think of movie soundtracks. Can anyone hear the "da-dum-da-dum-da-dum" from *Jaws* without thinking a shark attack is immanent?

The other class of figures, the schemes, catalogue different ways writers can structure their sentences. When used to analyze cultural forms other than language, they focus attention on how those forms are put together and organized. Jeanne Fahnestock has found analogues for several schemes in diagrams and illustrations appearing in scientific treatises. As an example, Fahnestock selects a photograph of lines of force between two electrically charged plates. She describes this photo as a visual antimetabole, with one side of the photo serving as the mirror image of the other in an A:B::B:A pattern. Switching to music, we might note that jazz legend Thelonius Monk composed a tune based on epistrophe, although he used an alternate spelling for the tune's title, "Epistrophy." Like the scheme of the same name, the tune "Epistrophy" repeats the same (or a similar) sequence of notes at the end of successive musical phrases, creating a melody with a strong falling emphasis.

Rather than hunt for exact cultural analogues for individual schemes, it may be more fruitful to apply the general principles of organization upon which those schemes depend—namely, parallelism, balance, repetition, contrast, and inversion or reversal. These concepts are so flexible that they can apply to almost any cultural form: a comic book, a landscaped garden, a sports stadium, a web page, a dance performance, an article of clothing, a fancy dish on the food channel. Art critics often use schematic concepts when analyzing or reviewing the visual and plastic arts, just as artists and craftspeople learn to apply them in their practices of production. Contrasting color schemes in painting and photographic composition, symmetrical and asymmetrical balance in print design, repeated patterns in ceramics and fabric design all reveal the parallel relation of verbal scheming to visual design. Schematic patterns can also play important roles in music. A jazz soloist, for instance, may use repetition to establish a melodic motif and then, through improvisation, vary it by creating a new melodic line that parallels, contrasts with, or inverts the original. And it's not just a matter of determining how a given cultural form adheres to these principles; sometimes, the most interesting cultural form deviates from them. In the history of jazz, bebop artists like Charlie "Bird" Parker and Miles Davis created their distinctive styles by leading listeners into familiar landscapes of sound and then introducing discordant surprises that to the untrained or conventional ear would sound like mistakes. Composers like Stravinsky created a similar effect in classical music, with performances that sometimes resulted in actual riots among the usually placid audience of concert goers. Cultural expression matters to people, and, strange as it may seem, stylistic variation can be risky.

Conclusion: From Competence to Creativity

Whether we are talking about language, fashion, music, film, pottery, or painting, *style* is the performance of identity using a recognized form within a cultural context. As we acquire competence within cultural forms, we use conventions to identify with established groups, and we deviate from convention to assert individuality or a social identity at odds with the established norms of the "mainstream" or dominant group. We engage in performative play, troping and scheming with conventions to invite audiences into the process of testing limits, making meaning, negotiating identity—the processes usually grouped under the heading of *creativity*. The creative use of the trends of analysis and composition covered in this book point toward ever wider fields of application, beginning with the performance of prose in the writing classroom but ultimately extending into every field of study and into the broadest array of cultural practices.

Exercises

1. Using our analysis of clothing as a model, pick a cultural practice (bowling, for instance, or shopping, sitting in class, walking in the park, posting to a message board, watching a movie in a theater) and describe the conventions that participants typically observe when performing it. Are there any variations in these conventions depending on who is performing this practice or on where or when he or she is performing it? If so, include those in your analysis. Next describe possible deviations from these conventions and explain how these deviations allow participants to form distinctive or stylized identities.

2. Pick a cultural artifact (a specific building, garden, laptop, painting, car, sofa, etc.) and characterize the footing it takes up with respect to potential spectators or users. How does that artifact position itself in its immediate setting, and how does it position those spectators and users?

3. Select another cultural practice or artifact, one that is distinctly patterned. Analyze your selection by drawing on the five structural principles embodied in the schemes: parallelism, balance, repetition, contrast, and inversion or reversal. Don't feel obliged to use all five; instead, use only those that allow you to analyze your selection best. After completing your analysis, use the schemes to compose written analogues for each of the patterns you singled out—analogues that both describe and enact the pattern. For instance, if the practice or artifact you chose is dominated by patterns of repetition and reversal, you might describe one of its repeating patterns in the form of an anaphora or an epistrophe, while describing an inverted pattern with anastrophe. If repetition and inversion combine in a single aspect of your selection, you might use antimetabole, which consists of both repetition and inversion.

4. Over the course of this semester you have created your own cultural artifact: your commonplace book. Imagine that you are an archeologist from the future who discovers your notebook or file. What will she make of it? What patterns (or conventions) will she be able to discern in its design? Will she note any deviations within these patterns? What information will it reveal about you as a member of early twenty-first-century

culture? More specifically, what will she be able to tell about the kinds of sentences (and the stylistic moves they make) you valued enough to copy down, imitate, and comment upon? Write up your answer to these questions in short essay. For fun, you might even assume the persona of this future archeologist.

Appendix on Grammar / Notes / Works Cited / Index

Appendix on Grammar

As defined in chapter 1, grammar is the set of rules (written and unwritten) by which a language functions. It should be distinguished from *style*, which itself has two common meanings:

1. *editorial style*, the rules developed to govern conventions of printing and manuscript presentation (how many spaces to put after a period, whether to use one or two quotations marks, whether to put the period inside or outside the quotation mark, etc., things decided by publishers and other corporate forces that often have little or nothing to do with the history of usage that gives rise to grammar).
2. *rhetorical style*, the set of decisions any author makes about word choice and sentence structure (such as whether to use active or passive voice, how long to make a sentence, whether to use technical jargon) while remaining within the rules of grammar.

To know how to use editorial style and to make good decisions in rhetorical style, you need to have a command of grammar. You need to know what choices are available within the grammatical system of a language. Many writers know grammar not as a set of rules but as a set of practices. They have absorbed a kind of tacit understanding from their extensive reading and writing practice. They can't tell you the rules, though they can usually abide by them. But if you want to move to the next level of stylistic performance, one way is to get inside the language and become more conscious of what's going on.

If we think of writing as performance, a knowledge of grammar and how to use it operates at the level of *competence*. A performer must first of all be competent within the medium of choice. A musician, for example, must be able to play relatively error-free scales and tunes before beginning to improvise or compose. If the audience hears a mistake, it could ruin an entire performance. It can stick in the mind and distract attention away from the rest of the performance, no matter how good it may be. Multiple errors are unthinkable among professional musicians or even educated or well-rehearsed amateurs.

Beyond the embarrassment of incompetence, however, a thorough knowledge of grammar—a deep competence—allows a writer greater flexibility and freedom in the act of writing. If a musician has deep competence, a missed note might become part of an innovative riff back into the scale or tune being played. A good writer will likewise know many moves within the rules of grammar to allow the best choice in sentence structure and word choice to emerge either in the process of drafting or editing the work.

Deep competence, or mastery, comes only with years of practice. At best, this appendix provides the basis and the encouragement for you to get a foothold in grammar and work your way toward a more complete mastery. For some readers, it will be a review; for others, a demystification of what may have seemed the obscure rules by which English functions. In either case, we hope it will move you to further study and awareness of English grammar and provide some common language to use when you need to talk about the functions of words and sentences.

Word Forms (Morphology)

If grammatical competence is a baseline for performing prose, it's important to know that what counts as competence changes over time or even from one writing occasion to the next. Geoffrey Chaucer and Virginia Woolf, for instance, are both virtuoso writers of English, although they worked within different mediums of competence (Chaucer in Middle English, and Woolf in Modern English). The criteria of competence also change with setting: when text-messaging or IM-ing your friends, for instance, expectations for writing grammatically "correct" English are usually relaxed, while those expectations are in full force when writing a paper for your English professor or a memo to your boss. To illustrate the variability of grammar over time, let's begin with a brief history of word forms (or morphology) in English. In the section that follows this one, we'll review in greater detail the criteria of grammatical competence you will be expected to have for most of the writing occasions you will encounter in your classes and your career—that is, a command of Standard American Edited English.

Historians of language tell us there are two kinds of grammars: synthetic and analytic.

- *Synthetic grammars* show the functions of words within a sentence by using inflections—either endings added to the word (such as -*s* or -*ed*) or alterations in word form (*is* versus *was*, for example). In synthetic grammars, all nouns are declined to show whether they perform as a subject, an object, or a modifier of another noun; and all verbs are conjugated to indicate changes in tense, mood, and number.

- *Analytic grammars* show word function through word order and other word classes that perform the same kind of work that inflections do in synthetic grammars. For instance, whether a noun is a subject or an object depends on its placement with respect to the verb (some languages move from subject to verb to object, while others move from subject to object to verb). To indicate tense, mood, and number, analytic grammars use auxiliaries (*will* versus *would*, for instance, and *has* versus *have*).

English is a little of both. Some very old version of Anglo-Saxon must have been fully synthetic. The versions of Old English that we read in *Beowulf* are more fully inflected than Modern English, but even in these ancient texts, the inflections had begun to simplify. Simplification usually results from contact among cultural and national groups, multiculturalism if you please. About a century or so after *Beowulf* was written, beginning in 1066, simplification rapidly increased when the Normans, who spoke French, invaded England. As the Normans tried to speak Old English and the Anglo-Saxons tried to speak French, they simplified word forms and endings. The result was that in Modern English we have a mix of Old French and Old English and only remnants of the inflectional system. In our pronouns, for example, we still distinguish between cases. We say *he* or *she* (the *nominative* form) to indicate subjects of verbs, as in "*he* drove" and "*she* grew sick," but *him* or *her* (the *objective* form) to indicate objects of verbs or prepositions, as in "he drove *her* crazy" and "she grew sick of *him*." Pronouns change to indicate number as well, from *he* or *she* to *they*, and to indicate possession, as in *his* or *her*.

The inflections (endings and form changes) of nouns disappeared almost completely. Nouns still change to indicate number—typically by adding an *-s* ending, though occasionally by preserving an old form—*brother* becomes *brothers*, but most people still understand the old form of *brethren*. Some of the most frequently used plurals retain their old forms, as in *men*, *women*, and *children*, suggesting that frequency of use is a key to preservation: think of the verb *to be*, the most irregular in English and the most frequently used.

Beyond plurals, the one true remnant of the old case system for English nouns is the possessive form, indicated by the -*'s* or plural -*s'*, as in "the boy's doll" or "the boys' trucks." The apostrophe may indicate the loss of a letter from the old -*as* genitive ending in Old English. It may also be that advertisers can't ever get their apostrophes right because they are (unconsciously) participating in the continuing simplification of the old synthetic grammar of English.

As English inflections have simplified and disappeared, sentence order has rigidified. Even with the possessive ending, for example, we must keep the possessive noun or pronoun in the position before the modified word: "the boy's doll" and "their trucks," not "the doll boy's" or "trucks their." In fact, one of the reasons for the tendency of the apostrophe to disappear is that it's really not needed. Many novelists and poets these days omit it in the possessive and let the context correct for any confusion that might arise between "the boy's trucks" and "the boys' trucks." They do the same thing with the other use of apostrophes: contractions. Even big-time English stylists like William Faulkner and Cormac McCarthy write "cant" (meaning "can't," short for "cannot," not trivial political language [also "cant"]). The automatic spelling corrector won't let us write "won't" without the apostrophe so we'll have to let "cant" suffice as an example.

The Basic Sentence

The basic sentence in English divides into two major parts: the subject and the predicate. The subject forms the topic of the sentence; the predicate makes a comment about that topic. It says what the subject is or what the subject does. Consider this example from Lawrence Ferlinghetti's poem "Dog" (from *A Coney Island of the Mind*, a personal and sentimental favorite of ours):

> The dog trots freely in the streets.

The subject is "The dog." It announces what or who the sentence is about. The predicate is "trots freely in the streets," and it tells us, in this case, what the subject is doing. Both subject and predicate divide into smaller parts. The subject consists of a simple subject and its modifiers, while the predicate includes a verb, its modifiers, and for two important classes of verbs (transitive verbs and linking verbs), its complements. In the Ferlinghetti sentence, "dog" is the simple subject, and the definite article "the" is its modifier. The verb "trots" is intransitive and does not take complements, but it can have modifiers—in this case, "freely" (an adverb expressing manner) and "in the streets" (a prepositional phrase acting like an adverb: it expresses *where* the dog trots). Let's sum up:

Subject	Predicate
simple subject + modifiers	verb + modifiers + complements

Congratulations! You now have a firm grasp on the basic sentence in English. It's really that simple. All other sentences result from elaborating on this basic pattern or from combining two or more basic sentences to form larger structures. We'll examine those larger structures below, but before we do, let's explore each element of the basic sentence more fully.

Simple Subjects

In the Ferlinghetti sentence (as in most sentences), the simple subject is a noun ("dog"), but other grammatical structures can fill that role. To put it somewhat differently, just as the prepositional phrase "in the streets" can act like an adverb, other structures can act like and fill the role of nouns. One such structure is the gerund, a verbal formed by adding *-ing* to the base verb: walking, skipping, dancing, laughing, and so on. Listed by themselves, gerunds are indistinguishable from another type of verbal: the present participle. What distinguishes the two is the role each plays in a sentence: gerunds act like nouns, while participles act like adjectives (see below). Like nouns, gerunds can serve as simple subjects in sentences: "Barking is fun." They can also have modifiers, as in "The dog's loud barking startled the cop," where the definite article ("The"), the possessive ("dog's"), and the adjective ("loud") modify "barking." Another structure that can fill the role of simple subject is the infinitive—also a verbal, but this time formed by adding "to" in front of the base verb: "To bark is fun." Infinitives can only be modified by adverbs that appear after the infinitive phrase: "To bark loudly is fun," and "To bark at the cop is fun" (note that "at the cop" is another prepositional phrase acting like an adverb).

The final grammatical structure that can serve as a simple subject is the noun clause. Noun clauses are usually introduced by words such as "what," "that," or "how": "What the dog hears is very discouraging," or "That the dog is barking loudly is noted by the cop." As you might notice, using noun clauses as subjects might sound a tad formal, even stilted. If these clauses are lengthy, they delay the appearance of the sentence's main verb and, as a result, may frustrate comprehension. In other words, issues of performance (in this case, level of formality and readers' ease of understanding) can emerge in response to grammatical choice. To avoid delivering such stilted and obtuse performances, writers often prefer to reserve lengthy noun clauses for the ends of their sentences: "The cop notes the dog's loud barking," or "The cop notes the loud barking of the dog" (the difference between these two variants is that, in the first, "barking" receives the main emphasis, while "the dog" receives it in the second).

Simple Subjects	
Nouns	dog, Bob, chair
Gerunds	barking, laughing, reading
Infinitives	to bark, to laugh, to read
Noun clauses	what startles the cop

Verbs

Although several grammatical structures can fill the role of simple subject in a sentence, only verbs can serve as verbs. There are three main verb classes: intransitive, transitive, and linking. In our original sentence, the verb "trots" is intransitive: it reports an action but does not take a direct object—all the action resides, so to speak, with the dog. Because intransitive verbs do not have direct objects, they and their subjects can stand alone as complete sentences: "The dog trots." Consider a sentence in which the verb is transitive: "The dog chews a bone." Like "trots," the verb "chews" reports an action, but unlike an intransitive verb, the reported action of a transitive verb carries through or extends to a direct object, the "bone." Transitive verbs can also change voice from active to passive: "The bone is chewed by the dog." With passive constructions, the subject receives the action and is thus passive, while the agent is either displaced into a prepositional phrase (a *by*-phrase) or omitted altogether: "The bone is chewed."

The passive voice offers a good test for deciding whether a verb is intransitive or transitive. If a sentence can be revoiced as a passive, then the verb is transitive. Start by moving the subject into a *by*-phrase, change the verb into its passive form, and see if a meaningful sentence emerges:

The dog chews the bone.
The bone is chewed by the dog.

The dog trots freely in the streets.
??? is trotted freely in the streets by the dog

If a sentence cannot be revoiced as a passive (as with the second pair of sentences above), then there's a good chance that the verb is intransitive, unless it's a member of our final class of verbs—linking verbs.

Linking verbs are not verbs of action but verbs of, well, being. As the name implies, a linking verb establishes a connection—a "link"—between the subject and the information that comes after the verb. "The dog is a beagle" links the subject ("dog") to another noun ("beagle") and thus identifies him with that noun. Linking verbs can also connect subjects to adjectives and adverbs (grammarians have special names for nouns, adjectives, and adverbs that follow linking verbs, but we'll discuss those in the next section). Consider "The dog is brown" and "The dog is here." The first identifies the dog with an attribute (its color), the second with his location ("here"). Linking verbs are also often followed by prepositional phrases acting like adverbs: "The dog is in the street," or "The dog is on the porch." In most cases, linking verbs appear as some form of the verb "to be," but there are other possibilities: "The dog seems tired," "The dog smells musty," "The streets appear wet." In all three of these sentences, the verb creates a link between the subject and an attribute of that subject.

Verbs change to indicate number, person, and tense. Number and person work together and must match (or agree with) the number and person of the subject. When the subject is a gerund, infinitive, or noun clause, the verb is third-person singular: "Barking is fun," but not "Barking are fun." When the subject is a noun (or pronoun), its number and person determines the verb form. In the present tense, most verbs have only one variation. Here's how they are conjugated:

Singular:
    1st person: I *trot*.
    2nd person: You *trot*.
    3rd person: She, he, or it *trots*.

Plural:
>   1st person: We *trot*.
>   2nd person: You *trot*.
>   3rd person: They *trot*.

In conjugation, notice that only the third-person singular form of the verb changes. The -*s* is added. That inflection causes problems for many students who do not produce its sound in their spoken dialects. It probably go the way of the 'postrophe, dig? It eventually fall off or be simplifyin. (But now you know that the "error" makes sense. Indeed, many errors have a logic or pattern that a little analysis will reveal. This kind of analysis is very useful for teachers of English and for writers trying to get rid of errors.)

Verbs change to indicate tense, or time, as well. In English, we have three simple tenses: the present, past, and future:

The dog trots.
The dog trotted.
The dog will trot.

Some verbs, like *trotted*, add the -*ed* to indicate past tense; others change form: The dog stinks; the dog stunk. Verbs indicate future tense by adding the auxiliary verb "will" in front of the verb: I will trot; you will trot; she, he, or it will trot. Some sticklers insist on using "shall" when the subject is "I" or "we," but for most occasions, "shall" sounds overly formal or even British, as in "I shall trot freely in the streets." In other words, the writer who uses "shall" with first person pronouns delivers a different kind of performance than the writer who opts for the less formal (and perhaps more egalitarian) "will."

Beyond the three simple tenses, we have verb phrases that combine tense and aspect to form the complex tenses. English has nine complex tenses—add those to the simple tenses and that is twelve tenses in all! Here are the present-tense versions of the complex tenses. You can derive the rest by adding past and future versions of each:

- The dog is trotting (*present progressive* to distinguish an act in progress from an act that is presently habitual, which is the most common function of the simple present "trots").
- The dog has trotted (*present perfect* to indicate continuing actions).
- The dog has been trotting (*present perfect progressive*).

Why so many tenses? You would think the simple tenses were enough to locate all actions in time: something is happening now, something already happened, or something will happen. But it's not that simple. We often need to express different nuances of time: for instance, to report an action that began in the past but continues through the present, to distinguish between two past events that occurred at different times, or to background one action against another:

- The dog has run away. (The action began in the past but *continues* through the present.)
- The dog had chased a cat up a tree when the dogcatcher arrived on the scene. (The dog treed the cat *before* the dogcatcher arrived.)
- While the dog is eying the cat, the dogcatcher makes his move. (The action of eyeing the cat is backgrounded against the action of the dogcatcher.)

You may have been told to pick a tense and stick with it. This advice may be good for novice writers, but more accomplished stylists—those with deep competence—capitalize on our tense system and its flexibility to capture many gradations and distinctions in time.

Complements

A complement is a word, phrase, or clause that *completes* a grammatical structure. The word "complement" usually names what follows a verb, but as we'll see shortly, complements can also follow prepositions, infinitives, present participles, and gerunds. The kind of complement that follows or completes a verb is governed by the type of verb used. Transitive verbs allow for three possibilities: direct object, indirect object, and object complement. Intransitive verbs take no complements: a subject plus an intransitive verb is complete unto itself ("The dog trots"), although this base form may be fleshed out by modifiers ("The dog trots *freely in the streets*"). Linking verbs also allow for three possibilities: predicate noun, predicate adjective, and predicate adverb.

We have already seen an example of a direct object when we discussed the transitive verb in "The dog chews the bone," where the noun "bone" is a direct object that completes the action reported by "chews." Other possibilities included phrases and clauses serving as direct objects: "The dog likes *to bark*," and "The dogcatcher sees *what the dog is up to*." A good way to identify the direct object is to turn the sentence into a question: "What does the dog like?" and "What does the dogcatcher see?" The answer in both cases is the direct object: "to bark" and "what the dog is up to."

Some transitive verbs can have two complements: either a direct object and indirect object, or a direct object and an object complement. Transitive verbs that allow direct and indirect objects often involve actions in which something is transmitted from one person or object to another person or object. In such cases, the indirect object plays the role of recipient of the action: "The dogcatcher gives the dog a bone." Here "bone" is the direct object, while "dog," the recipient of the action, is the indirect object. Other transitive verbs that take direct and indirect objects involve actions in which some item is made or obtained for the indirect object which, in this case, plays the role of beneficiary of the action: "The dogcatcher cooks the dog a steak," where "steak" is the direct object and "dog," the beneficiary of the action, is the indirect object. If you are unsure which of two complements is the indirect object, you can test if the sentence still works when you place a preposition in front of either complement (use "to" for verbs of transmission and "for" for verbs of creation). "The dogcatcher gives (to) the dog a bone" still works, but not "The dogcatcher gives the dog (to) a bone." Similarly, "The dogcatcher cooks (for) the dog a steak" works, but not "The dogcatcher cooks the dog (for) a steak." (We can imagine a context in which the second sentence might work, but we shudder to think about it). Another characteristic of an indirect object is that it is relatively mobile and can move to the end of a sentence so long as it appears with the appropriate preposition in front of it: "The dogcatcher gives a bone to the dog" and "The dogcatcher cooks a steak for the dog."

The other double complement combination is the direct object and object complement: "The dog likes his steaks rare," and "The dog considers the dogcatcher a pal." Just as the complements of verbs complete the action reported by the verb, an object complement completes the direct object by specifying or renaming it in some way. In the first example, the object complement "rare" (an adjective) specifies how the dog likes his steaks cooked. In the second, "pal" (a noun) renames "dogcatcher." Some linguists explain the relationship between direct objects and object complements by imagining an implicit linking verb between the two: "his steaks (are) rare," and "the dogcatcher (is) a pal."

Linking verbs have their own set of possible complements: predicate nouns, predicate adjectives, and predicate adverbs. Earlier, we saw examples of all three:

- The dog is a beagle (predicate noun).
- The dog is brown (predicate adjective).
- The dog is here (predicate adverb).

When a linking verb is followed by a prepositional phrase indicating place or time, linguists and grammarians call that prepositional phrase a "predicate adverbial" because it functions like an adverb: "The dog is *in the streets*" or "Lunch is *at noon.*"

Other grammatical structures include complements. Two of the most common are prepositional and gerundive phrases. The complement of a prepositional phrase typically appears right after the preposition:

- The dog trots freely in *the streets.*
- The dog is fond of *barking.*
- The dog barks over *there.*

Note how the complement of a preposition can be, among other things, a noun phrase ("the streets"), a gerund ("barking"), or an adverb ("there"). Gerunds can also take complements:

Catching *the dog* proved difficult.

Here the complement acts much like the direct object of a verb. In fact, if that complement were a pronoun, it would take the objective (and not the nominative) form: "Catching *him*," but not "Catching *he.*"

Modifiers

Adjectives and adverbs are the two main single-word modifiers in English. Adjectives modify nouns. Adverbs modify verbs, adjectives, and other adverbs, and tell how, when, why, or where. Both kinds of modifiers, when used judiciously, add specificity and precision to our writing. Not just any old "dog," but a "brown dog"; not just a "brown dog," but a "happy brown dog"; and so on. The same goes for adverbs: the dog doesn't just "trot," he "trots freely in the streets."

You may have heard professional writers or teachers tell you to avoid adjectives and adverbs at all costs. This advice strikes us as too absolute. What they probably mean is to avoid using adjectives and adverbs as substitutes for careful word choice. In other words, it's a problem at or near the level of competence. Why, for instance, write "bad experience," when English offers more precise or evocative nouns to choose from: "disappointment," "embarrassment," "fiasco," or even "bummer"? Or why write "speaks loudly," when "shouts," "bellows," "shrieks," or "roars" would be more apt? If you do notice that your prose seems overly laden with adjectives and adverbs, check the nouns and verbs they modify. If those nouns and verbs are too general in scope (like "experience" and "shouts"), try to find a more precise single-word substitute.

In addition to adjectives and adverbs, we have other words, phrases, and clauses that can modify. Even though these other modifiers are not, strictly speaking, adjectives and adverbs, they act as if they were either one or the other—as adjectives when modifying nouns, as adverbs when modifying verbs. Participles and participial phrases, for instance, act like adjectives and modify nouns:

- The *barking* dog trots freely in the streets.
- *Barking a happy tune*, the dog trots freely in the streets.
- The *exhausted* dog stops for a rest.
- The dog, *exhausted with trotting*, stops for a rest.

A few observations. First, participles come in two forms: the present participle (ending in *-ing*), and the past participle (ending in either *-ed* or *-en*). Second, when participles act as single-word modifiers, they appear before the noun, just like adjectives: "the *barking* dog," and "the *exhausted* dog." When they are part of a participial phrase, they become more mobile and can appear (set off by commas) before or after the noun phrase they modify:

- The dog, *barking a happy tune*, trots freely in the streets.
- *Exhausted with trotting*, the dog stops for a rest.

Participial phrases can even come at the end of the sentence:

- The dog trots freely in the streets, *barking a happy tune*.
- The dog stops for a rest, *exhausted with trotting*.

Wherever they appear, one rule must be observed: the implied grammatical subject of the participle must be the same as the grammatical subject of the clause in which it appears. Otherwise, you have a dangling modifier:

Exhausted with trotting, the day comes to an end.
Or a misplaced modifier:
Barking a happy tune, the dogcatcher chases the dog.

In the first sentence, the implicit grammatical subject of "exhausted" is "dog," but "dog" is nowhere to be found, so the modifier dangles. In the second sentence, the "dog" is there alright, but he's not the grammatical subject of the sentence—"dogcatcher" is! Thus the sentence implies that it's the dogcatcher who barks a happy tune. But this doesn't make much sense. The modifier must be misplaced.

Prepositional phrases also modify. Unlike participial phrases which can only act as adjectives, prepositional phrases can serve as either adjectives or adverbs. Functioning as an adjective, the prepositional phrase usually comes right after the noun it modifies in a fairly rigid formation. You say, "The dog *with the brown spots* trots freely in the streets," but not "With the brown spots, the dog trots" or "The dog trots with the brown spots," etc. Functioning as adverbs, the phrases are more mobile: "*In the streets*, the dog trots freely" or "The dog trots *in the streets* freely." If you were to say, "The dog *in the streets* trots freely," the prepositional phrases ceases to work as an adverb and, instead, serves as an adjective. Which dog? The one "in the streets." In this case, the phrase's position with respect to the noun "dog" determines the role it plays in the sentence.

Clauses that serve as dependent clauses in sentences also modify. Dependent clauses have the same structure as a basic sentence (a simple subject plus its modifiers and a verb plus its complements and modifiers), but they cannot stand alone as independent sentences. Instead, they must work as modifiers along with independent clauses. They come in two basic forms: *subordinate clauses*, which function as adverbs, and *relative clauses*, which function as adjectives and as nouns.

Subordinate clauses are formed by adding a subordinating conjunction such as *when, if, because, while,* or *whereas* in front of what would otherwise be an independent clause, as in "When the dog trots freely in the streets." Such a clause, being adverbial, is relatively mobile and can go at the beginning of the sentence (in which case it is followed by a comma, by the way) or at the end (in which case it is not preceded by a comma): "When the dog trots freely in the streets, the mail carrier steps cautiously." Or "The mail carrier steps cautiously when the dog trots freely in the streets."

Writers use subordinate clauses to show how events or bits of information are related in terms of time, cause-effect, importance, and so on. For instance, if we removed the subordinating conjunction from the sentence above and expressed both clauses as independent ones, we'd have "The dog trots freely in the streets, and the mail carrier steps cautiously." What are the consequences of this revision? For one, since "subordinate" suggests "less important," the revision elevates the once subordinate clause to the same level of importance as the main clause: the information that each expresses is now presented as equal in significance. Another consequence of this revision is that we lose explicit guidance on how these two events relate in terms of time and causation. In other words, the subordinating conjunction *when* makes it clear that these two events (the dog trotting and the mail carrier steeping cautiously) happen at the same time. There's also the sense that the first event causes the second one. To put it somewhat differently, writers use subordination to process and interpret the events and information they present. Writers who rarely use subordination (Ernest Hemmingway, for instance) leave it up to readers to work out the connections between the events and bits of information conveyed. And that may be precisely their goal—that is to at least create the illusion of an unfiltered, unmediated reality.

Relative clauses function as adjectives and sometimes as nouns and, again, predictably, are less mobile within the sentence. Relative clauses are formed by using a relative pronoun—*that, who, whom,* or *which*—as a functioning part of the clause. "The dog *that trots freely in the streets* is a nuisance to the mail carrier *who fears being bitten.*" Notice that these two adjectival relative clauses come right after the noun they modify, in the same way that prepositional phrases do when they function as adjectives. Both also use the relative pronoun—"that" or "who"—for the subject of the clause. The independent clause in the first example is "The dog is a nuisance to the mail carrier." The relative clauses—"that trots freely in the streets" and "who fears being bitten"—are embedded within the independent clause.

We don't use commas to set off this clause because it is, depending on which handbook you use, called an "essential clause" or "restrictive clause," which suggests that the meaning of the sentence changes radically if the clause is omitted. Without the commas, the sentence suggests that the free trotting is the problem, not just the dog in and of itself. To use commas—"The dog, which trots freely in the streets, . . ."—would suggest that the dog is a nuisance no matter what he does.

In most texts of Old English, the relative pronoun *that*, which never changes its case no matter what, does the work of all relative pronouns in modern English. By the eighteenth century, however, English grammarians appear to have grown jealous of the French who had *qui* and *que* to show the difference between subject and object and the difference between people and things in relative clauses and so went digging in some ancient English and found the linguistic ancestors of *who* and *whom*, two of the most troublesome words in English, as well as the equally troublesome *which*. Now we have to use *who* to indicate the subject or nominative function, as in "who fears being bitten," and *whom* to indicate the objective, as in "the congressman whom the dog bit." Notice that when the relative pronoun serves as object, it moves to the front of the clause before the subject. If you have doubts about whether to write *who* or *whom*, put it in the order of an independent clause: "the dog bit him" (whom).

The relative pronouns *that* and *which* are more or less interchangeable in historical English, but in the last few decades, editorial styles have suggested that you use *that* for restrictive clauses (not set off with commas) and *which* for nonrestrictive clauses that are to be set off with commas. Most grammar checkers in computer programs follow this convention as well.

Sentence Types

Now we have the basic elements of all types of English sentences:

- *Simple*—only one independent clause, a subject and predicate with one-word and phrasal modifiers: "The dog trots freely in the streets." (You can have compound subjects or verbs in simple sentences: "The dog and mail carrier walk the streets," or "The dog trots in the streets and sees many things.")
- *Compound*—two or more independent clauses linked with coordinating conjunctions (*and, or, nor, for, but*): "The dog trots freely in the streets, and he sees many things."
- *Complex*—one independent clause and at least one dependent clause: "When the dog trots in the streets, the mail carrier cringes," or "The dog that trots freely in the streets strikes fear in the heart of the mail carrier."
- *Complex-Compound*—two or more independent clauses linked with coordinating conjunctions and containing at least one dependent clause: "The dog that trots freely through the streets may frighten the mail carrier, but he is actually quite harmless."

We can analyze all of these sentence types in terms of the basic sentence in English. A simple sentence is just your basic sentence: a simple subject plus its modifiers, and a verb plus its complements and modifiers. If a simple sentence has a compound subject, just add another subject plus its modifiers to the formula; if it has a compound predicate, add another verb plus its complements and modifiers. A compound sentence is two or more basic sentences joined with coordinating conjunctions. A complex sentence is a basic sentence with at least one more basic sentence attached in a relationship of dependence (either through a subordinating conjunction or relative pronoun). A compound-complex sentence consists of two or more basic sentences joined with coordinating conjunctions with at least one subordinate or relative clause thrown into the mix.

A Note on Sources: If you are not yet sick of the dog sentences and want to read the poem "Dog" by Lawrence Ferlinghetti, go to http://boppin.com/poets/ferlinghetti.htm, which also has a nice recent picture of the old beatnik poet.

Notes

Preface

1. Here, for instance, is how James D. White defines that final step in the writing process: "Focusing on sentence-level concerns, such as punctuation, sentence length, spelling, agreement of subjects and predicates, and style" (107). It is not clear what White thinks style is, but his placement of it in this parallel series suggests it is no more complex or compelling than spelling and subject-verb agreement—the all-too-common confusion these days of style with grammar and other matters governed by mechanical rules.

2. Motives of Style

1. An excellent introduction to the functions of word classes is Scott Rice's *Right Words, Right Places*. We also discuss these word classes in the appendix on grammar.

2. For simplicity's sake, we're using "subordination" here as a cover term for both subordinate and relative clauses. For a fuller treatment, see the appendix.

Works Cited

Abbey, Edward. "Canyonlands and Compromises." In *Voices for the Earth: A Treasury of the Sierra Club Bulletin*. Ed. Ann Gilliam. San Francisco: Sierra Club, 1979. 391–93.

Armstrong, William H. *Sounder*. New York: Harper Trophy, 1972.

Attridge, Derek. *Peculiar Language: Literature as Difference from the Renaissance to James Joyce*. New York: Routledge, 2004.

Atwan, Robert, ed. *Best American Essays: College Edition*. 4th ed. Boston: Houghton, 2004.

———, ed. *Best American Essays: College Edition*. 5th ed. Boston: Houghton, 2008.

Balester, Valerie. *Cultural Divide: A Study of African-American College-Level Writers*. Portsmouth, NH: Boynton Cook, 1993.

Barnhill, David Landis, ed. *At Home on the Earth*. Berkeley: U of California P, 1999.

Barry, Anita K. *English Grammar: Language as Human Behavior*. 2nd ed. Upper Saddle River, NJ: Prentice Hall, 2002.

Barthelme, Donald. *Sixty Stories*. London: Penguin Classics, 2003.

Bass, Rick. "From *The Ninemile Wolves*." In Finch and Elder, eds. 1114–19.

———. "On Willow Creek." In Barnhill, ed. 211–26.

Beard, Jo Ann. "Werner." In Wallace, ed. 1–21.

Blix, Hans. *Thirteenth Quarterly Report of the Executive Chairman of the United Nations Monitoring, Verification, and Inspection Commission*. New York: United Nations. 30 May 2003. http://www.un.org/Depts/unmovic/new/documents/quarterly_reports/s-2007–106.pdf.

Blood, Rebecca. "SXSW 'blogger love-in' eyewitness." http://wmf.editthispage. com/discuss/msgReader$364?mode=day.

———. "Weblogs: A History and Perspective." In *Rebecca's Pocket*. http://www. rebeccablood.net/essays/weblogistory.html.

Bragg, Rick. *All Over but the Shoutin'*. New York: Vintage, 1997.

———. *Ava's Man*. New York: Vintage, 2001.

Britt, Suzanne. "That Lean and Hungry Look." In Hickey, ed. 64–66.

Brooks, Max. *World War Z: An Oral History of the Zombie War*. New York: Crown Books, 2006.

Bryson, Bill. *In a Sunburned Country*. New York: Broadway, 2001.

———. *A Short History of Nearly Everything*. New York: Broadway, 2003.

Burke, Kenneth. *A Grammar of Motives*. Berkeley: U of California P, 1969.

———. "Literature as Equipment for Living." In *The Philosophy of Literary Form*. Berkeley: U of California P, 1973. 293–304.

———. *A Rhetoric of Motives*. Berkeley: U of California P, 1969.

Burroughs, Franklin. "Compression Wood." In Hoagland and Atwan, ed. 38–54.

Bush, George W. Address. U.S. Capitol, Washington, DC, 20 Sept. 2001. http:// www.presidentialrhetoric.com/speeches/09.20.01.html.

Carpenter, William J. "Rethinking Stylistic Analysis in the Writing Classroom." In Johnson and Pace, ed. 181–97.

Carr, Nicholas. "Is Google Making Us Stupid?" *Atlantic*, July/August 2008, 56–63.

Cicero. *De Oratore*. Trans. E. W. Sutton and H. Rackam. Loeb Classical Library 349. Cambridge, MA: Harvard UP, 1977.

Cisneros, Sandra. *The House on Mango Street*. New York: Vintage Books, 1984.

Clements, Peter. "Re-Placing the Sentence: Approaching Style through Genre." In Johnson and Pace, 198–214.

Connors, Robert J. "The Erasure of the Sentence." *College Composition and Communication* 52, no. 1 (2000): 96–128.

Conover, Ted. "The Road Is Very Unfair." In Sims and Kramer, eds. 303–42.

Corbett, Edward P. J. *Classical Rhetoric for the Modern Student*. 2nd ed. New York: Oxford UP, 1971.

Cornwell, Bernard. *The Winter King: A Novel of Arthur*. New York: St. Martin's Griffin, 1995.

Crenshaw, Paul. "Storm Country." In Orlean, ed. 21–27.

CSIRO. "Treating toxic waste with sound waves." http://www.csiro.au/solutions/ ps9b.html.

Davis, Sheila. "Metonymy." In Enos, ed. 444–46.

———. "Synecdoche." In Enos, ed. 712–713.

Denby, David. "High-School Confidential." *New Yorker*, May 31, 1999, 95–98.

Dickens, Charles. *A Tale of Two Cities*. New York: Penguin, 2003.

Dickinson, Emily. *The Complete Poems of Emily Dickinson*. Ed. Thomas H. Johnson. Boston: Little, Brown, 1960.

Didion, Joan. "Marrying Absurd." In DiYanni, ed. 89–93.

Dillard, Annie. "Living like Weasels." In DiYanni, ed. 94–99.

———. "The Stunt Pilot." In Atwan, ed., 5th ed., 180–92.

DiYanni, Robert, ed. *Fifty Great Essays*. 2nd ed. New York: Penguin, 2005.

Doyle, Brian. "Joyas Voladoras." In Orlean, ed., 28–30.

Du Bois, W. E. B. "Battle for Humanity." *In Our Own Words*. Ed. Robert Torricelli and Andrew Carroll. New York: Kodansha International, 1999.

Dundes, Alan. "The Number Three in American Culture." In *Every Man His Way*. Ed. Alan Dundes. Englewood Cliffs, NJ: Prentice-Hall, 1968. 410–24.

Erlich, Gretel. "Spring." In Atwan, ed., 4th ed.

Emerson, Ralph Waldo. "Compensation." *Essays and Lectures*. Washington, DC: Library of America, 1983. 283–302.

Enos, Theresa, ed. *Encyclopedia of Rhetoric and Composition: Communication for Ancient Times to the Information Age*. New York: Garland, 1996.

Fagone, Jason. "Horseman of the Esophagus: Among the Super Gluttons, on the Frontlines of Competitive Eating." *Atlantic*, May 2006, 86–93.

Fahnestock, Jeanne. *Rhetorical Figures in Science*. New York: Oxford UP, 1999.

Fakundiny, Lydia. *The Art of the Essay*. Boston: Houghton Mifflin, 1991.

Faulkner, William. "Nobel Prize Acceptance Speech." http://www.rjgeib.com/thoughts/faulkner/faulkner.html.

Ferlinghetti, Lawrence. *A Coney Island of the Mind: Poems*. New York: New Directions, 1968.

Finch, Robert, and John Elder, eds. *Nature Writing: The Tradition in English*. 2nd ed. New York: Norton, 2002.

Flower, Linda, John R. Hayes, and Heidi Swarts. "Revising Functional Documents: The Scenario Principle." In *New Essays in Technical and Scientific Communication: Research, Theory, Practice*. Ed. Paul V. Anderson, John Brockmann, and Carolyn R. Miller. Amityville, NY: Baywood, 1983. 51–68.

Foss, Sonja K. "Ambiguity as Persuasion: The Vietnam Veterans Memorial." *Communication Quarterly* 34, no. 3 (1986): 326–40.

Franzen, Jonathan. "The Comfort Zone." In Orlean, ed., *The Best American Essays* 37–55.

Frazer, Ian. "If Memory Doesn't Serve." In Orlean, ed., *The Best American Essays* 56–61.

Freud, Sigmund. *Jokes and Their Relation to the Unconscious*. Trans. James Strachey. New York: Norton, 1963.

Goffman, Erving. *Forms of Talk*. Philadelphia: U of Pennsylvania P, 1981.

Gordon, Emily Fox. "Faculty Wife." In Lopate, ed. 115–32.

Gould, Stephen Jay. *Bully for Brontosaurus*. London: Hutchinson Radius, 1991.

Grealy, Lucy. "My God." In Lopate, ed. 173–88.

Greenbaum, Sidney. *Oxford English Grammar*. Oxford: Oxford UP, 1996.

Grief, Mark. "Against Exercise." In Orlean, ed., *The Best American Essays* 62–73.

Gutkind, Lee, ed. *In Fact: The Best of Creative Nonfiction*. New York: Norton, 2005.

Hack the Planet. http://wmf.editthispage.com/discuss/msgReader$364?mode =day.

Hall, Meredith. "Shunned." In Gutkind, ed. 49–70.

Halliday, M. A. K. *An Introduction to Functional Grammar*. 2nd ed. London: Arnold, 1994.

Hauck, Charlie. "My Plan to Save Network Television." *New York Times*, 16 Sep. 2006: A15.

Heimel, Cynthia. *If You Can't Live Without Me, Why Aren't You Dead Yet?!* New York: Grove, 2002.

Hemingway, Ernest. *The Short Stories*. New York: Macmillan, 1986.

Hickey, Dona. *Developing a Written Voice*. Mountain View, CA: Mayfield, 1993.

Hoagland, Edward. "Wild Things." In Lopate, ed. 315–35.

Hoagland, Edward, and Robert Atwan, eds. *The Best American Essays 1999*. Boston: Houghton Mifflin, 1999.

Hubbell, Sue. "A Country Year." In Barnhill, ed. 201–7.

Hunt, Douglas, ed. *The Dolphin Reader*. 6th ed. Boston: Houghton Mifflin, 2003.

Jackson, J. B. "Ghosts at the Door." In Lopate, ed. 211–23.

Jerome, Jerome K. *Three Men in a Boat*. London: Penguin, 1957.

Johnson, Samuel. *Johnson's Dictionary: A Modern Selection*. Ed. E. L. McAdam Jr. and George Milne. New York: Pantheon, 1963.

———. "The Vanity of Human Wishes." *Samuel Johnson: The Major Works*. Ed. Donald Greene. Oxford: Oxford UP, 2000. 12–21.

Johnson, T. R. *A Rhetoric of Pleasure: Prose Style and Today's Composition Classroom*. Portsmouth, NH: Boynton/Cook, 2003.

Johnson, T. R., and Tom Pace. *Refiguring Prose: Possibilities for Writing Pedagogy*. Logan: Utah State UP, 2005.

Joyce, James. *A Portrait of the Artist as a Young Man*. New York: Penguin, 2003.

Keizer, Garret. "Loaded." In Wallace, ed. 137–43.

Kennedy, John F. *The Greatest Speeches of John F. Kennedy*. Ed. Brian R. Dudley. West Vancouver, BC: Titan, 2000.

Killingsworth, M. Jimmie. *Appeals in Modern Rhetoric: An Ordinary-Language Approach*. Carbondale: Southern Illinois UP, 2005.

———. "Birdwatcher." *ISLE* 16, no. 3 (2009): 591–603.

———. *The Cambridge Introduction to Walt Whitman*. Cambridge, UK: Cambridge UP, 2007.

Killingsworth, M. Jimmie, and Jacqueline S. Palmer. *Ecospeak: Rhetoric and Environmental Politics in America*. Carbondale: Southern Illinois UP, 1992.

King, Martin Luther, Jr. "Eulogy for the Young Victims of the Sixteenth Street Baptist Church Bombing." *A Call to Conscience: The Landmark Speeches of Dr. Martin Luther King, Jr*. Ed. Clayborn Carson and Kris Shepard. New York: IPM/Warner, 2001. 95–99.

———. "I Have a Dream." http://www.americanrhetoric.com/speeches/Ihaveadream. htm.

———. "Letter from Birmingham Jail." In DiYanni, ed. 216–33.

Kinneavy, James. *A Theory of Discourse*. New York: Norton, 1971.

Klosterman, Chuck. *Sex, Drugs, and Cocoa Puffs*. New York: Scribner, 2003.

Koch, Kenneth. *Making Your Own Days: The Pleasures of Reading and Writing Poetry*. New York: Scribner, 1998.

Kolln, Martha. *Rhetorical Grammar*. New York: Macmillan, 1991.

Kolln, Martha J. *Rhetorical Grammar: Grammatical Choices, Rhetorical Effects*. 5th ed. New York: Longman, 2007.

Komunyakaa, Yusef. "The Blue Machinery of Summer." In Atwan, ed., 5th ed., 86–95.

Kostelnick, Charles, and Michael Hassett. *Shaping Information: The Rhetoric of Visual Conventions*. Carbondale: Southern Illinois UP, 2003.

Kothari, Geeka. "If You Are What You Eat, Then What Am I?" In Lightman, ed. 91–100.

Krakauer, Jon. *Into the Wild*. New York: Anchor, 1997.

Lakoff, George, and Mark Johnson. *Metaphors We Live By*. Chicago: U of Chicago P, 1980.

Lanham, Richard. *Analyzing Prose*. New York: Scribner, 1983.

Lapham, Lewis H. "Adagio, ma non troppo." *Harper's*, August 1995, 9–11.

Lee, Chang-Rae. "Coming Home Again." In DiYanni, ed. 244–55.

Leech, Geoffrey N., and Michael H. Short. *Style in Fiction: A Linguistic Introduction to English Fictional Prose*. London: Longman, 1981.

Levy, E. J. "Mastering the Art of French Cooking." In Orlean, ed., *The Best* 121–30.

Lightman, Alan, ed. *The Best American Essays 2000*. Boston: Houghton Mifflin, 2000.

Lincoln, Abraham. "The Gettysburg Address." *Selected Speeches and Writings: Abraham Lincoln*. New York: Vintage, 1992.

Lopate, Philip, ed. *The Anchor Essay Annual: Best of 1998*. New York: Anchor, 1998.

McCarthy, Cormac. *All the Pretty Horses*. New York: Vintage, 1993.

McCourt, Malachy. *A Monk Swimming*. New York: Hyperion, 1998.

Melville, Herman. *Moby Dick*. New York: Barnes and Noble Classics, 2003.

Mitchell, Joseph. "The Rivermen." In Sims and Kramer, eds. 37–73.

Mori, Kyoko. "Yarn." In Atwan, ed., 5th ed., 232–41.

Munro, Alice. *Selected Stories*. New York: Vintage, 1997.

Norris, Kathleen. "Celibate Passions." In Root and Steinberg, eds. 13–34.

O'Brien, Tim. *The Things They Carried*. New York: Broadway, 1990.

Ohmann, Richard. *English in America*. New York: Oxford UP, 1976.

Ong, Walter J. *Orality and Literacy: The Technologizing of the Word*. London: Methuen, 1982.

Orlean, Susan. "The American Man at Age Ten." In Sims and Kramer, eds. 99–109.

———. "Show Dog." *New Yorker*, February 20 and 27, 1995, 161–69.

Orlean, Susan, ed. *The Best American Essays: 2005*. Boston: Houghton Mifflin, 2005.

Orwell, George. "Politics and the English Language." In Hunt, ed. 156–69.

Parker, Dorothy. *The Poetry and Short Stories of Dorothy Parker*. New York: Modern Library, 1994.

Perillo, Lucia. "When the Body Begins to Fall Apart on the Academic Stage." In Root and Steinberg, eds. 139–41.

Peterson, Linda H., John C. Brereton, and Joan E. Hartman, eds. *The Norton Reader: An Anthology of Nonfiction Prose*. Shorter 10th ed. New York: Norton, 2000.

Pope, Alexander. *The Dunciad*. Whitefish, MT: Kissinger, 2004.

Provost, Gary. *100 Ways to Improve Your Writing*. New York: New American Library, 1985.

Putnam, Robert D. "Bowling Alone: America's Declining Social Capital." In Hunt, ed. 197–214.

Quammen, David. *The Flight of the Iguana*. New York: Simon and Schuster, 1988.

———. "Strawberries under Ice." In Sims and Kramer, eds. 197–208.

Quintilian. *Institutio Oratoria*. 4 vols. Cambridge, MA: Harvard UP, 1972.

Quirk, Matthew. "Calendar." *Atlantic,* September 2007, 33.

Rankin, Elizabeth D. "Revitalizing Style: Toward a New Theory and Pedagogy." *Freshman English News* 14 (1985): 8–13.

Rawlins, Jack. *The Writer's Way*. 2nd ed. Boston: Houghton Mifflin, 1992.

Raymo, Chet. In Root and Steinberg, eds. 148–51.

Rice, Scott. *Right Words, Right Places*. Belmont, CA: Wadsworth, 1993.

Root, Robert L., Jr., and Michael Steinberg, eds. *The Fourth Genre: Contemporary Writers of/on Creative Nonfiction*. 2nd ed. New York: Longman, 2002.

Rosin, Hanna. "The Reverend." *Atlantic*, September 2006, 38–40.

Sanders, Scott Russell. "The Inheritance of Tools." In Atwan, ed., 5th ed., 131–39.

———. "Settling Down." In Barnhill, ed. 77–92.

Schwartz, Lynne Sharon. "At a Certain Age." In Lightman, ed. 134–39.

Sedaris, David. *Naked*. New York: Little, Brown, 1997.

Shakespeare, William. *The Complete Works*. 3rd ed. Ed. David Bevington. London: Scott, Foresman, 1980.

Simic, Charles. "Dinner at Uncle Boris's." In Gutkind, ed. 85–91.

Simpson, Sherry. "Killing Wolves." In Gutkind, ed. 133–61.

Sims, Norman, and Mark Kramer, eds. *Literary Journalism*. New York: Ballantine, 1995.

Singer, Mark. "Predilections." In Sims and Kramer, eds. 259–300.

Smith, Charles Kay. *Styles and Structures: Alternative Approaches to College Writing*. New York: Norton, 1974.

Snyder, Gary. *Turtle Island*. New York: New Directions, 1974.

Staples, Brent. "Mr. Bellow's Planet." In Sims and Kramer, eds. 179–93.

Strunk, William, Jr., and E. B. White. *The Elements of Style*. 4th ed. New York: Longman, 1999.

Tannen, Deborah. *Gender and Discourse*. Oxford: Oxford UP, 1994.

Teague, Matthew. "Double Bind." *Atlantic,* April 2006, 53–62.

Tolkien, J. R. R. *The Fellowship of the Ring*. Boston: Houghton, 1994.

Traugott, Elizabeth Cross, and Mary Louise Pratt. *Linguistics for Students of Literature*. New York: Harcourt Brace Jovanovich, 1980.

Trillin, Calvin. "First Family of Astoria." In Sims and Kramer, eds. 77–95.

Tuft, Virginia. *Artful Sentences: Syntax as Style*. Cheshire, CT: Graphics Press, 2006.

Twain, Mark. "Journalism in Tennessee." In *The Complete Short Stories of Mark Twain*. Ed. Charles Neider. Toronto: Bantam, 1983. 27–32.

Vickers, Brian. *In Defense of Rhetoric*. Oxford: Oxford UP, 1989.

Wales, Katie. *A Dictionary of Stylistics*. London: Longman, 1997.

Wallace, David Foster. "Consider the Lobster." In Orlean, ed. *The Best* 252–70.

Wallace, David Foster, ed. *The Best American Essays 2007*. Boston: Houghton Mifflin, 2007.

Watson, James D. *The Double Helix: A Personal Account of the Discovery of the Structure of DNA*. New York. Mentor, 1969.

Watson, J. D., and F. H. C. Crick, "Molecular Structure of Nucleic Acids." http://www.nature.com/genomics/human/watson-crick/index.html.

White, E. B. "Once More to the Lake." In DiYanni, ed. 379–86.

White, James D. *Preparing to Teach Writing: Research, Theory, and Practice*. 3rd ed. Mahwah, NJ: Lawrence Erlbaum, 2003.

Whitman, Walt. *Complete Poetry and Collected Prose*. New York: Library of America, 1982.

Wideman, John Edgar. "Looking at Emmett Till." In Gutkind, ed. 24–46.

———. "Whose War: The Color of Terror." *Harper's*, March 2002, 33–38.

Wilde, Oscar. *The Complete Works of Oscar Wilde: Stories, Plays, Poems, and Essays*. New York: Harper Perennial, 1989.

Williams, Joseph. *Style: Toward Clarity and Grace*. Chicago: U of Chicago P, 1990.

Williams, Terry Tempest. "A Shark in the Mind of One Contemplating Wilderness." In Lightman, ed. 221–17.

Wilson, Robert McLiam. "Sticks and Stones: The Irish Identity." In Lopate, ed. 280–85.

WiseGeek. "What Are Hummingbirds?" http://www.wisegeek.com/what-are-hummingbirds.htm.

Zoellner, Robert. "Talk-Write: A Behavioral Pedagogy for Composition." *College English* 30 (1969): 267–320.

Index

Chris Holcomb is an associate professor of English at the University of South Carolina, where he teaches rhetoric and composition. His previous publications include *Mirth Making: The Rhetorical Discourse on Jesting in Early Modern England* and several articles on style and performance.

M. Jimmie Killingsworth is professor and head of the English department at Texas A&M University, where he teaches American literature and rhetoric. His recent publications include *Appeals in Modern Rhetoric: An Ordinary Language Approach* (2005) and *The Cambridge Introduction to Walt Whitman* (2007).